JIHAD

ALSO BY AHMED RASHID

THE RESURGENCE OF CENTRAL ASIA: ISLAM OR NATIONALISM? (1994)

TALIBAN: ISLAM, OIL AND FUNDAMENTALISM IN CENTRAL ASIA (2000)

JIHAD

The Rise of Militant Islam in Central Asia

AHMED RASHID

A WORLD POLICY INSTITUTE BOOK

YALE UNIVERSITY PRESS   NEW HAVEN & LONDON

Designed by Rebecca Gibb and set in Electra and The Sans types.

Printed in the United States of America by R. R. Donnelley & Sons Co.

Library of Congress Cataloging-in-Publication Data

Rashid, Ahmed.

Jihad : the rise of militant Islam in Central Asia / Ahmed Rashid.

p. cm.

Includes bibliographical references and index.

ISBN 0-300-09345-4 (alk. paper)

1. Asia, Central—Politics and government. 2. Islam and politics—Asia, Central. 3. Islamic fundamentalism—Asia, Central. 4. Jihad. I. Title.

DS329.4 .R38 2002

958'.0429—dc21   2001006898

A catalogue record for this book is available from the British Library.

The paper in this book meets the guidelines for permanence and durability of the Committee on Production Guidelines for Book Longevity of the Council on Library Resources.

10   9   8   7   6   5   4   3   2   1

FOR ANGELES AND HER LOVE,

AND IN MEMORY OF JOHNNY DAS AND PHILIPPE TOPALIAN,

WHO WOULD HAVE LOVED THIS VAST LANDSCAPE OF SKY AND STEPPE

CONTENTS

PREFACE

I first went to Central Asia in 1988, tracking the chimera of the war in Afghanistan. I wanted to learn more about Afghanistan's minority ethnic groups, who for the first time in their history were taking their place as arbitrators of their own destiny now that the Soviet army had pulled out. In order to understand these groups, I needed to understand their origins, which lay in Central Asia, then part of the collapsing Soviet Union. Three years later, when the Soviet Union finally fell apart, I was again in Central Asia, and I witnessed the emergence of the five new independent states there.

Subsequent trips to Central Asia led to my first book, published in 1994: *The Resurgence of Central Asia: Islam or Nationalism?* The question I posed—whether the newly independent Central Asian regimes would build a democratic order that used ethnic nationalism as a binding force or whether Islamic fundamentalism would take its place—was one that I could not directly answer at the time. This book is in part an attempt to answer that early question.

In the Introduction I explore the complex meaning of jihad—so often perceived simplistically in the West as a holy war—and how the new jihad movements arose. But Westerners are not the only people who misconstrue the idea of jihad. How the new fundamentalist and militant Islamic movements have distorted its greater meaning of an inner struggle to be a good and devout Muslim has much to say about the conflicts currently tearing Central Asia apart.

Part I deals with the history of Central Asia and its indigenous Islamic movements from the sixth century B.C. to the end of the Communist era. Only by going back in the past can we understand the present: the history of ethnic conflict, the growth of Islam, and the crucial part played by geography. I also summarize the first decade of independence in each of the Central Asian states, examining what the regimes have achieved—and how they have failed.

Part II is an investigation into the new phenomenon of radical Islam in Central Asia. Focusing on the three biggest movements—the Islamic Renaissance Party (IRP), the Hizb ut-Tahrir (HT), and the Islamic Movement of Uzbekistan (IMU)—I outline their origins, beliefs, influence, and activities. The most important discovery that emerges from this discussion is that although these movements began with different ideologies, agendas, and support bases, the situation in Central Asia—in particular the government repression of even the most moderate Islam—is pulling them together and into the orbit of other radical Islamic movements like the Taliban and Osama bin Laden's Al Qaeda. And they are spreading with incredible speed in what is basically alien territory because the local governments and the international community alike have failed the people of Central Asia, offering them little but massive repression, unemployment, poverty, disease, and war.

The two largest underground Islamic movements, the Hizb ut-Tahrir and the Islamic Movement of Uzbekistan, are shrouded in secrecy. They issue few press statements, give only a handful of interviews, and allow no photographs of their leaders. How has the IMU leader Juma Namangani become such a mythical, even heroic, figure in the Central Asian Islamic underground when hardly anyone even knows what he looks like? The search for Namangani and the even more elusive HT leaders—whose very names are unknown—is a large part of what this book is about. So if it sometimes reads like a poor detective story, with clues that lead nowhere, mysterious evidence, and inconclusive theories, it is because the ending has yet to be written.

Since my first visit I have traveled to Central Asia dozens of times, and even when I am away from that beautiful, stark land I have followed the events there with a fascination that has become little less than obsession. The vast, empty landscape dotted with oases of vibrant populations and political ferment, sitting on the world's last great untapped natural energy reserves, is still almost as unknown to Westerners as it was to Europeans in the Middle Ages. In fact, it is more so: the Europeans recognized its importance as the bridge between Europe and Asia, but now that no one travels the Silk Route, Westerners have relegated Central Asia to the realm of legend. The bloody civil wars and political unrest that have plagued the region for more than a decade have been poorly covered—and even less well understood—by the international media. Yet, as the world is finally recognizing, Central Asia is vital to future stability in South Asia, the Middle East, China, and Russia.

You can ask questions in Central Asia, but don't expect straight answers. Often you will get no answers at all. There are only moments of illumination, such as the one that came to me in 1993 while I was covering the civil war in Tajikistan. As I was enjoying a leisurely Sunday lunch in the garden of the Dushanbe home of a well-known Tajik journalist, a firefight broke out at both ends of his street that eventually developed into a three-way battle. As bullets zipped into the shrubbery, nobody knew who was killing whom or why. But the shocking part for me was that my hosts, a poet, a novelist, and a journalist—the cream of Tajikistan's liberal intelligentsia—suddenly pulled concealed pistols out of their pockets and fired back. We were stranded in the garden for six hours, but I never discovered who the combatants were, although dead bodies littered the street.

I hope this book helps explain who today's combatants in Central Asia are and why they are fighting. Until the international community understands that the future of Central Asia can affect the future of the rest of the world, things are unlikely to improve. I have tried to identify the key players and the major issues. But do not expect this book to answer all your questions.

This book could not have been written without the help of many friends in Central Asia who have to remain anonymous. They include government officials, diplomats, journalists, academics, mullahs, businessmen, aid workers, and ordinary people. Foreign humanitarian relief organizations like the United Nations, the Agency for Technical Co-operation and Development (ACTED), the Aga Khan Foundation, and the Soros Foundation have provided enormous encouragement and support to my work over the years, but they are not responsible for any of my conclusions. Foreign journalists and diplomats working in the region have unstintingly given me time, insight, and information.

Two people in particular must be singled out for the breadth of knowledge, experience, and friendship they have shared with me over the years—Barnett Rubin and Olivier Roy. I have absorbed so many of their ideas over the years that I no longer know which are mine and which are theirs. I hope they will forgive me if I appear at times to be stealing from them.

I would also like to thank Ivo Petrov and Hiroshi Takahashi of the U.N. Tajikistan Office for Peace Keeping, and Lakhdar Brahimi and Francesc Vendrell and their staffs at the U.N. Special Mission for Afghanistan, for their kindness, hospitality, and experience, from all of which I have learned much. Their support for my efforts to highlight the crises in both Afghanistan and Central Asia was backed by practical help—for example, rides in U.N. planes to places that were otherwise inaccessible. Writers and mountain climbers Nancy and John Bouchard emerged from an unexpected quarter to provide help and friendship. Frederic Roussel, the constantly active head of ACTED, has been a friend of long standing and provided much-needed support at a critical moment.

I would also like to thank the publications I work for, which have given me the time, the funds, and the space in print to explore Central Asia, asking few questions about what I was doing in a part of the world that only a few of their readers were initially interested in. Over the years I have tried to whet their appetites for more on Central Asia. For nearly twenty years *The Far Eastern Economic Review* and its wonderful, long-time editors Nayan Chanda and Michael Vatikiotis have given me the kind of space to write about Central Asia that has been the envy of my fellow journalists—and have rarely questioned my judgments. At times I have returned from a long journey in Central Asia and explained that I had a story that was far too complicated to explain; they should just trust me to write it. Invariably, they have done so.

In London the *Daily Telegraph* and before that *The Independent* have had no doubts about the worthiness of covering Central Asia. The present foreign editor of the *Daily Telegraph*, Alec Russell, has himself become an aficionado of the region, and he has given me enormous encouragement. In Pakistan I have to thank Arif Nizami of *The Nation* newspaper for the coverage he has given my articles from the region and my attempts to educate Pakistani readers to the idea that there are more ways than one to look at Central Asia and Afghanistan.

A special thanks is owed to Karl E. Meyer, editor of *World Policy Journal*, who asked me to write an article about the first ten years of independence of the Central Asian Republics. Aided by his magnificent managing editor, Linda Wrigley, the *Journal* published two articles and graciously gave me permission to use some of that material here.

This book had just gone into editing at Yale University Press when the Pentagon and the World Trade Center were attacked. Those tragic events have underscored how urgently Westerners need to understand the situation in Central Asia. I would like to thank my editor Larisa Heimert, who all along insisted that I do this book and has given me constant encouragement, and Liz Pelton, who has done so much to bring both my previous book on the Taliban and this new book before the public. And a special thanks to manuscript editor Susan Laity for her meticulous, scrupulous editing and for the trouble she has taken to learn about Central Asia before tackling the difficult task of editing my work.

This book could not have been written without the support of my wife, Angeles, and our two children, who have put up with a great deal, in particular my constant absences from home. There is no sufficient way to thank them.

Lahore
October 2001

MAPS

MAP 1: CENTRAL ASIA

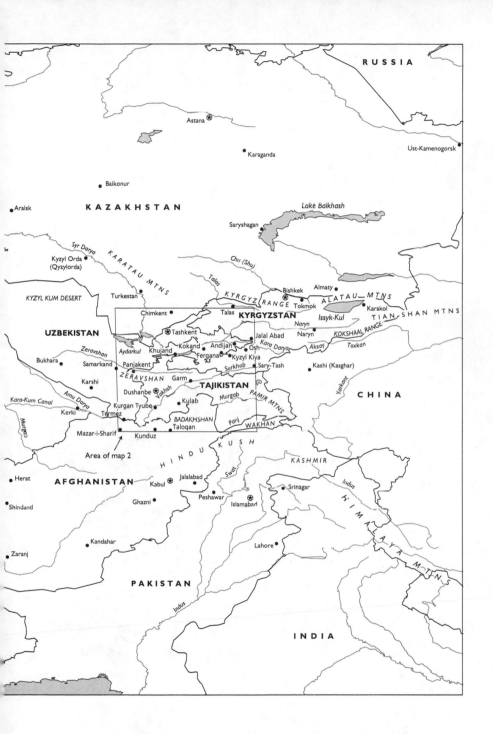

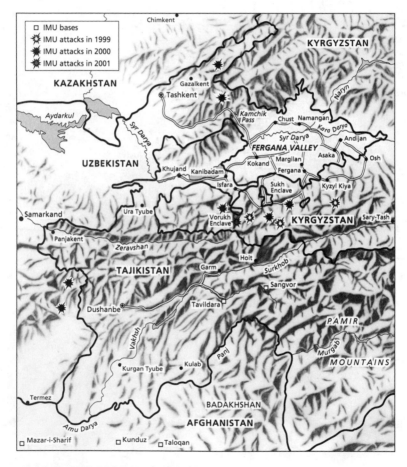

MAP 2: THE FERGANA VALLEY REGION

1   Introduction: Central Asia's Islamic Warriors

THE HISTORY OF ISLAM is a story of change and adaptation. Throughout Muslim history, movements have arisen periodically that seek to transform both the nature of Islamic belief and the political and social lives of their adherents. Since the seventh century, followers of The Prophet Muhammad have fanned out to spread His message throughout the known world. Muslim nomadic tribes—often originating in Central Asia—carried the word across the steppes and mountains of the vast Eurasian landmass, some peacefully as they drove their caravans of goods along the ancient Silk Route, others by conquest. The conquerors would transform the vanquished empire, but in time their empires would change and become urbanized, until each was in its turn conquered by new nomadic Muslim tribes. The changes the conquerors wrought—religious, political, social—have often been driven by the concept of jihad.

In Western thought, heavily influenced by the medieval Christian Crusaders—with their own ideas about "holy war"—jihad has always been portrayed as an Islamic war against unbelievers. Westerners point to the conquest of Spain in the eighth century by the

Moors and the vast Ottoman Empire of the thirteen through twentieth centuries, and focus on the bloodshed, ignoring not only the
enormous achievements in science and art and the basic tolerance
of these empires, but also the true idea of jihad that spread peacefully throughout these realms. Militancy is not the essence of jihad.

The greater jihad as explained by The Prophet Muhammad is
first inward-seeking: it involves the effort of each Muslim to become
a better human being, to struggle to improve him- or herself. In
doing so the follower of jihad can also benefit his or her community.
In addition, jihad is a test of each Muslim's obedience to God and
willingness to implement His commands on earth. As Barbara Metcalf described it, "Jihad is the inner struggle of moral discipline and
commitment to Islam and political action."[1] It is also true that Islam
sanctions rebellion against an unjust ruler, whether Muslim or not,
and jihad can become the means to mobilize that political and social struggle. This is the lesser jihad. Thus, Muslims revere the life
of The Prophet Muhammad because it exemplified both the greater
and the lesser jihad—The Prophet struggled lifelong to improve Himself as a Muslim in order both to set an example to those around
Him and to demonstrate His complete commitment to God. But
He also fought against the corrupt Arab society He was living in,
and He used every means—including but not exclusively militant
ones—to transform it.

Today's global jihadi movements, from the Taliban in Afghanistan
to Osama bin Laden's worldwide Al Qaeda to the Islamic Movement
of Uzbekistan (IMU), ignore the greater jihad advocated by The
Prophet and adopt the lesser jihad as a complete political and social
philosophy. Yet nowhere in Muslim writings or tradition does jihad
sanction the killing of innocent non-Muslim men, women, and children, or even fellow Muslims, on the basis of ethnicity, sect, or belief.
It is this perversion of jihad—as a justification to slaughter the innocent—which in part defines the radical new fundamentalism of
today's most extreme Islamic movements.

These new Islamic fundamentalists are not interested in transforming a corrupt society into a just one, nor do they care about providing jobs, education, or social benefits to their followers or creating harmony between the various ethnic groups that inhabit many Muslim countries. The new jihadi groups have no economic manifesto, no plan for better governance and the building of political institutions, and no blueprint for creating democratic participation in the decision-making process of their future Islamic states. They depend on a single charismatic leader, an amir, rather than a more democratically constituted organization or party for governance. They believe that the character, piety, and purity of their leader rather than his political abilities, education, or experience will enable him to lead the new society. Thus has emerged the phenomenon of the cults of Mullah Muhammad Omar of the Taliban, Osama bin Laden of Al Qaeda, and Juma Namangani of the Islamic Movement of Uzbekistan.

The new jihadi groups are equally obsessed with implementing *sharia* (Islamic law). However, they see sharia not as a way of creating a just society but simply as a means to regulate personal behavior and dress codes for Muslims—a concept that distorts centuries of tradition, culture, history, and even the religion of Islam itself. The hallmark of the Taliban, Al Qaeda (The Base), and the IMU is the rejection of all historical experience, scientific experiment, and other forms of knowledge that Muslims (and other societies) have developed over the past 1,400 years. Thus the Taliban have tried to rewrite Afghan history in order to justify their repression of women and minority ethnic groups or their destruction of statues of Buddha. The new Islamic order for these jihadi groups is reduced to a harsh, repressive penal code for their citizens that strips Islam of its values, humanism, and spirituality. If God and the Islam of The Prophet Muhammad offer sustenance for devout Muslims to search their souls and seek meaning in today's ever-changing, complex world, the new jihadi groups reduce Islam to the length of one's beard and the question of whether burka-clad women are allowed to expose their ankles.

Before September 11, 2001, this new phase in the long history of Islamic fundamentalism had gone largely unnoticed in the Western world. The unprecedented events of that day in New York and Washington, D.C.—when nineteen Al Qaeda militants trained in Afghanistan took over the controls of four aircraft and flew three of them into the commercial and military heart of America, killing close to six thousand people—changed the world forever. The civilized nations' battle against terrorism may well define the twenty-first century just as Nazism and the Cold War defined the twentieth.

But to define these attacks solely as acts of terrorism misses the point of the new political phenomenon at work amongst small groups of extremists around the Muslim world. When a U.S.-led military alliance began bombing Taliban defenses and Al Qaeda training camps on October 7, few reports of the defenders mentioned that the man who was reputedly commanding the Taliban forces in Taloqan, in northeastern Afghanistan, was Juma Namangani, the military leader of the IMU. Still largely unnoticed amongst the many Islamic fundamentalist groups that have set up operational bases with the Taliban over the past few years, the IMU presents one of the biggest threats, for it aims to topple the regime of neighboring Uzbekistan's President Islam Karimov as part of a jihad that will reach across Central Asia.

Comprising the republics of Kazakhstan, Kyrgyzstan, Tajikistan, Turkmenistan, and Uzbekistan, Central Asia is almost certain to become the new global battleground. Its history has been marked by more than two thousand years of conflict, as the great empires of the past fought to control the commercial lifeline linking Europe and Asia, the Silk Route. (Almost the only empire that did not at one time or another rule part or all of Central Asia was the Roman Empire.) But today's conflicts differ from the struggles of the past, and they stem largely from the changes wrought in the region by the Soviet Union—and from the chaos that accompanied its dissolution in 1991.

For the majority of the people in Central Asia, independence from the Soviet Communist system did not immediately translate into an urge for democracy, the market economy, or Western culture and consumerism, as was the case elsewhere in the former Soviet Union, for example Russia and the Baltic republics. Instead, Islamic revival swept through the region. One of the key tenets of the Soviet system had been that religion was incompatible with communism, and the Communists methodically set about repressing all forms of religious expression within the country. As the Soviet empire fell apart, the people of Central Asia, who had been forced to renounce or hide their religion for seventy-four years, at last saw an opportunity to reconnect spiritually and culturally with their Islamic past.

The Central Asians embraced Islam not only to reestablish their own ethnic and cultural identity but to reconnect with their Muslim neighbors to the south, who had been cut off from them ever since Stalin closed the borders between the Soviet Union and the rest of the world. Almost the first new visitors to the independent Central Asian republics were Islamic missionaries from Pakistan, Saudi Arabia, Turkey, and elsewhere, who helped build hundreds of new mosques and distributed free copies of the Koran translated into Russian and other native languages. Millions of Central Asians emotionally seized this opportunity to rediscover their identity and heritage, all of which they linked intimately with Islam. As I traveled through the region in that first heady year of independence, I was besieged by people wanting to know about the world of Islam outside their valleys and mountain villages. Few people knew about the Islamic revolution in Iran in 1979, the depth of the Palestinian resistance to Israel, or the mini-wars that had been waged by Islamic militants in Kashmir, Algeria, Egypt, and the Philippines. Many had forgotten their prayers and other rituals of Islam, even though an underground movement of itinerant preachers, as well as local mystics and teachers, had kept alive traditions of the faith, and the cultural and social mores that this faith fostered.

What Central Asians did know about, however, for many of them had experienced its effects firsthand, was the Soviet Union's invasion of Afghanistan in 1979 and the ten-year war that followed. Thousands of young men had been conscripted into the Soviet Army and sent to fight the Afghan Mujahedeen (Islamic fighters). Contrary to Soviet expectations, many young men returned home with admiring stories of the sacrifices and Islamic zeal of their opponents. Even though some of their comrades had come back in zinc-lined coffins, the survivors spoke with glowing pride the Mujahedeen guerrillas' success and bravery against the overwhelming firepower of their own Soviet forces. Sipping tea, men of an older generation compared the Afghans to Central Asia's own Mujahedeen—the Basmachis—who had resisted the 1917 Bolshevik Revolution for more than a decade. Their hatred for the Soviet army and political system was obvious. The fact that they shared an ethnic and linguistic affinity with many of the people they were fighting made them realize even more deeply how the Soviet Communist system had deprived them of their common heritage and national pride.

When independence came, with its rush of excitement and religious fervor, Central Asians nonetheless realized that the policies and actions of their governments would determine both the political and economic future of their fragile states and the future of their Islamic revival. Would the rulers embrace popular Islam and democracy and rejoin the wider Islamic world with its culture of tolerance, or would they continue the Communist policies of political, social, and religious repression—thereby ensuring greater resistance from the newly aroused population? Such critical decisions would determine whether the Central Asian countries moved towards stability and progress or tumbled into instability and civil war.

The choice was there, but it quickly became apparent that the Central Asian leaders—all but Kyrgyzstan's President Askar Akayev apparatchiks from the Communist era—were never going to consider these options. Instead, these highly centralized, bureaucratic post-Soviet ruling elites lumbered along the well-trodden path they knew best—the suppression of dissent, democracy, popular culture, and eventually the Islamic revival. (Even in Kyrgyzstan the majority of the ruling elites were stalwarts of the old Communist government.)

Central Asian's reemergence into the world brought global conflicts as well. The region's enormous oil and gas reserves, which had lain largely untapped because Moscow preferred to exploit the resources of Russian Siberia, now became a battleground for the competing interests of Russia, the United States, and neighboring countries Iran, Turkey, Pakistan, and China. In what analysts quickly came to call the "new Great Game" (after the nineteenth-century rivalry between the empires of tsarist Russia and Great Britain for control of Asia), Russia, China, and the United States struggled to establish pipelines that would give them both access to natural resources and influence over the people of Central Asia.

Afghanistan, which had been a pawn in the Cold War U.S.-Soviet rivalry since 1979, found itself still caught in the middle, despite the breakup of the Soviet Union. But the money the United States had funneled via Pakistan's secret service to the most extremist of the anti-Soviet Islamic fighters during the war started a movement that would change the game altogether. A new group, the Taliban, rose to power and set in place a model of extremist Islamic fundamentalism unknown in the Muslim world. With the financial and military help of the Saudi extremist Osama bin Laden, Taliban-ruled Afghanistan became a base for Islamic militants of every kind, who trained with the Taliban forces before returning to their homes to spread instability across the region.

Helping the militants' cause were the shortsighted hard-line policies of the Central Asian regimes. The refusal of the leaderships to consider democratic or economic reforms in countries that had lost their main economic support (the Soviet Union), combined with their repression of religion, pushed moderates and political reformers into the camps of the radicals. The Central Asian regimes launched repeated crackdowns against Islamic activism, in which not only militants but thousands of ordinary practicing Muslims were jailed, tortured, and sentenced to long prison terms in new gulags set up in remote corners of their countries. For five years (1992–97) a bloody civil war pitting Islamic rebels and Tajik democrats against the Tajik regime engulfed Tajikistan, ultimately claiming more than fifty thousand lives.

Hope emerged in Tajikistan with the end of the war, as the rebels and the government forces both accepted a peace accord in which a representative, coalition government was established. That fragile coalition has been threatened by four years of economic hardship and the incursions of Islamic extremists from neighboring Uzbekistan, but as of this writing it still holds—and carries the best hope for Central Asian stability in its model of a democratically elected government in which legal Islamic parties are represented.

One of the greatest threats to Tajikistan's stability—and Central Asia's—is the Islamic Movement of Uzbekistan. Formed in 1998 by extremists who were dissatisfied with the moderation of the Islamic Renaissance Party and determined to topple the government of Central Asian strongman Islam Karimov, the IMU launched guerrilla attacks against the regimes from bases in Tajikistan and Afghanistan in 1999, 2000, and 2001. Under the military leadership of the charismatic Juma Namangani, the IMU has extended its jihad to the whole of Central Asia.

The key target of Namangani's repeated guerrilla forays is the Fergana Valley, which is divided between the three states of Uzbekistan, Kyrgyzstan, and Tajikistan. Each of these countries now faces a direct military threat, therefore, and even the states like Kazakhstan that are not centers of fighting have increased their military spending to meet the perceived threat of an expanded war. Meanwhile, a new round of competition for influence has been touched off between the United States, Russia, and China as each pours in military aid, advisers, and training to fight the guerrillas, painting increasingly dire scenarios about the future of the region. But the big powers do little to improve the horrific economic, political, and social conditions in these countries, allowing the regimes to continue their policies unchecked. (Indeed, as I discuss in Chapter 11, since the October 7 bombings, Uzbekistan's Karimov has increased his human-rights abuses, secure in his position as an essential ally to the U.S.-led military alliance.)

The result is that the IMU is growing. Namangani is now recruiting dissidents from all of Central Asia's major ethnic groups, as well as Chechens and Dagestanis from the Caucasus and Uighurs from China's Muslim province of Xinjiang. With little to offer except the deposition of the current regimes and the institution of sharia, the IMU has nonetheless become a transnational group. Support flows in from across the region, and funding comes from as far away as Saudi Arabia—as well as from the narcotics and weapons trade out of Afghanistan.

Another even more widespread Islamic movement, the Hizb ut-Tahrir al-Islami (HT; the Party of Islamic Liberation) has also taken root in Central Asia. If the IMU says little about its ultimate aims, the HT produces an abundance of literature about its goals, including a Web site (www.hizb-ut-tahrir.org). Unlike the IMU, the HT, which has also declared jihad in Central Asia, seeks to reunite the Central Asian republics and eventually the whole Muslim world by nonviolent means with the eventual aim of establishing a caliphate similar to that established after the death of The Prophet Muhammad in seventh-century Arabia. But the HT resembles the IMU in its complete lack of a social, economic, or political plan for governing this caliphate. Nonetheless, its utopian aims are becoming popular amongst college and university students throughout the region. And because the regimes equate all Muslims with militants, the HT's recruits are now filling the jails and penal colonies of Central Asia.

Although every act of state repression has pushed these movements into taking more extreme positions, distorting their original
message, it remains true that the Islamic ideologies of the IMU and
the HT are based not on the indigenous Islam of Central Asia, the
birthplace of Sufism (the tolerant form of Islamic mysticism) and
nineteenth-century Jadidism (the modernist interpretation of Islam),
but on imported ideologies. Their message of extremism originated
with the Taliban in Afghanistan, the militant madrassah culture of
Pakistan (where many IMU and HT adherents studied), and the extreme Wahhabi doctrine of Saudi Arabia. Contrary to Central Asia's
Islamic traditions and history, *jihad* in its simplest form rather than
ijtihad (reinterpretation and consensus) has become the primary
aim of these groups as they seek to mobilize popular support.

The severe censorship practiced by the Central Asian regimes
has made it difficult to uncover or verify any information about these
Islamic movements. But rumor, myth, and the ancient Central
Asian tradition of storytelling have created a different reality, adding
to the mystique of these movements. In the villages of Central Asia,
people speak of how the advance guard of IMU guerrilla groups consists of beautiful female snipers, who, armed with the latest scopes
and night-vision goggles, can either seduce or kill a soldier from a
long distance; of how the guerrillas' knapsacks are filled with dollar
bills which they distribute to the farmers who feed them; of how two
guerrillas held an entire battalion of Uzbek troops at bay; of how the
guerrillas have been blessed by Muslim saints to make their bodies
impervious to wounds or, conversely, to keep their bodies sweet
smelling after death; of how the militants are funded by Saudis, Pakistanis, Turks, Iranians, and Osama bin Laden. The need to sift
through the tales to separate fact from fiction is in part what prompted me to write this book.

What is clear, however, is that Central Asia's problems are primarily internal, and they will not be solved simply by defeating the IMU.
The lack of economic reform or development, the absence of

democracy or free expression, the centralized controls of a Soviet-minded bureaucracy, and the growing cancers of corruption and public cynicism have made the situation in these countries increasingly fragile. As the leaders age, the population gets younger: more than 60 percent of the region's 50 million people are under the age of 25. This new generation is unemployed, poorly educated, and hungry—how long will it continue to tolerate the decline in living standards and the lack of rudimentary freedoms? A social and political explosion seems inescapable unless the demands of the young are addressed.

But the ruling elites cling to power at the expense of all else. Indeed, their regional jealousies, rivalries, and competition have kept them from even the most basic measures of self-protection. They cannot agree on the formation of a joint security belt, much less a common Central Asian market that would have a chance to improve the well being of their people.

Meanwhile, religion and ethnicity remain intensely combustible issues. At the heart of Central Asia lies a cultural vacuum, which cannot be filled with imitations of Western culture. By ignoring their heritage, which has given so much to their own people and to the wider Islamic world, Central Asia's rulers deny their people a chance to create a modern identity from their own past. By refusing to accommodate traditional Islam, democracy, and interethnic harmony, the Central Asian governments fuel the fires of extremism.

The Central Asian regimes now have a new chance to reverse this trend. By joining the U.S.-led alliance against the Taliban and Osama bin Laden, they have given their countries a tremendous opportunity for change, economic development, and democracy. The gratitude of the West, of Russia, and of China can be called upon in future resource-development deals, assistance with the creation of new political institutions, and a better life for their people. The chance is there. It is for Central Asia—and the world—to take it.

PART I Islam and Politics in Central Asia, Past and Present

2 Conquerors and Saints:
The Past as Present

THE ETHNIC, POLITICAL, AND RELIGIOUS factions now vying for
control in Central Asia have a history almost as old as the Central
Asian civilizations themselves. Since around 500 B.C., when Darius
I added the region known as Transoxiana (present-day Uzbekistan
and Tajikistan) to the Persian Empire, to the 1920s, when Stalin
forcefully divided the region into the five socialist republics that cor-
respond to the current independent republics, Central Asia has
been a center for war and empire, art and culture, religion and
commerce.

Much of the reason for Central Asia's rich history is geographical: its huge landmass lies at the heart of the Eurasian continent. In
ancient times it was considered the center of the world, linking
China with Europe by means of the famous Silk Route. In reality
this consisted of several routes, forged to allow merchants to carry
goods by camel caravan across the two continents. But the travelers
transported more than silk or spices; they also spread new technologies—such as papermaking, gunpowder, and silk weaving—new
ideas, and new religions. The religion of the ancient Greeks, Bud-

dhism, Judaism, Zoroastrianism, Nestorian Christianity, Hinduism, Manichaeanism, and most of the major ideas of Islam have at one time or another found a home in Central Asia. It is the prevalence of the various ideas on Islam, in particular, and how they have been received by the various rulers of the Central Asian landmass, that are essential to an understanding of the conflicts that threaten the region today.

The Importance of Geography

Central Asia's greatest strength in the past—and its greatest problem today—is that it is landlocked, bordering Iran and Afghanistan to the south, China to the east, and Russia to the north and west. The vast Central Asian steppe is bounded by the Caspian Sea in the west, the Hindu Kush and the Pamir Mountain ranges in the south, and the Tian Shan Mountains in the west along the border with China. There are no clear geographical boundaries in the north, where the Kazakh steppe merges into Siberia.

Central Asia was once known as "the land between the two rivers" for the two major rivers, the Amu Darya (Oxus) and the Syr Darya (Jaxartes), that bounded much of its territory before emptying into the Aral Sea. These two rivers have created formidable geographical, cultural, and political boundaries that separated Central Asia from the rest of the world even as the Silk Route connected it. The Amu Darya, for example, divided the nomadic Turkic and Mongol empires in Central Asia from the Persian Empire to the south, and helped act as a buffer—along with an independent Afghanistan—between the British Empire in India and tsarist Russia. Recently it has marked the border between Taliban-ruled Afghanistan and Central Asia. The Syr Darya has protected Central Asian kingdoms from periodic invasions from Mongolia, Siberia, and the Gobi Desert.

Rivers are not the only natural boundaries. Central Asia lies at the crossroads of the world's highest mountain ranges: the Pamir Mountains, which cover 93 percent of today's Tajikistan; the Tian Shan Mountains, stretching to the east and north of the Pamirs; the Himalayas to the southeast; and the Hindu Kush to the south. The legendary traveler Marco Polo crossed the Pamirs in 1273 on his way to China, dubbing the range the Roof of the World. "Ascending mountain after mountain, you at length arrive at a point, where you might suppose the surrounding summits to be the highest lands in the world. . . . So great is the height of the mountains, that no birds are to be seen near their summits. Here there live a tribe of savage, ill disposed and idolatrous people, who subsist upon the animals they can destroy and clothe themselves with the skins," wrote Polo in his memoirs.[1]

In the center of this vast, magnificent landscape of mountains and steppe are two of the largest deserts in the world. In the south, covering much of Turkmenistan, is the Kara-Kum (black sands) Desert: more than 135,000 square miles where rain falls approximately once a decade. To the north, in Uzbekistan, lies the Kyzyl Kum (red sands) Desert. But between these bleak wastes lush, well-irrigated valleys provide oases around which settlements and cities have grown, each oasis a self-contained economic community whose citizens traded with the local nomads and caravans that passed through. The harsh, sparsely populated landscape made Central Asia ripe for conquest but difficult to rule: empires rose and fell periodically throughout its history.

The geographical face of Central Asia remained largely untouched until the late nineteenth and twentieth centuries, when the region became part of the Russian Empire and then the Soviet Union. The Russians and later the Soviets changed the landscape, building massive irrigation networks flowing from huge reservoirs to support cotton agriculture between the Amu and Syr Darya rivers. Although in the process they created irretrievable environmental damage and pollution that have eventually resulted in acute water shortages, the drying up of lakes and rivers, and further desertification, the water routes were for many years essential sources of agriculture and food. Today those irrigation networks lie broken, hostage to the political battles that divide the region.

Central Asia currently comprises five independent republics: Kazakhstan, Uzbekistan, Turkmenistan, Kyrgyzstan, and Tajikistan, whose fiercely disputed boundaries were drawn by Stalin as part of his divide-and-rule campaign. Its landmass of 1,542,200 square miles hosts a population of just 52 million people, representing more than one hundred ethnic groups, from the predominant Uzbeks, Kazakhs, and Tajiks to Germans, Koreans, and Tibetans. The largest ethnic group is the Uzbeks, who make up 72 percent of Uzbekistan's 22 million people as well as substantial minorities in all the other Central Asian republics. Before the breakup of the Soviet Union, there were also some 10 million Russians, comprising one-fifth of the population, many the result of forced relocation by Stalin, as another means of weakening the power of the region's ethnic groups. A large number of these Russians have migrated to Russia since 1991.

But the heart of Central Asia has always been the Fergana Valley. Just two hundred miles long and seventy miles across at its widest point, the fertile valley has for centuries been the home for the largest concentration of people. Today it has 10 million inhabitants, 20 percent of the total population of Central Asia. The emperor Babur, who conquered Afghanistan and founded the Mogul Empire in India in the fifteenth century, was born in the Fergana Valley, describing it in his memoirs as the closest place to Paradise on earth. From his splendid palaces in Delhi, Babur would recall the 140 varieties of grapes and watermelons produced in Fergana. Valley horses were prized as cavalry mounts by nomadic tribes and empire builders as far away as China.[2]

More than crops and livestock flourished in the Fergana Valley. Fergana has also traditionally been the center of Central Asia's political and cultural Islam, producing saints, scholars, mystics, and warriors whose knowledge and learning spread across the Muslim world.

The bordering city of Osh, today the second-largest city in Kyrgyzstan, was a seat of Islamic learning in the tenth century. Legend has it that the large mountain in the center of the town was blessed by King Solomon; it still bears the name Takht-i-Sulaiman (Seat of Solomon) and was long a site of Muslim pilgrimage. To the west lie the ancient Muslim capitals of Bukhara and Samarkand. The 360 mosques and 113 madrassahs (Islamic religious schools) of medieval Bukhara produced scholars who spread their faith throughout Russia, China, South Asia, and the Middle East. In the words of a medieval proverb: "The sun does not shine on Bukhara, it is Bukhara that shines on the sun." Even after Bukhara became a Russian protectorate in 1868 there were still 100 madrassahs in Bukhara, with some 10,000 students.

A History of Conquest

The history of Central Asia is a tale of conquest, of Mongol "hordes" and Arab holy warriors who swept across its steppes and crossed its mountains and, for a time, enfolded it within the largest empires in the world. Alexander, Tamerlane, Genghis Khan: at one time each of these conquerors added the territories of Central Asia to his vast empire, founding dynasties that survived for centuries—until the next invader arrived.

Early Central Asian history is dominated by the rivalry between the Persians to the south and the Turkic tribes to the north, who vied for control of the rich oasis cities. The Persian Empire under Darius I added Transoxiana to its territory around 500 B.C. but the Persians were ousted for a time by Turkic nomadic invasions from Siberia and Mongolia. These tribes had originally (beginning in about 1000 B.C.) inhabited the Alatau Mountains in eastern Central Asia. (The Chinese began using the word *Tur* or *Turkic* to identify all the nomadic tribes who posed a threat to their empire—the ancient origins of the word *Turkistan* [home of the Turks], used even today to identify Central Asia.) The resurgent Persians next fell victim to Alexander the Great, who conquered Bactria and Sogdiana (ancient Uzbekistan, Tajikistan, and Afghanistan) between 329 and 327 B.C., founding the modern-day city of Khujand. Alexander consolidated his control by urging his men to marry local women; he himself married a Sogdian princess, Roxana.

Alexander's Greco-Sogdian heirs created the Bactrian Empire, which governed a large part of Central Asia and Afghanistan between 300 and 140 B.C. The western region of Central Asia (present-day Turkmenistan) was ruled by the Parthians, a tribal dynasty based on the Saka tribes, whose empire lasted until A.D. 226, when they were defeated by the Persian Sassanids. Meanwhile, the north of Central Asia was invaded in the last century B.C. by successive waves of Sakas, who in time were driven out by another tribal group of nomads from the Gobi Desert: the Hsiung-nu, the forefathers of the Mongols. The Hsiung-nu had spread west after defeating the Uighurs, another tribal confederation who at that time ruled present-day Xinjiang Province and western China. Continuing their westward march across Central Asia, the Huns, as they were now called, reached the Volga River by A.D. 400. Their empire—the first nomadic Mongol empire—now stretched from Korea to the Volga.

In the fifth century the Huns invaded Europe under their chief Attila and marched on Rome. As the Huns moved westwards the vacuum in eastern Central Asia was once again filled by invading Turkic tribes, who continued their incursions for several centuries. These nomadic invasions from Mongolia and western China have left behind few traces of their empires or culture, and little is known about the political system they erected to rule their vast landmass. Invariably, they would arrive to conquer and then move on eastwards whilst other tribes arrived to take their place.

One nomadic empire did leave some impressive traces: the Kushan Empire, which dates from the first and second centuries A.D. and also included northern India, Iran, and present-day Xinjiang Province in China. In the second century the great Kushan king Kanishka became a patron of the Mahayana school of Buddhism, which was the first to humanize the figure of Buddha. (Previously Buddha had been depicted only by symbols, such as the prayer wheel.) Massive and beautiful stylized Kushan Buddha statues have been unearthed in archaeological digs in the twentieth century in Afghanistan and Tajikistan. It is also noteworthy that in keeping with the religious tolerance that has always characterized Central Asia, the Kushans allowed Zoroastrianism and Hinduism to flourish alongside Buddhism.

For the first several centuries A.D., then, various groups contended over Central Asia: Huns, Sassanians, Turks, and Chinese, who invaded the Fergana Valley. But the next important series of incursions began around 650, when the first Arabs came, bringing with them the new faith of Islam. During the next hundred years they sent invading forces into Transoxiana, capturing Bukhara and Samarkand. In 751 an Arab army defeated a Chinese army at Talas, in present-day Kyrgyzstan, decisively ending Chinese ambitions and establishing Islam in Central Asia, although the Arabs themselves did not remain to found substantial kingdoms in the region.

Independent Muslim kingdoms sprang up in the oasis cities. The most significant of these was the empire of the Persian Samanids (874–999), who made their capital at Bukhara. With a well-organized bureaucracy and army the Samanids regulated and expanded the Silk Route, spreading the Persian language and making Bukhara a trade, transport, and cultural center of the Islamic world. Physicians such as Ibn Sina, mathematicians like Al Biruni, and poets such as Firdausi ensured that the Samanid court would leave an indelible mark on the development of the Persian language and culture, an importance that would not be eroded in Central Asia for centuries.

The Samanid Empire came to an end with the arrival of a new wave of Turkic tribes. The Ghaznavids (based in Ghazni, Afghanistan) took over Khurasand, the Qarakhanids captured Bukhara, and later the Seljuks arrived to defeat them and conquer Central Asia and Turkey.

By 1055 the Seljuk chief Turhril was standing outside the gates of Baghdad. For the next two hundred years the Seljuks ruled the area from the Pamir Mountains and the borders of China to Iraq, uniting Central Asia with the Persian and Arab worlds for the first time under Turkic hegemony.

The Mongol hordes (*ordas*) were the next to sweep through the region. In 1218 the Seljuks had executed an envoy of the Mongol ruler Genghis Khan and murdered 450 merchants who had been trading with the Mongols. The infuriated Mongols set out to conquer the Seljuks, and historians have subsequently blamed Seljuk high-handedness for the Mongol onslaught that followed. Under Genghis Khan the Mongols captured Bukhara in 1220, killing thirty thousand people. Standing before a pile of heads in Bukhara, Genghis Khan declared, "You ask who I am, who speaks this to you. Know, then, that I am the scourge of God. If you had not sinned God would not have sent me hither to punish you." The Mongols continued eastwards, adding Russia and parts of Eastern Europe to their empire. Then, having conquered this vast area, they settled down to exploit it. They developed the Silk Route, which had broken down during the incessant invasions, building resthouses along the way and instituting a postal service. Under the Mongols it was possible for caravans to travel in safety from Istanbul to present-day Beijing. For the first time since the conquests of Alexander the Great, Europe was linked with Asia. After the death of Genghis Khan, Central Asia was ruled by his son Chagatai, whose descendants divided the region into two khanates: Transoxiana in the west and Turkistan in the east.

The last great explosion out of Central Asia was to leave the most significant cultural influence in the region. Timur (Tamerlane), who did not begin his conquests until he was forty years old, created the first indigenous empire in Central Asia. Timur was a Barlas Turk who had been born near Samarkand, and he made the city his capital in 1369. After he had conquered Central Asia, he added India, Persia, Arabia, and parts of Russia to his empire. Samarkand was already one of the largest cities in the world, with a population of 150,000, and under Timur it became one of the architectural marvels of the world as well, for Timur brought in artisans and architects from all the conquered regions. By now, after almost four hundred years of Turkic rule, the region had become established as the center for Turkic influence in Central Asia and of resistance to Persian cultural and political domination. Timur even replaced Persian with the Jagatai dialect of Turkish as the court language.

The Shaybani Uzbeks, who traced their genealogy back to Uzbek Khan, a grandson of Genghis Khan, created the last of the great nomadic empires in Central Asia. In 1500 they defeated the Timurids (descendants of Timur) and set up their capital in Bukhara. Under Shaybani rule Turkic (Uzbek) language and literature flourished. The great Uzbek poet Mir Alisher Navai (1441–1501) created the first Turkic script, which replaced Persian.

After the sixteenth century, weakened by the decline of the Silk Route as sea routes opened linking Europe to Africa and India, the Shaybani Empire began to erode. Large empires and strong rulers were no longer needed to ensure the safety of the Silk Route, whilst the dramatic loss of income from the traffic in trade meant that rulers were no longer capable of keeping large standing armies and expanding their kingdoms. In addition, the conservative ulema (Islamic scholars, who had enormous influence over daily life) banned innovations in education and science, further marginalizing Central Asia. The Shaybani Empire gradually degenerated into a collection of small, squabbling, city-based fiefdoms. In the seventeenth and eighteenth centuries these emerged as three separate but weak khanates—Khiva, Kokand, and Bukhara—in which the khans (rulers) later established dynasties: the Kungrad in Khiva, the Mangyt in Bukhara, and the Ming in Kokand. The impoverished khans survived by the slave trade and the imposition of exorbitant taxes on the population.

It was inevitable that the tsars, seeking to expand their Russian empire, should eventually look to Central Asia. By 1650 the Russians had annexed Siberia and reached the Pacific Ocean. In the next two centuries Russia moved to conquer the Caucasus and Central Asia. Peter the Great invaded the Kazakh steppe in 1715 and began building Russian forts, the first at Omsk in 1716. By 1750 all the Kazakh khans, who saw the Russians as their best security against the marauding Uzbeks, had signed treaties with Moscow.

The Russian expansion was fueled by the empire's vast military-bureaucratic apparatus, which had subdued the Caucasus and was now without a role even as the tsars eyed the potential resources of Central Asia: minerals and cotton. When the American Civil War (1861–65) cut off vital cotton supplies to Russian factories, the urge to conquer Central Asia was irresistible. At the same time Russia was watching with apprehension the steady expansion of the British Empire in India from Bengal towards Afghanistan. This was the era of the Great Game—the vast power struggle between Russia and Great Britain for control of Asia that used Central Asia and Afghanistan as pawns in their efforts to outmaneuver each other, building influence. At the end of the nineteenth century, Afghanistan was established as an independent buffer between the two empires of Russia and Britain.

In the brief period between 1865 and 1876, Russian armies captured Tashkent and much of modern-day Uzbekistan, Turkmenistan, and Tajikistan, although the border between Afghanistan and Tajikistan remained open, and tribal leaders and bandits frequently took refuge in one another's territories—a tradition that is being revived today amongst the Islamic extremists of Central Asia and the Taliban. The Russians established the province of Turkestan, whose capital was Tashkent and which was ruled by a governor general appointed by Moscow. They left the khanates of Bukhara and Khiva as autonomous political units, dependent on Russia. Whilst the settled regions were easily conquered, the nomadic tribes continued to resist for several decades, and periodic revolts broke out in the Fergana Valley. In 1885 Russian troops crushed a revolt in the valley towns of Osh, Margilan, and Andijan led by a Sufi Dervish, Khan Tura. The most serious threat to Russian rule arose in May 1898, when twenty-two Russian soldiers were killed in Andijan by Islamic rebels. The revolt spread to other towns before Russian troops arrived and brutally quashed the rebellion.

As a way of controlling the region, the Russians began resettling Central Asia with ethnic Russians and Cossacks and turning the rest of the land over to cotton production; in 1891 alone more than a million Russian and Cossack farmers were settled on Kazakh lands adjoining Siberia. The Russians developed large cotton plantations by means of vast irrigation projects. New industries manned by Russian workers were also introduced, and Central Asia was linked with Russia through a railway network that for the first time brought the Russian Empire up to the borders of Afghanistan, Iran, China, and British India.

Tsarist rule ended in a holocaust of suffering for the peoples of Central Asia. In 1916, with the region facing a massive famine, a revolt broke out after Moscow tried to draft Central Asians to fight for the tsarist army in World War I. The government also increased taxes and forcefully appropriated wheat from the region. The Kazakh and Kyrgyz nomads, who saw no reason why they should fight in Europe for the tsar, were the first to rebel, and the revolt soon spread across Central Asia. But as with previous rebellions, tsarist troops brutally suppressed it, killing tens of thousands of people in the process. In the Tian Shan Mountains a Cossack army carried out reprisals against the Kyrgyz, slaughtering flocks, burning down villages, and forcing huge numbers of Kyrgyz to flee across the border into Chinese Turkestan. Even today the Kyrgyz identify the 1916–17 repression as the worst period in their history, in which as much as a quarter of the Kyrgyz population was slaughtered or forced to flee.

But when the Russian Revolution broke out in 1917, Central Asia had no desire to become part of the new Soviet Union. Central Asians resisted Sovietization more fiercely than most other regions, with the Muslim Basmachis ("bandits"), as the Bolsheviks termed them, leading the struggle. By 1929, however, when the Basmachis were finally defeated, the map of Central Asia had been forcibly redrawn into five soviet republics, and the centuries of wars for control of the region seemed to have come to an end. That too was to change.[3]

Islam in Central Asia

The people of Central Asia are predominantly Sunni Muslims of the Hannafi sect. Shia Muslims make up a small minority in some of the great trading cities, like Bukhara and Samarkand, as well as in Tajikistan, where the Ismaeli sect, whose spiritual leader is the Aga Khan, can be found in the Gorno-Badakhshan region of the Pamir Mountains. (The Ismaelis also occupy adjacent areas south of the Pamirs in modern-day Afghanistan and Pakistan.) Since 1991 Central Asia has also seen a meteoric rise of militant Islamic sects, each with its own brand of orthodoxy and sharia (Islamic law), and this phenomenon has obscured one of the most important aspects of traditional Central Asian Islam—its tolerance. Characterized by major advances in philosophy, ethics, legal codes, and scientific research under largely liberal political rulers, and spread through a vast region by Arabs, Mongols, and Turks, the Islam of Central Asia took many forms. Early Central Asian Muslims coexisted in relative peace not only with one another but also with the Jews, Buddhists, Hindus, Zoroastrians, and Nestorian Christians who had established pockets of civilization in the region.

Perhaps the most important Islamic movement to arise in Central Asia was Sufism: a form of Islamic mysticism that preached direct communion with God and tolerance towards all other forms of worship. Sufism originated in Central Asia and Persia soon after the Arab invasions. The name derives from the rough woolen cloaks worn by the early Sufi brothers (*sufi* means "wool" in Arabic), who inherited some of the symbols of pre-Islamic nomadic mystics. The Sufis encouraged popular participation in Islam through their opposition to authority, intellectualism, and the mullahs (clergy). Sufis urged all Muslims to experience God directly, without the intervention of priests or scholars—an important factor in the spread of Islam amongst Central Asia's sparse, nomadic population. The Sufi orders, or *tariqas* ("the way"), are best defined as "brotherhood[s] of Sufis who have a common pedigree of spiritual masters, . . . in which elders initiate disciples and grant them formal permission to continue a common school of thought and practice."[4] Sufis invoke God through the *zikr*, vocal (or sometimes silent) prayers, chants, songs, and even whirling dances, which the Dervishes—another Sufi sect—perfected into an art form. Many of the tariqas evolved into secret societies with their own codes of behavior and prayer. The tariqas played a major role in reviving Islam in the thirteenth century after the Mongol destruction, and they continued to sustain Islamic faith and practice centuries later in the Soviet era, when Islam was driven underground by the authorities.

The most important tariqas are Naqshbandiyya, Qadiriyya, Yasawiyya, and Kubrawiyya. The Qadiriyya, probably the oldest extant order, was founded by Abd al-Qadir. A minor tariqa in Baghdad in the twelfth century, the Qadiriyya moved to Central Asia, becoming particularly strong during the thirteenth century, and then spread to Afghanistan and India. Central Asian Qadiris were centered mainly in the cities of Transoxiana. Kubra, the founder of Kubrawiyya, was martyred in the Mongol massacres in Central Asia in 1221. The Kubrawiyya order took strong hold in Khorezm (present-day Uzbekistan). The Yasawiyya order was founded by the poet and mystic Ahmed Yasawi, who died in 1166 and is buried in southern Kazakhstan. Their main influence was in the Fergana Valley and amongst the southern Turkic tribes. Muhammad ibn Baha ad-Din Naqshband (1317–89), the founder of the Naqshbandiyya tariqa, is still the most revered mystic and saint in Central Asia and Afghanistan. Even today his tomb outside Bukhara is the most important place of pilgrimage in Central Asia. Unlike other Sufi sects the Naqshbandis, though mystics, believe in active missionary work and political activism; many led revolts against the tsar and the Communists. The leader of the 1898 revolt in Andijan was a Naqshbandi.

The Sufi orders spread their message to China via the Fergana Valley and to India and the Arab world through Afghanistan. Sufi spiritual leaders, especially the Naqshbandis, vied with the traditional ulema, who tended to be fiercely opposed to them, for influence amongst local rulers. And influence they had: the rulers of the Turkic dynasties would seek validation for their rule from the leading Sufi saints. The relationship of ruler and mystic, in the words of Islamic scholar Bruce Lawrence, tended to be "fraught with tension," for Sufi mystics saw themselves as eternal rulers, more powerful than the most autocratic temporal ruler.[5] In the eighteenth and nineteenth centuries the leading Naqshbandi families (leadership in the sect was frequently passed down from father to son) served as political advisers and spiritual guides to many of the khans who governed the increasingly fragmented Central Asia. Some of these Sufi families became rulers themselves. Many became rich and corrupt in the process, one of the reasons for the Jadid reforms in the nineteenth century. In the twentieth century Naqshbandi political activism played a major role in influencing militant Islamic movements in Afghanistan, Chechnya, and most recently the Fergana Valley.

But beyond the oasis towns and valleys, the spread of Islam on the Central Asian steppe was slow and sporadic. Islam did not come to the Kazakh steppe until the seventeenth century, and even then the predominant Sufism incorporated ancient shamanistic traditions of the nomadic culture, such as the veneration of animals and nature. Although Zoroastrianism, the religion of the Persian kings, was discouraged by the Islamic invaders, elements continued to thrive on the steppe, taking on an Islamic coloring, as well as in Iran and India. Thus, early on in the history of Islam two branches of the religion emerged in Central Asia: the traditional, conservative, scholarly Islam of the settled areas and the oasis cultures that was dominated by local rulers and the ulema, and the much looser, less restrictive Islam of the nomads that still favored Sufism and pre-Islamic traditions. As historian Fernand Braudel noted, "Islam is essentially an urban religion. So Islam consists of a few densely populated regions, separated by vast stretches of empty space."[6] Even today the nomadic Kazakh, Kyrgyz, and Turkmen tribes are far less Islamicized—and much less susceptible to Islamic radicalism—than their ethnic counterparts in the settled oasis areas.

The Arabs who brought Islam to Central Asia were soon displaced by Persian and Turkic tribes, each of whom adopted Islam. Of the two, for many centuries Persian was the dominant influence, lasting until the Safavid dynasty came to power in Persia around 1500. The Safavids changed Persia's state religion from Sunni to Shia Islam—a step that considerably reduced Persian influence in Central Asia. In addition, Persia became preoccupied with combating the challenge of the Ottoman power in Turkey on its western borders, and Persian leaders therefore paid less attention to Central Asia.

Nevertheless, the earlier Persian empires had left an enormous legacy in Central Asia in the arts, language, poetry, and sciences. Not until the Shaybani Uzbeks, who aggressively made their empire more Turkic, did Persian control and influence in Central Asia wane. The only vestiges of Persian ethnicity remaining in Central Asia today are the Tajiks, who speak Persian and are proud of their Persian culture and heritage. But the tension between Persian and Turkic culture continues, both in the competition for influence in Central Asia between Iran and Turkey and in the ongoing disputes between Tajikistan and Turkic Uzbekistan over Tajiks in Uzbekistan and Uzbeks in Tajikistan, and over borders. Many Tajiks assert that the cities of Bukhara and Samarkand, which Stalin handed over to Uzbekistan, should rightfully belong to Tajikistan for they are Tajik cultural and historical centers.

Central Asian Islam became less dynamic under the tsars, not because Central Asia's new Russian masters tried to interfere with the Islamic clergy, law, or practices but because they wooed them with modern advances: industry, education, technology. The Russians also supported the ultra-conservative ulema, whilst at the same time settling millions of ethnic Russians in the region to try and make good Russians out of Central Asians.

But the new colonial masters were only partly successful. The introduction of Western ideas and sciences paved the way for a modernist reinterpretation of Islam by the Jadids, a reform sect of Tartars whose inspiration was Ismail Bay Gasprinski (1851–1914), founder of the influential Tartar-language newspaper *Tercuman* in 1883. Based on *Usul-i-jadid* (new educational principles), Jadidism was one of the many intellectual Islamic reform movements that swept the colonized Muslim world in the late nineteenth century. All sought in varying degrees to reconcile the problems associated with exposure to Western modernism with Muslim religion and culture, particularly for Muslims who lived in colonies ruled by non-Muslims. These movements, in India, Egypt, Turkey, and Afghanistan, were primarily anticolonial and pan-Islamic, but they also advocated religious reform, modern education, and an understanding of the sciences.

Jadid teachers and scholars in Tashkent and the Fergana Valley founded new schools with modern curricula: math, the sciences, theater, poetry, and Russian and Turkic literature, as well as traditional Islamic subjects. They staged plays and operas and published a number of newspapers that helped revive the Turkic languages and develop a modern Turkic culture. The literature they generated analyzed local history, culture, and politics in a modern way for the first time. This embrace of modernism brought the Jadids into conflict not just with the Russians but also with the ulema, whom they considered reactionary and obscurantist. For their part the Russians had encouraged the ulema to continue their practice of a conservative interpretation of the sharia as a way of countering anti-Russian Islamic and nationalist movements.

For all their success the Jadids remained an intellectual rather than a mass movement, divided over ideology and politics. When the 1917 revolution came, some Jadids backed the Bolsheviks because they sought to throw over the tsarist empire and saw in the Communist ideology a chance of greater freedom, the adoption of modern ideas, and education whilst others resisted them because of their lack of respect for Islam. The Jadids who joined the Communist Party after 1917 played a critical role in helping build indigenous Communist parties in Central Asia, but it did them little good. The Soviets termed the Jadids bourgeois reformers and banned their literature. When Stalin came to power he began a steady purge of Jadids; the last Jadids were eliminated in the massacres of 1937. During the brief cultural flowering after independence in 1991, Uzbek intellectuals attempted to republish and popularize Jadid writings, but they were quickly suppressed. Uzbek President Islam Karimov discourages all attempts to renew interest in Jadidism, although the movement has immense relevance in today's discussion of the way Islam, nationalism, and democracy can coexist in Central Asia.

3   Islam Underground in the Soviet Union

WHEN THE BOLSHEVIKS seized power in St. Petersburg and Moscow in 1917, Central Asia was already in deep ferment as a result of the acute famine of 1916–17, the suppression by tsarist troops of revolts against conscription, and the growing politicization of the population and strong anti-Russian feeling fomented by Islamic intellectuals. Initial support for the Bolsheviks came only in Tashkent, where the large ethnic Russian working class and some Muslims set up the Tashkent Soviet. Tashkent Bolsheviks created the Turkestan Autonomous Soviet Socialist Republic in April 1918, but it controlled little beyond the city.

In 1917 the Bolsheviks had published a declaration of rights, granting all national groups the right to self-determination. Potentially the Bolsheviks' best chance to win support from the millions of non-Russians in the former tsarist empire, the declaration also gave Muslims the freedom to practice Islam.

However, in Central Asia, at least, it quickly became apparent that the theory of self-determination was going to be defined extremely narrowly. It was not based on actual self-determination or the right of secession for non-Russian national groups. Instead, self-determination would be the right of only one class, the proletariat—and there was no Central Asian proletariat at the time. The Bolsheviks were prepared to acknowledge "rights" of self-determination only if they did not undermine the status of Greater Russia; the Russian proletariat could decide not to be part of the tsarist empire by overthrowing the government, but the non-Russian regions could not decide to secede from the Bolshevik empire that was taking its place. A Western writer who was in Tashkent in 1918 later summed up the situation: "The Bolshevik program included self-determination and the native Mohammedan population considered that this referred to them with their 95% majority. They soon discovered that self-determination in the Bolshevik view did not refer to Turkestan."[1]

The Brief Flowering of Ideological Ferment

Nevertheless, the revolution created intense political debate, and for a time there was a mass reawakening amongst the different peoples of the former tsarist empire, in which many divergent political trends and ideas emerged. (Significantly, many of them have reemerged in one form or another since independence.) For the first time Central Asians discovered nationalism and began to consider the benefits of forging a greater commonality of interest within their own clans and ethnic groups. Coupled with Islamic revival—also prevalent at that time—this nationalist fervor was translated into a number of new political movements.

Pan-Turkism, advocated by the Jadids and other urban intellectuals, sought to unite the Turkic-speaking peoples of Central Asia into a single state, Turkistan, that would be free of Russian control and governed by Islamic precepts. Amongst the nomadic ethnic groups a form of tribal or clan nationalism emerged. The Kazakh ordas, for example, created Alash Orda, a political party that was actually allowed to govern much of the Kazakh steppe from 1917 to 1920.

Alash Orda's nationalism was both anti-Russian and opposed to ethnic groups regarded as oppressors of the Kazakhs, such as the Uzbeks. Meanwhile, the traditional ulema and mullahs, who had been left alone under the tsars, feared a loss of power in either a Bolshevik or an ethnic nationalist state. Nonetheless, they too saw a political opportunity in the turmoil of the times and called for the creation of an Islamic state governed by sharia (Islamic law).

Some Central Asian Muslims even embraced communism. When the Bolsheviks summoned Muslim organizations to a major congress at Baku, Azerbaijan, in 1920, Muslim delegates, adopting the slogan East Is Not West, Muslims Are Not Russians, demanded that they be allowed to set up a Muslim Communist Party. The foremost advocate of the new Muslim party was Mir Said Sultan Galiev, a Tartar journalist and writer from Kazan who joined the Bolsheviks and helped enlist 250,000 Muslims into the Red Army to fight the tsarist (White) forces still rampaging through Central Asia and the Caucasus. Galiev believed that the national struggle had to supersede the class struggle in Central Asia and that only a separate Muslim Communist party and army could prevail against Russian chauvinism. He tried to persuade the Bolsheviks that Marxism and Islam could coexist as long as Muslims were given some degree of autonomy.[2]

The Bolsheviks tolerated such ideas only until they had won the civil war against the White armies in 1923. They then set out to reconquer Central Asia and enforce single-party rule. They arrested not only Galiev but everyone else who opposed Bolshevik orthodoxy—Muslim Communists, Jadids, mullahs, clan and tribal leaders, and nationalists like the Alash Orda leaders. The reconquest of Central Asia was accomplished at the expense of thousands of lives. In later events, such as Stalin's forced land-resettlement and collectivization programs (in which nomadism was virtually wiped out), the political purges, and the suppression of Islam, millions more died.

Whilst in other colonial states in the Muslim world Islamicists grappled with new political ideas that involved throwing off their colo-

34

nial yoke and creating independent Muslim states, in Central Asia one form of colonialism replaced another. The ferment of ideas between 1917 and 1923—in particular the debate about how Islam should evolve alongside the competing ideologies of communism, nationalism, Pan-Turkism, and modernism—subsided after the Bolshevik reconquest. The resultant political vacuum was soon filled by the official state party, the Russian Communist Party (Bolshevik) (later renamed the Communist Party of the Soviet Union). For the next seven decades Central Asia was cut off from contact with the outside world, as the Soviet Union closed its borders with Iran, Turkey, Afghanistan, and, later, China. Until perestroika in the 1980s began to open some of these closed channels, Central Asians learned nothing about the political ideas that shaped the twentieth century, including developments in Islamic thinking and political movements that were going on just across the border. When independence finally came, in 1991, the Central Asians, ideologically speaking, were still back in the 1920s. The crisis in Central Asia today is directly related to this stunted political and ideological growth, which the Communists ensured by their actions in 1923 and afterwards.

Sovietization had not come about unopposed, however, even amongst the peasants and working class. In February 1918 an Islamic revolt led by mullahs and clan leaders erupted. The first of the Basmachi rebellions, it consisted of a number of independent guerrilla groups in regions as far apart as Turkmenistan and Tajikistan. These Muslim groups were fighting for a variety of causes: jihad, sharia, Turkic nationalism, anticommunism. Throughout the sporadic fighting that continued until 1929, the Basmachi leaders remained divided by clan and tribal loyalties, and never developed a coherent leadership or ideology. This divisiveness weakened their ability to stand up to the Soviets, although individual leaders and bands kept the rebellion going for more than ten years. Muhammad Qurban Junaid Khan, a wealthy landlord belonging to the Yomut tribe who was appointed paramount leader of the Turkmen tribes, waged a heroic resistance until 1927, when he was forced into exile in Afghanistan. The Basmachis were supported in their revolt by the British, who sought to undermine Soviet power and sent the Basmachis camel caravans of arms and ammunition from India.

The last of the Basmachi rebellions was finally put down in 1929, in Tajikistan. Many Basmachi leaders, and tens of thousands of their Uzbek, Tajik, and Turkmen supporters, fled to Afghanistan. Fifty years later Basmachi ideals once more sparked rebellion, this time motivating the Afghan Mujahedeen to resist the Soviet invasion of Afghanistan. History repeated itself, too, in the response of Great Britain, now joined by the United States, who backed a clandestine program to undermine the Central Asian regimes by supporting the Mujahedeen in the hope of stirring up Islamic unrest—and hence political rebellion—in Soviet Central Asia.

The Repression of Islam

Whilst the Basmachi revolts were still simmering across Central Asia, Stalin decided that the best way to quell unrest was to isolate the rebels. He consequently redrew the map of Turkestan, dividing the region into five socialist republics and demarcating borders not along geographical or ethnic lines but in ways that seemed likeliest to suppress dissent.

The Fergana Valley was split amongst three republics, and borders were created to divide clans, villages, and ethnic groups. The Tajiks were given their own republic, but its distinguishing feature was that it did not contain the Tajik cultural and economic centers, Bukhara and Samarkand, which went to Uzbekistan. Meanwhile, numerous Tajiks in other cities found themselves residents of republics that were dominated by other ethnic groups. The Turkmen republic was for decades governed entirely by Russians. Far from ending dissent, these artificial divisions became the source of many of the ethnic conflicts, border and water disputes, and infrastructure problems that plague Central Asia today.

The collectivization of the late 1920s and the 1930s, like the crushing of Islamic resistance, targeted the freewheeling Kazakh, Kyrgyz, and Turkmen nomads. Tens of thousands of Kazakhs and Kyrgyz fled to China during the forced collectivization of their livestock in 1930–31. According to some experts Kazakhstan lost 1.5 million people through migration, murder, starvation, or other causes—one-third its entire population. Herdsmen would kill their livestock rather than see it appropriated by the state. The number of cattle in Kazakhstan shrank from 7.4 million head in 1929 to 1.6 million in 1933, the number of sheep from 22 million to 1.7 million.[3] Many Kyrgyz nomads had already fled to China in 1924, when the Red Army arrived to carry out a census of their flocks and herds. A European witness recorded the flight of half a million Kyrgyz with their herds of yaks, horses, camels, and sheep to China. "To an enormous distance I could see camel train after camel train; the entire horde was on trek, flying from officials of the Soviets. . . . I little suspected at the time that I had been the witness of the last march of the free Kyrgyz."[4] In the ten years between 1917 and 1927, an estimated one-quarter of the Kyrgyz population died.

However, for all the repression they bought, the Soviets also carried out progressive reforms, in the availability of mass education and health care, the growth of industry, the development of mechanized methods of farming and irrigation, and the creation of a communications infrastructure that was fully integrated with Russia. Of course, the point of these improvements was to enable Central Asia's produce, raw materials, and minerals to flow into Russia. Central Asia thus became a colony for Russian industry and, later, for its excess population, as millions of Russians were forcibly resettled in Central Asia to farm the land and run the factories.

Having consolidated their power, the Soviets launched punitive campaigns to eliminate the practice of Islam in Central Asia. The Communist Party considered all religious observance "bourgeois

37

decadence" and had already clamped down on all religions in the new Communist Russia. However, Islam was particularly targeted because it was considered backward and reactionary, and because the Soviets feared it, having seen during the Basmachi revolt that it had the potential to create a nationalist and religious resistance to Communist rule. They depicted Islam as a reactionary, mullah-led force supported by British imperialists that was trying to undermine the revolution and prevent progress and education.

Mosques were shut down and converted into workshops, Muslim worship and ceremonies were banned, women were forbidden to wear the veil, and children were not allowed to read the Koran. Even the collectivization programs had a strong anti-Islam content. Whereas in 1917 there had been some twenty thousand mosques in the Russian Empire, by 1929 less than four thousand were operative, and by 1935 only sixty registered mosques remained in Uzbekistan, four in Turkmenistan, and twenty in Kazakhstan. Millions of people had no local mosque to attend, whilst madrassahs were banned altogether.[5]

Ironically, the situation improved slightly after Hitler invaded the Soviet Union in 1941. Needing everyone he could get for the war effort, Stalin appeased the Muslims by setting up four Islamic spiritual directorates—carefully organized to allow Moscow to mobilize and better control the Muslim population at the same time. The Islamic Directorate for Central Asia and Kazakhstan was based in Tashkent; the others were located in Ufa, Russia (European Russia and Siberia), Baku, Azerbaijan (Transcaucasia), and Buinaksk, Dagestan (Northern Caucasus). During the war years Central Asia also benefited from the large-scale development of industry, for Stalin had the Russian factories moved brick by brick from the front lines to Central Asia, to be safe from German bombing.

But Stalin was also using Central Asia as a dumping ground for entire ethnic groups the Soviets considered potential German sympathizers. These populations were removed en masse from the Caucasus and Ukraine. On February 23, 1944, Stalin deported half a million Chechens to Central Asia and Siberia, a third of whom died in transit or whilst in exile. As with the creation of the Central Asian republics, these policies later accentuated ethnic tensions in the region, causing problems that continue today.

Once World War II ended, the repression against Islam continued. Even before war's end, in May 1944, the government had created the Council for Affairs of Religious Cults by special decree, which later became the leading Soviet state organ dealing with Islam and Muslims. By its means, the Soviets had reduced Islam to the legal status of a cult. As Moscow launched a powerful campaign to eliminate all vestiges of Islamic culture and practice even more mosques were closed down. Although there was a brief period of liberalization between 1955 and 1958 under Nikita Khrushchev as part of his campaign to liberalize some of Stalin's harsh policies, another crackdown soon followed.

In the 1960s, however, the Soviets tried a new tack. Seeking to win support for Soviet foreign policy in the wider Muslim world, Moscow had to show that it tolerated Islam in its own country, specifically in Central Asia. A policy that came to be known by its critics as "official Islam" was developed, and the government opened two "official" madrassahs, in Tashkent and Bukhara, in which mullahs would train in both Islamic and Soviet studies. These state-approved mullahs would then be appointed to a registered mosque. Some students were allowed to go abroad (usually to Al Azhar University in Cairo) for further study. Muslim holy days were respected, and a few Muslims were even allowed to perform the hajj (pilgrimage to Mecca) and visit other Muslim shrines in the Middle East. The Soviets invited foreign Muslim dignitaries to Tashkent to see how compatible Islam was with socialism.

The last anti-Islamic crusade was launched by Mikhail Gorbachev under his "liberalizing" program of perestroika, in which Islam was perceived as the enemy of modernization and a rallying point for anti-Russian feelings amongst Central Asia's ethnic groups. Gorbachev's own anti-Muslim views were reinforced by the Central Asian leaders, who feared that any Islamic revival amongst the population would lead to demands for greater democracy and freedom, posing a threat to their grip on power.

Islam Underground

But throughout the Soviet period it was the "unofficial" Islam that sustained the true faith, even though it had gone underground. Unregistered mosques flourished clandestinely; if a mosque was closed down by the authorities, another would spring up somewhere else. It is estimated that Uzbekistan had six hundred unregistered mosques in 1945, whilst Tajikistan had more than five hundred shrines, served by seven hundred unregistered mullahs, where tens of thousands of people would gather on holy days. People ran madrassahs in their homes, joined together to pray and perform religious ceremonies at night, and visited shrines and tombs—camouflaging their visits by going during Communist holidays. Underground mosques and madrassahs appeared in graveyards, where both the living and the dead could be attended to.

Itinerant mullahs and fakirs carried religious rites from region to region, surviving through donations from the communities they visited. By 1960 it was estimated that there were some six thousand unregistered mullahs in Tajikistan alone. The Fergana Valley was also a center for itinerant mullahs, who spent their lives crossing the length and breadth of Central Asia, avoiding the authorities. The valley also hosted a large number of clandestine home madrassahs. Children from all over Central Asia came to Fergana to study.[6]

The Sufi secret societies, or tariqas, contributed enormously to the survival of Islam during this period, and itinerant preachers did much to increase Sufi numbers and popularity. The well-organized Sufi sects clandestinely published religious literature, which was widely circulated. This samizdat literature, similar to the writings produced by Soviet dissidents in Russia, has largely been ignored by Western and Islamic scholars.

Even within the local Communist parties, some officials continued to hire mullahs and Sufis secretly to perform Islamic rites for important occasions—marriages, births, and deaths. (Mixed marriages with Russians were rare except amongst the educated Kazakh and Kyrgyz city dwellers, who were less religious.) In 1989 I attended one such clandestine Muslim wedding at a collective farm in the Fergana Valley. The marriage was registered at the local Communist Party office, as the law demanded, and the bride dressed in white. But after the couple returned home, the bride changed into traditional Uzbek costume, and an unregistered mullah solemnized the wedding according to Islamic law. That night a sheep was slaughtered in secrecy, and everyone stayed up cooking, dancing, and singing. The marriage feast was held at the crack of dawn to avoid the security police—but the local Uzbek Communist Party officials had been invited as well, and they joined the farmworkers in the traditional wedding pilaf. Everyone then went to work, pretending they had just woken up. The dowry and bride price, banned under Soviet law, were paid by the boy's family in jewelry, furniture, and sheep rather than cash.

Women also played a major role in keeping Islam alive. Not only were they leaders in sustaining Islamic traditions and culture in the home, but they also secretly served, cleaned, and maintained the Sufi shrines, where people would gather on weekends to pray. In the 1990s I visited several of these Sufi shrines in the Pamir Mountains. I noticed that the local villagers treated the women who had maintained them during the worst days of Soviet oppression with enormous respect and devotion.

The Soviet authorities in Moscow either pretended to ignore what was going on under their noses or, more likely, had little idea of the continuance and spread of Islam amongst the population. Local members of the Central Asian Communist parties who were Muslims themselves certainly knew about the underground Islam, but they kept their knowledge secret from Moscow. In part, they did not wish to annoy their fellow citizens and the mullahs, but they also took great pride in snubbing the Russians. The Soviets were never able to bridge the gap between the Muslim and the non-Muslim world, any more than they bridged the gulf between Russians and Central Asian ethnic groups.

Islam played a key role in sustaining the clan, regional, and ethnic solidarity amongst the people of Central Asia. Whilst the Communist system set out to destroy such vestiges of the past, the local Communist parties—many of whose members were Muslims—were in reality built on regional and clan alliances. In Uzbekistan the traditional rivalries between the Uzbek elites from regions such as Samarkand, Tashkent, and the Fergana Valley continued unabated even within the Communist Party of Uzbekistan, where the Central Committee had to balance regional representation in all its appointments. In Kazakhstan and Kyrgyzstan the local Communist parties also maintained a fine balance between the different ordas, whilst in Turkmenistan the three largest tribes were given due representation in the Communist Party. In Tajikistan, with its high mountains and isolated valleys, the mix of Uzbeks and Tajiks created a sharp regionalization of clans and ethnic groups. The collectivization of land into single large farms did nothing to halt this process; instead, collective farms became a means to enforce clan solidarity by employing peasants from a single clan or region.

The Rise of Islamic Militancy Under Perestroika

In the mid-1980s President Mikhail Gorbachev unveiled his policy of perestroika (restructuring), with its liberal—or at least more liberal—social and political policies. These did not include lifting restrictions against religious practices, but people all across Russia interpreted this differently, and there was an immediate revival in all the religions. In particular, the Soviet nomenklatura (ruling elite) were shocked to discover that one of the first consequences of this move was a sudden explosion of interest in Islam in Central Asia. Thousands of mosques were built, Korans and other Islamic literature were brought in from Saudi Arabia and Pakistan and distributed free amongst the population, and itinerant mullahs became public prayer leaders overnight in collective farms and villages.

The main reason for this "explosion" was, of course, that Islam had never disappeared, not even during the worst repression of the Soviet era. The more the Soviets tried to stamp it out, the more it spread throughout Central Asia as an act of ethnic and regional as well as religious resistance. But there were external factors as well that contributed to the revival of Islam in this period. And these new factors led to a disturbing new trend in Central Asian Islam, one that is still dominant—the rise of Islamic militancy. Significantly, this new Islamicism was based on ideas from the Islamic world outside Central Asia rather than an outgrowth of traditional Central Asian Islam.

In the 1980s thousands of Central Asians were drafted into the Red Army to fight the Afghan Mujahedeen, who were still resisting the 1979 invasion of their country by the Soviet Union. Central Asian Muslims were thus reintroduced to the wider *umma* (Muslim world) through a war against their coreligionists, and many were deeply affected by the Islamic dedication of their opponents. Central Asian soldiers who were taken prisoner often joined the Mujahedeen. As the war continued, it grew broader in scope, drawing in the United States, Great Britain, Pakistan, and Saudi Arabia, amongst other interested parties.

In 1986 the secret services of the United States, Great Britain, and Pakistan agreed on a plan to launch guerrilla attacks into Tajikistan and Uzbekistan, which were supplying the Soviet troops in Afghanistan. Afghan Mujahedeen units crossed the Amu Darya

River in March 1987 and launched rocket attacks against villages in Tajikistan. Meanwhile, hundreds of Uzbek and Tajik Muslims clandestinely traveled to Pakistan and Saudi Arabia to study in madrassahs or to train as guerrilla fighters so that they could join the Mujahedeen. This was part of a wider U.S., Pakistani, and Saudi plan to recruit radical Muslims from around the world to fight with the Afghans. Between 1982 and 1992 thirty-five thousand Muslim radicals from forty-three Islamic countries fought for the Mujahedeen. Tens of thousands more studied in the thousands of new government-funded madrassahs in Pakistan. Eventually more than a hundred thousand Muslim radicals from around the world had direct contact with Pakistan and Afghanistan.

But soon these Muslims began to envision a fight beyond Afghanistan. During the late 1980s leading Deobandi madrassahs in Pakistan began to reserve places specifically for Central Asian radicals, who received a free education and a living allowance. Before long every Deobandi madrassah boasted a large contingent of Central Asian students who had arrived clandestinely, without passports or visas, and were given scholarships. These students were being prepared for a larger war; Uzbek and Tajik radicals whom I met in Afghanistan in 1989 were convinced that an Afghan victory would lead to Islamic revolutions throughout Central Asia.[7]

The sect in which they were training, Deobandism, was a Sunni Islamic revivalist sect that had been established in British India in the nineteenth century. Along with several other branches of Sunni Islam, Deobandism helped radicalize Islamic thought in Pakistan, Afghanistan, and later the Fergana Valley. Deobandis abhorred Shiaism and took a restrictive view of the role of women, but their most significant ideological contribution to Sunni Islam was the reintroduction of jihad in the latter half of the twentieth century. The concept of jihad had previously been dominated by Shia Iran following the Iranian revolution. In the 1990s, however, Pakistan's Deobandi madrassahs played a major role in educating the Taliban leadership, and jihad was a key part of their program. But Deobandism met with resistance amongst other Central Asian Muslims, even militant ones. Whereas the Deobandi-Taliban influence over the new generation of Islamic militants who later formed the Islamic Movement of Uzbekistan played a key role in the evolution of the IMU's political ideology and its ideas on jihad, Tajikistan's Islamic opposition was inspired by the Afghan Tajik military commander Ahmad Shah Masood, whose Islamic model was closely linked to Tajik nationalism. Thus the long-standing split between Uzbek and Tajik—Turkic and Persian—in Central Asia continued to play out even in the realm of the new ideologies of radical Islam. The Uzbek militants gravitated to the radicalism of the Pakistan-Afghan Pashtuns led first by Gulbuddin Hekmatyar and later by the Taliban; the Tajiks saw their model within the Afghan Tajik milieu. And both Pakistan and Afghanistan continued to involve themselves in spreading Islamic radical ideas in Central Asia.

The other major Sunni Islamic sect that began to find a foothold in Central Asia as a result of the Afghan war and the later collapse of the Soviet Union was Wahhabism. The strict Wahhabi creed has its roots in the eighteenth-century movement under Abdul Wahab of Saudi Arabia to eliminate Sufism amongst the Arab bedouin. In the twentieth century the Saudi royal family adopted Wahhabism as state law, and after the oil boom in the 1970s, Saudi Arabia made spreading Wahhabism a major plank of its foreign policy. Although Wahhabis had first arrived in Central Asia in 1912, when a native of Medina, Sayed Shari Muhammad, set up Wahhabi cells in the Fergana Valley, the austere creed—which opposed not only Sufism but worship at shrines—was never particularly popular, for it broke with the moderate Islamic traditions of Central Asia. But in the 1980s, as Saudi funds flowed to Wahhabi leaders of the Afghan Mujahedeen and later of Central Asia (many of whom trained in Saudi madrassahs), Wahhabism began to play an increasingly influential role in these regions.

As they have done to exacerbate so many of the problems of Central Asia, the regimes of the various republics have given Wahhabism a boost by their shortsighted, tyrannical reaction to it. In 1992, for example, the Uzbek government began to label anyone who was perceived to be an adherent of radical Islam or held anti-government sentiments as part of his Islamic beliefs, a Wahhabi. By 1997 the government was labeling as Wahhabis even ordinary Muslims who practiced Islam in unofficial mosques or engaged in private prayer or study. Any Muslim who associated with unregistered prayer leaders or taught children how to read the Koran was also termed a Wahhabi. Today the government uses *Wahhabi* to undermine all Muslim believers by associating them with the Wahhabis' record of extremism. Such mislabeling, whilst demonstrating the lack of real knowledge about Islam amongst the ruling elites, enables them to suppress all Islamic activity merely by naming it Wahhabi. But it has also given the sect a popular mystique, allowing Muslims to regard Wahhabis as persecuted Muslim faithful, that goes far to overcome its lack of compatibility with Central Asian Islam and keeps the movement vital in the region.

Central Asia in the Waning Years of the Soviet Union

On December 12, 1991, the presidents of the five Central Asian Soviet republics—Nursultan Nazarbayev of Kazakhstan, Rakhmon Nabiev of Tajikistan, Askar Akayev of Kyrgyzstan, Islam Karimov of Uzbekistan, and Saparmurad Niyazov of Turkmenistan—sat down together in Ashgabat, the capital of Turkmenistan, to discuss the crisis that had erupted a continent away. Four days earlier Presidents Boris Yeltsin of Russia, Leonid Kravchuk of Ukraine, and Stanislav Shuskevich of Belarus (formerly Byelorrussia) had signed the Minsk Treaty, which formally disbanded the Soviet Union and created a new Commonwealth of Independent States (CIS). The Slavic presidents had not bothered to consult with their counterparts in Central Asia before taking this momentous step.

As I watched the presidents arrive at Ashgabat airport that cold, snowy evening, I could detect even from a distance their sense of anger, betrayal, and frustration. They knew that the Russia on which they had come to depend had now abandoned them. Since the August 1991 coup attempt against President Mikhail Gorbachev, the Central Asian leaders had been in the forefront of the hard-liners, demanding that a strong center be preserved even as the Soviet Union was dissolving. They were deeply concerned that the republics' security, economics, and social services—all of which were completely enmeshed with Russia's—would be destroyed if the Soviet Union fell apart. Now it had happened.

At the end of their meeting, the Central Asian leaders announced that the republics would be willing to join the CIS as long as they were granted complete equality with the other member nations. In fact, they begged Russia to let them into the new group. Ten days later, on December 21, in Almaty, then the capital of Kazakhstan, a new CIS was formed, comprising eleven of the fifteen former Soviet republics. (The three Baltic republics and Georgia refused to join.) Thus in three rapid historical transformations spanning a single century, the Central Asian people had been forcefully absorbed into tsarist Russia, forcefully Sovietized into socialist republics, and forcefully reorganized into independent republics. The only difference was that whereas the first two transformations had been bloody, the third was peaceful.

The mood amongst the Central Asian leaders was one of mourning rather than celebration, however. By millions of threads, from electricity grids to oil pipelines to roads and military bases, the Central Asian states were tied to Russia. Their industry and agriculture depended on Russian imports whilst their exports went mainly to Russian markets. Every international telephone line to Central Asia went through Moscow. The republics had no independent armed forces, and many of the poorer states, such as Tajikistan, survived on Soviet subsidies, which would now be cut off. But the Central Asian

47

leaders tried to put a brave face on the crisis, calling for a Central Asian common market and community to save them from what they feared could be individual state ruin.

The men chosen to lead these new republics were deeply conservative Communists, whose view of the outside world had depended on Moscow. They had reviled Gorbachev's attempts at reform because anything that weakened the centralized government would also threaten their power bases and stir up dormant nationalism amongst their people. Brought up and educated in the Soviet system, many could not even speak their national language. Their privileges and promotions depended on Moscow; their security lay in the presence of the Soviet army, which now threatened to withdraw; their economies rested on trade ties to the Soviet Union; and the only thing keeping their underfunded social systems, such as education and health facilities, functioning was massive Soviet financial aid.

The Central Asian leaders dreaded independence from Moscow as much as their people welcomed it. Now each faced the prospect of running an autonomous country and would have to deal with problems of inflation, job creation, economic development, foreign policy, and security. The crisis they faced worsened when millions of Russians, who held critical jobs in the army, bureaucracy, and the economic sectors of all five of the republics, began to migrate back to Russia. An enormous management crisis blew up in the Central Asian states.

But what frightened these leaders most was the challenge of dealing with public expectations about political freedom, free expression, democracy, and Islam. Gorbachev's attempts to open up the Soviet system had exposed Central Asians to new political ideas and new religious trends. Amongst the ideas taking hold were Western-style democracy, advocated by Russian liberals and influenced by the struggles of the Baltic Republics; Pan-Turkism, whose adherents hoped to create a unified Turkic state from the borders of China to Turkey; free market capitalism; and Islamic fundamentalism, which sought to impose sharia. Gorbachev had unwittingly opened a Pandora's Box, which the Central Asian leaders desperately wanted to shut again.

One of the problems facing these men was that none of them had had long to consolidate his power. Gorbachev's accession to power in March 1985 had coincided with the loss within the space of four years of all five of the first secretaries of the Central Asian Communist parties. Each had enjoyed close to twenty years of undisputed power, but by the end of 1986 all five had either died or been ousted from their positions of power. Grasping what appeared at first to be an ideal opportunity to bring Central Asia more firmly under Soviet (Russian) control, Gorbachev had tried to install Russians in the vacant positions. The plan was not a unilateral success.

In December 1986, for example, Gorbachev replaced Kazakhstan's Communist party chief Dinmukhamed Kunayev, an ethnic Kazakh who had ruled the republic since 1964, with the Russian Gennady Kolbin. A few days after Kolbin took office, riots broke out in Almaty, which quickly spread to other towns. Seventeen people were killed and hundreds injured in the most public demonstration of anti-Russian, and anti-Communist, feeling since World War II. This naked expression of popular protest—and power—shocked the Soviet nomenklatura. Kolbin was replaced by Nursultan Nazarbayev, an ethnic Kazakh. Gorbachev had more success stacking the governments with Russians in the other Central Asian states (except Uzbekistan), but the leaders continued to be drawn from Central Asian ethnic groups.

Once considered the peaceful, docile backwater of the Soviet Union, Central Asia was responding to economic deprivation, ethnic tensions, and growing anti-Russian feeling by a wave of violence. In May 1988 there were riots in Ashgabat as young people complained of the lack of jobs. In June 1989 dozens of people were killed in the Fergana Valley in battles between Uzbeks and Meskhetian Turks over land and housing. In February 1990 there was bloody rioting between Tajiks and Armenians in Dushanbe, again over housing shortages. In June 1990 the most violent ethnic clashes yet took place in southern Kyrgyzstan at the eastern edge of the Fergana Valley between Uzbeks and Kyrgyz. Hundreds of people were killed in an orgy of ethnic violence in which the bodies of farmers were hung up on meat hooks in Osh bazaar. The riots ended only when Soviet troops arrived to restore law and order. In September 1991 Islamic militants led another rebellion in Namangan in the Fergana Valley against President Islam Karimov. Meanwhile, in the Caucasus a war had broken out between Azerbaijan and Armenia over the disputed territory of Nagorno-Karabakh. Thirty thousand people eventually died in that conflict.

The Central Asian communist elite had managed to restore order only with the help of Soviet troops and support from Moscow, and these incidents stoked fears that even greater ethnic and economic conflicts would explode once independence came. At the same time the ruling elite felt betrayed by Gorbachev's decision in 1988 to withdraw Soviet troops from Afghanistan—a decision in which they were not consulted. (They had also not been consulted when Soviet troops invaded Afghanistan in 1979.) Unlike the rest of the Soviet Union, where antiwar feeling was growing as thousands of soldiers returned home in body bags, Central Asia—or at least its regimes— had regarded the war with favor because the region had benefited economically from its position as supply base for the Soviet army in Afghanistan. Moreover, the ruling elite also feared the outcome of the battle for power in Kabul between the Afghan Communist regime and the Islamic Mujahedeen. They were right to worry—in April 1992, just four months after the breakup of the Soviet Union, Kabul fell to the Mujahedeen.

By 1990 the leaders in Central Asia were contending with a worsening economic crisis as food prices shot up and shops were emptied of consumer goods because Russian factories refused to fill orders without cash payments. Because of its own economic crisis Russia was no longer demanding raw materials from Central Asia like cotton and minerals, and the leaders had no idea how to attract new buyers from outside the Soviet Union. Soviet subsidies for their social systems were suddenly withdrawn, leaving the governments unable to pay salaries or pensions. Yet the Central Asian leaders refused even to consider economic reform as a way to obtain Western aid. Unlike the Slav republics, Central Asia had no influential reformers advocating a reorientation to a market economy. In March 1991 Kazakhstan was paralyzed by a coal miners' strike that resulted in seventy thousand workers being laid off for several months as salaries and pensions went unpaid.

In Russia, however, the prevailing mood was one of open hostility to Central Asia. Once considered an undisputed part of the Great Soviet Motherland, the region was now regarded as culturally, racially, and religiously separate from Russia, whilst economically it was seen as a financial burden rather than a resource base. "Why should we bail out these strife-torn regions of Central Asia, who share nothing with us—least of all our religion? We would be much better off on our own," grumbled an aide to Russia's deputy prime minister Yegor Gaidar. Even the dissident Alexander Solzhenitsyn, famous for his opposition to the Soviet regime, argued in a widely read essay that Russia would be strong only after "it has shed the onerous burden of the Central Asian underbelly."[8] Moscow did not even seem to care about the large Slav minorities the government had seded into each Central Asian state, though the Russian citizens in these states were crying out for protection.

This mood became more pronounced after Boris Yeltsin was elected president of Russia in June 1991 with 60 percent of the Russian vote after a campaign that pushed opposition to empire and promotion of Slav chauvinism. With Yeltsin's accession threatening the country as a whole, Gorbachev spent a desperate summer attempting to negotiate a new treaty that would devolve powers from Moscow to the republics and prevent the breakup of the Soviet Union. A day before the treaty was due to be signed, on August 20, 1991, hard-liners in Moscow staged a coup, seeking to keep the nation's government firmly entrenched in Moscow. The coup was crushed a few days later, but the union treaty died with it.

Whilst the other Soviet republics condemned the coup, the reaction in Central Asia was just the opposite. The leaders of Turkmenistan, Uzbekistan, and Tajikistan openly endorsed the coup makers for saving the Soviet Union, whilst Kazakhstan's President Nazarbayev said nothing for the first two days after the attempt. Only Kyrgyz president Akayev condemned the coup and moved troops into Bishkek to protect his government. When the coup failed and a triumphant Gorbachev returned to Moscow, the Central Asian leaders faced a major credibility crisis at home as the fledgling opposition parties demanded their resignations. The leaders quickly moved to reassert control, now following Gorbachev's lead assiduously. When Gorbachev dissolved the Communist Party of the Soviet Union on August 24, the Central Asian leaders promptly dissolved their own Communist parties. In Tajikistan, however, opposition parties in Dushanbe staged anti-government rallies, which on September 7 forced Kakhar Makhanov, the first secretary of the Tajikistan Communist Party, to resign—a step that was to lead to civil war six months later.

Thus when independence came in December, Central Asia was already in deep crisis, with a leadership that appeared to be directionless and fearful of the future. Yet for the people of Central Asia independence was a joyous affirmation of their national and ethnic identities, and many hoped that their leaders would submerge their individual ambitions and jealousies in a five-way union that would not only stand up to Russia but guarantee security at home and allow the republics to develop their crisis-hit economies. There was enormous, if naive, public expectation that the leaders would move in the direction of an economic common market, joint security provisions, and joint overtures to the outside world. Many Central

Asian intellectuals saw these steps as the only way to keep in check the myriad problems each individual state suffered from. Although the leaders voiced initial approval of such plans and advocated the need for a Central Asian common market and joint positions in international forums, they did not allow any public participation or voice in discussions about the future course of action for their republics. Turkmenistan and Uzbekistan began to censor even the incoming Moscow press and television, which were more open than their own state-run media.

As the leaders stepped up political repression and censorship, they retreated into narrow policies of individual state building, which they saw as the only guarantee for their own political survival. Unable to jointly tackle their pressing economic and security problems, they were helpless to solve the growing internal problems. Meanwhile, Russia was adding to Central Asia's problems. Russian troops withdrew from the republics, leaving fledgling local armies with few indigenous officers of high rank. Russian economic planners demanded international prices for their exported consumer items and finished goods, whilst they pressured the Central Asian states to sell them cotton, minerals, and oil for the same low prices they had paid during the Soviet era. Moscow stopped all loans, aid, and subsidies to the region and then demanded that Central Asia pay back its enormous past debts to Russia in U.S. dollars. Attempts to open up to the outside world were stymied by the lack of diplomats, knowledge of foreign languages, availability of foreign exchange, and know-how. Central Asia had no trained senior civil servants, specialists, and factory managers because these posts had all been occupied by Russians, and they were all leaving.

The result was a dramatic economic decline across Central Asia as living standards plummeted, inflation galloped upwards, unemployment grew, and critical raw materials for industry and agriculture became unattainable. Economic problems, in turn, heightened local political and ethnic tensions, which led to an escalation of ethnic and border disputes between states. The leaders banned opposition parties, placed tight controls on the media, and outlawed public discussion and debate on future policy. They were counting on the semi-dormant, subservient attitudes and political inactivism that had been forced on the populace during the Soviet era to prevent widespread uprising or protests. Yet by turning their own political survival into state policy, the leaders only ensured that the politically active elements—intellectuals, mullahs, new political parties—would be forced, like the Islam of the Soviet era, to go underground. And as with the Islamicists, all these groups would eventually become radicalized and violent.

Meanwhile, as the few democrats in Central Asia looked to Russia and the Baltic republics for political inspiration, many young people looked to Islam and the Muslim countries of Pakistan, Iran, Turkey, and Saudi Arabia for new ideological inspiration. The rapid resurgence of Islam in Central Asia during the past few years had reinforced local ethnic ties and anti-Russian nationalism. It had also reminded many people of what they had lost during the Soviet era—and what they had to gain.

The speed of the Islamic resurgence caught the elite by surprise, increasing the gulf between the leaders and the people and between the local Muslim populations and the Central Asian Russians. Yet because devout Muslims had been forced underground, relying on itinerant mullahs and local worship to keep their religion alive, they had no mass-based parties to put forth an organized political opposition. For their part the ruling elites had no more idea about how to deal with the Islamic resurgence than they did about how to solve the political and economic crises or deal with the new political parties.

Even before the breakup of the Soviet Union, there had been a huge spurt in the building of mosques. In October 1990 Kyrgyzstan had fifty new mosques compared to a total of fifteen a year earlier; Turkmenistan, thirty compared to five; Tajikistan, forty compared to seventeen; and Kazakhstan, ninety compared to thirty-seven. A year later—October 1991—there were more than a thousand new mosques in each republic, and a new mosque was opening every day. Sufism flourished. Collective farms rebuilt local Sufi shrines, which quickly became centers for weekend meditation, prayers, parties, and picnics by families whose younger members learned about the mystic powers of the shrine and were taught Sufi rituals by their elders. Adult women set up home schools, where they taught children the correct way to pray.

This indigenous Islamic revival was quickly radicalized by the arrival of outsiders. Korans, other Islamic literature, and money arrived with preachers from Saudi Arabia, the Arab Gulf states, Pakistan, Turkey, and Iran as everyone in the Muslim world tried to win new adherents to their particular interpretation of Islam in what was regarded as virgin territory. These preachers saw themselves as pioneers bringing Central Asian Muslims who had been forced to abandon the faith back to the bosom of the Islamic umma—and to their own particular sectarian beliefs.

In the beginning the Central Asian leadership tried to adapt to the new situation by making many of the necessary cosmetic changes that were being made in the other former Soviet republics. In addition to political reforms—banning the local Communist parties and reinventing themselves as socialists or peoples' representatives, nationalizing Communist property, and opening ties with the outside world by appointing ambassadors to important foreign countries—they tried to present themselves as born-again Muslims, reciting prayers or verses from the Koran before public speeches and cabinet meetings. But the leaders depended on the old "official Islam" network of mosques and mullahs to keep the Islamic resurgence under control, and the official Islam had no money or influence; the people mistrusted it because it was considered part of the former Communist system. The Central Asian leaders made no attempt to encourage the revival of Sufism or other forms of popular Islam; initially they even refused to declare Islamic holy days as days off work.

The states also forbade any political expression of Islam, placing a ban on any party that promoted Islamic ideas or ideology. Only in Tajikistan did the regime legalize the popular Islamic Renaissance Party (IRP) in response to the worsening political crisis. By 1992 the repressive measures of the Central Asian regimes began to further encourage the imported, well-funded ideologies of Islamic radicalism from outside the region as local movements went underground in order to avoid arrest and harassment by the police. The Central Asian governments tried to seal off these contacts—just as they sought to clamp down on political freedoms that Central Asians had begun taking as their right and to muzzle the increasingly outspoken media—but they were too slow. In many areas the seeds for militant Islam had been sown. The Soviet Union was no more, but Central Asia's problems were far from over.

4 The First Decade of Independence

WHEN THE SOVIET UNION ceased to exist, on December 8, 1991, the Central Asian states faced their greatest challenge and their brightest opportunity. The republics' ethnic populations had never been happy in the Russian-dominated Soviet Union, and rebellions, led by the Muslim Basmachis, had continued long after the rest of the former Russian Empire had succumbed to the Bolsheviks. The Soviet policies of closed borders, forced cotton agriculture, farm collectivization, population relocation, and—most significant—Stalin's redrawing of the map of Central Asia to create five incongruous states had left the region economically hard-pressed, ethnically and politically divided, and forced to practice its majority religion—Islam—in secret. But on the plus side, each of the republics sat on land that was rich with natural resources: oil, gas, minerals. The world's last great untapped energy reserve, Central Asia beckoned to international investors. The leaders of the five governments were thus uniquely positioned to take Central Asia out of Russian hibernation and reconnect their republics with the international community. Yet they failed to do so.

Some leaders tried. Kyrgyzstan's Askar Akayev adopted an International Monetary Fund (IMF) program and privatized businesses; Kazakhstan's Nursultan Nazarbayev negotiated with U.S. oil companies and managed to complete a significant new pipeline from the Tenghiz oil fields to the Black Sea; and even Uzbekistan's repressive Islam Karimov briefly allowed strong opposition parties to be represented in elections and sought international development deals. But at the end of their first decade of independence the Central Asian countries found themselves facing enormous political unrest, endemic poverty, and rampant unemployment, whilst a completely new problem—Islamic militancy—threatened the stability of the entire region. Even their magnificent resources have brought only limited international investment. Until the Central Asian regimes can find a way to stabilize their economies and their political situations, investors will seek safer, if less rich, territories.

Kazakhstan: Vast Resources Wasted

The nomadic Kazakh tribes migrated from southern Siberia to the vast Kazakh steppe in the twelfth century under their legendary-mythical founder, Alasha Khan. Their political system consisted of three ordas, composed of tribal, clan, and family units ruled by a khan, or chief. Although the ordas often warred with one another, they would unite to fight encroaching outsiders, such as the Chinese to the east and the Uzbeks to the south. Late converts to Islam, the Kazakhs came under the influence of Tartar mullahs only in the seventeenth century. (This, coupled with the weak sense of ethnic identity amongst the Kazakhs, explains why Islamic extremism is still rare in the country. Although the Kazakhs have become more conscious of Islam and more devout since independence, support for militant movements comes largely from Uzbeks living in the south.) In the eighteenth and nineteenth centuries, as Russia expanded its empire, the Kazakh steppe was the first to be incorporated. Forts were spread across the landscape, warring Kazakh khans were subdued, and treaties were made to settle the region. The government sent Russian and Cossack farmers to the steppe to cultivate wheat and cotton and restrict Kazakh nomadism—in 1891 alone, more than a million Russians were settled in northern Kazakhstan, which has remained predominantly Russian since then.

The Soviets continued the Russian policies of seeding the steppe with Russian and Cossack farmers, bloodily suppressing local rebellions, and seizing or destroying Kazakh flocks. As late as 1954 Moscow continued to claim northern Kazakhstan as virgin territory on which Russian farmers could be settled. The Soviets also set up the Baikonur cosmodrome in the north as a missile test site and rocket pad, and made Semipalatinsk the main testing ground for nuclear weapons. These bases have left a legacy of horrendous environmental, ecological, and health problems for the local population. Radiation levels are still very high.

The brutal personal subjugation, along with the repression of their fledgling political organizations, has made the Kazakhs, who have no literary tradition other than oral epic poetry to sustain a nationalist culture, the most Russified of the Central Asian peoples. By 1991 many Kazakhs did not speak their native language, Kazakh, and ethnic Kazakhs were more comfortable intermarrying with Russians than were other Central Asian nationalities.

In fact, at the time of independence Kazakhstan's huge landmass of some 1.6 million square miles, stretching nearly two thousand miles from west to east, was populated by only 17 million people, and the Kazakhs were in the minority—41 percent of the population was Russian compared to 38 percent Kazakh. Moreover, a hundred other ethnic groups, including Germans, Chechens, Koreans, and Chinese, inhabited the region, making ethnic relations the most pressing political problem facing the republic. Today Kazakhs hold a slim majority (52 percent), largely because some ethnic groups, such as Russians and Germans, have returned to their native lands.

Their departure has shrunk the total population by 8 percent. Fewer Russians have fled Kazakhstan than the other Central Asian states, however, owing to the accommodationist policies of President Nursultan Nazarbayev.

One of the most controversial things Nazarbayev has done to curb separatist tendencies amongst the Russian population is move the capital from the large and beautiful nineteenth-century city of Almaty, in the far east, to Astana, a small village in the center of the country adjacent to the belt of Russian settlers in the north, allocating massive funds to build a new city. The move has drained the sorely tried economy of Kazakhstan without significantly undermining the Russian and Cossack extremists, who demand to be allowed either to form a separate state or to rejoin Russia. Nor has it appeased Kazakh ultranationalists, who call for an end to Russian influence and the use of the Russian language.

As a consequence Nazarbayev—a Kazakh peasant from the Great Horde who won fame at school as a traditional wrestler before joining the Communist Party and rising to become the first secretary of the Communist Party of Kazakhstan in 1989 and later Kazakhstan's first president—has been in the forefront of Central Asian leaders in trying to maintain cordial ties with Russia. He has urged Moscow to make the Commonwealth of Independent States (CIS) stronger and more effective, advocating various plans to create closer economic and political unity amongst the Central Asian republics. But he has invariably lost these battles. Russia is unwilling to treat the Central Asian states as equal partners, whilst Uzbekistan's ambitious President Islam Karimov has thwarted Nazarbayev at every turn, owing both to personal rivalries and to Karimov's resentment over the attention Kazakhstan has received from the West because of its vast oil resources.

After independence the West courted Nazarbayev because he still held 104 Soviet-era SS-19 ballistic missiles with more than a thousand nuclear warheads, along with the testing sites at Baikonur and

Semipalatinsk. The United States plunged in, promising general economic aid and specifically to pay the cost of dismantling the missiles. Nazarbayev skillfully used the issue to build up a solid relationship with the United States and NATO countries whilst extracting the maximum financial benefit for Kazakhstan. By the time the missiles were dismantled, in 1995, the country had received some $400 million from Washington. But although Nazarbayev banned further nuclear tests, he continues to rent out the Baikonur launch site to Russia.

Fear has not been the only factor motivating Western interest in Kazakhstan since independence. Kazakhstan has enormous energy reserves, which remained largely untapped during the Soviet era because Moscow preferred to expand oil production in Russian Siberia. With estimated reserves of 100 billion barrels of oil and 85 trillion cubic feet of gas along its Caspian Sea coastline, Kazakhstan is probably the largest unexplored oil-bearing region in the world.

Kazakhstan has had mixed success in exploiting its greatest advantage, however. Nazarbayev became the first Central Asian leader to conclude a deal with a foreign oil company when after four years of negotiations he signed a joint venture with U.S. Chevron Corporation in May 1992 to develop the Tenghiz oil field and build a pipeline from the field to the Black Sea port of Novorossiysk, Russia. But work did not start on the $2.6 billion pipeline until 1997, and it was not until thirteen years after the negotiations began (March 2001) that the 948-mile pipeline was completed and began tests. When it officially opens, currently scheduled for the end of 2001, it will pump 560,000 barrels of oil a day to Novorossiysk.

After the Chevron deal was signed, international oil companies and embassies thronged to Almaty, at that point still the capital. Kazakhstan has signed lucrative exploration and export deals with oil companies from the United States, China, Europe, India, Japan, and Turkey that annually bring in $400–$800 million in foreign investment. But Western interest and investment in the oil sector decreased drastically in the mid-1990s because of low international oil prices and Russian objections to proposed Western pipelines that would travel south and avoid Russian territory. Oil production, which had been close to 526,000 barrels a day in 1991, when Kazakhstan was still part of the Soviet Union, rapidly declined over the decade, owing largely to Russian attempts to restrict the Kazakh oil fields by not allowing Kazakh oil exports through the existing Russian pipeline network, which extended to Europe. Western investment in Kazakhstan did revive in May 2000, after a Western oil consortium discovered a new oil field in the East Kashagan area in the Caspian Sea, reputed to be one of the biggest in the world.

Russia continues to act the role of spoiler in Kazakhstan, as the new Great Game plays out between the United States, Russia, and a third player, China, for control of Asia. Moscow has insisted that Kazakhstan build no new pipelines but rather use the existing Russian pipeline network to export its energy, thereby ensuring that Kazakhstan will remain dependent on Russia for exports to the West. Russia also demands a stake in every new joint venture the republic enters into with Western companies and disputes Kazakh claims to a share of the Caspian Sea. This last controversy has also pulled in neighboring Turkmenistan, Iran, and Azerbaijan, as each country tries to claim the water and oil wealth of the Caspian Sea. The dispute has become more heated with the discovery of yet more oil there.

Despite the pressures from Russia, Kazakhstan has continued to explore all possible export routes: east to China, south through Iran, and west to Turkey. But although there have been grandiose plans, the only pipeline that even started construction in the past decade has been the Tenghiz pipeline, which went to a Russian port. After China bought major stakes in Kazakh oil fields in 1999, Kazakhstan pushed for a pipeline to China, but nothing has come of these efforts as yet. China has made huge inroads in the region, however, becoming Kazakhstan's second-largest trading partner after Russia by 1993. At that time China and Kazakhstan began to demarcate and demilitarize their long borders, a process that was speeded up after the first summit meeting of the Shanghai Five (China, Russia, Kazakhstan, Kyrgyzstan, and Tajikistan) in April 1996.

Oil and gas are not the only strings to Kazakhstan's bow. The country has vast mineral resources—under the Soviets eighty different minerals were mined—and the steppe produces enormous quantities of wheat, all of which add to Kazakhstan's wealth and economic viability. These resources have induced international donor agencies like the International Monetary Fund (IMF) and the World Bank to lend Kazakhstan extensive funds to privatize industry and land—a process that began in April 1994 with the sale of fifty large state-owned companies to the private sector. However, these sales have been mired in scandal, as many of the companies were sold to Nazarbayev's cronies. And even this wealth has not been enough to resolve the economic crisis that began immediately after independence, when unemployment grew and the government had no money to pay salaries or pensions. The crisis became more acute in November 1993, when Russia forced Kazakhstan and other Central Asian states to leave the ruble zone. Kazakhstan established its own currency, the tenge, but the tenge has remained unstable and fluctuates wildly against the dollar.

The biggest problem facing Kazakhstan comes from its increasingly authoritarian and corrupt leadership, which has been frittering away Kazakhstan's natural resources and wasting its huge export potential. At the head is President Nazarbayev, who took—or rather kept—office immediately after independence. The first secretary of Kazakhstan's Communist Party, Nazarbayev obediently dismantled the party but immediately formed his own Unity Party, which, thanks to state pressure, widespread election rigging, and a refusal to allow opposition parties, has won all subsequent presidential and parliamentary elections.

The regime began by harassing opposition parties and newspapers; now these are banned, and opposition leaders have been jailed or forced to flee abroad. Corruption has become widespread at every level of government because the many oil companies offer huge bonuses and perks to local officials for the chance to take part in bidding contracts. In the midst of a political crisis in 1995, when opposition politicians were beginning to question high-level corruption, Nazarbayev followed the trend set by other Central Asia leaders and held a public referendum to extend his mandate as president until the year 2000. In June 2000 Nazarbayev strengthened his hand even further by getting parliament to pass a bill that conferred lifelong political and legal rights to him and his entire family granting blanket immunity against any charges that had already been made or that would be made in the future.

Nazarbayev appears to be setting up a family dynasty. His daughter, Dariga Naz, aged 37, is widely considered to be his potential successor. Naz already owns a vast television and newspaper empire that controls 80 percent of the country's media whilst her husband, Rakhat Aliyev, heads Kazakhstan's internal security agency. Nazarbayev's other son-in-law, Timur Kulebaev, and his nephew Kairat Satybalda have large business interests in Kazakhstan and are vying for power.

The blatantly corrupt political process has led to the rise of extremist opposition groups, as young Kazakhs as well as Uzbeks living in Kazakhstan join radical Islamic parties like the Islamic Movement of Uzbekistan (IMU), which ostensibly targets the government of Uzbekistan but in reality fights on many fronts (see Chapters 7 and 8) and the less political—and less militant—Hizb ut-Tahrir (HT), which seeks to impose sharia (Islamic law) on the whole of Central Asia (see Chapter 6). On the other side of the political spectrum Russian settlers in the north threaten to secede from the country. These movements and the political pressures they bring are posing new threats to Kazakhstan's security. In 2001 Kazakhstan doubled its military budget to $171 million (1 percent of gross domestic product), so that the army could create mobile fighting units to face possible guerrilla attacks by the IMU.

The politically restrictive environment has also led to the deterioration of human rights. Prisons overflow with disease-ridden inmates, despite the fact that Kazakhstan has the fourth-highest execution rate in the world. In 1995 alone a hundred prisoners were executed. Drug addiction has grown with the introduction of cheap heroin from Afghanistan. In 2001 thirty-seven thousand people in Kazakhstan were officially listed as drug users although estimates placed the number at tens of thousands more off the record. The rise in drug use and needle sharing has fueled an AIDS-HIV crisis; it is now estimated that there are three hundred thousand Central Asians infected with HIV, of whom the largest number live in Kazakhstan.

Corruption and incompetence have led to such wasteful projects as the construction of the new capital, Astana, and to growing disparities between the handful of well-connected party and business leaders and the rest of the population, who have seen few benefits from independence. Kazakhstan's huge advantage over the other Central Asian republics in terms of resources and space have so far been wasted, and public discontent is growing across the steppe.

Nevertheless, Nazarbayev's successful attempts to balance Russia and the West, and Kazakhstan's relative security and stability compared to those of its neighbors, have encouraged Western oil companies to step up their investments. In 2000 Kazakhstan's production was back up to 170 billion cubic feet of gas and 693,000 barrels of oil a day. The boost in oil exports led to a 9.5 percent growth in gross domestic product in 2000, compared to a 1.7 percent growth the year before. This was the biggest economic leap since independence, and with inflation down to 9 percent, consumer prices became relatively stable. With a steady flow of oil exports now secured by the Tenghiz pipeline, and a pledge that Kazakhstan will commit oil to the planned U.S. pipeline from Baku, Azerbaijan, to Ceyhan, Turkey—perhaps even build another pipeline to China—Kazakhstan will continue to receive foreign exchange in the years to come.

The question Kazakhstan faces is how this money will be spent. Living standards for most of the population remain desperately low, and the government still has not caught up in paying overdue pensions and salaries. The new oil-rich oligarchy drives Mercedes and BMWs in the tree-lined streets of Almaty, whilst the rest of the population struggles to afford a bus ticket. Little of Kazakhstan's new wealth has trickled down to the mass of ordinary people. This economic disparity, along with the lack of democratic representation and the repression of religious expression, are now fueling political unrest and driving more and more people to radical Islamic movements.

Kyrgyzstan: Caught in the Middle

The ethereal mountain ranges that cover 93 percent of Kyrgyzstan's 125,000 square miles have always hidden a harsher reality for its people. Daily life for the Kyrgyz nomads, who were once part of Genghis Khan's Golden Horde, has always been incredibly difficult. Their only resource has been their livestock. Kyrgyzstan's 4.8 million people (of whom the Kyrgyz constitute only 52 percent) are outnumbered five times by their flocks of goats, sheep, cattle, and horses.

The ancient center for these mountain tribes was the Tokmak plain northeast of Bishkek, where tribal chieftains held their councils. Southeast of Tokmak lies the lake of Issyk-Kul, situated in a fold in the Tian Shan Mountains—a vast inland sea beside which Genghis Khan and Timur both camped. The Soviets later turned Issyk-Kul into a resort for top Communist officials.

The Kyrgyz come from the same stock as the Kazakhs. Both migrated south from Siberia; the Kara-Kyrgyz, as the Kyrgyz were originally called, became the mountain dwellers, whilst the Kazakhs inhabited the steppe. Before 1917 the Russians called both groups simply Kyrgyz—it was Stalin who created the geographical and ethnic divisions that now exist between the two. Even today the customs, traditions, and language of the Kyrgyz and Kazakh remain similar.

The history of these mountain dwellers has come down through epic oral poetry and ballads, the most famous of which is the Manas, a lengthy chronicle of Kyrgyz history enfolded into the tale of the legendary hero Manas, who rode a winged horse and performed incredible feats for the Kyrgyz nation. The stunning landscape of high mountains and icy lakes is littered with such legends.

The Kyrgyz have survived on the edges of the great civilizations of Central Asia by increasing their numbers through the absorption of local tribes or new tribal migrations from China and Siberia that have intruded through the Fergana Valley. Like the Kazakhs, the Kyrgyz were latecomers to Islam, and elements of pre-Islamic Shamanism are still evident in many of their nomadic traditions.

Also like the Kazakhs, the Kyrgyz nomads were forced to flee their homeland or pushed into the far corners of the mountains by the Russian settlers, who had come to farm the small area containing fertile valleys. Many Kyrgyz joined the Basmachi rebels, resisting the Soviets until 1929. Even after the region had been subdued by Stalin's programs, few Kyrgyz joined the Communist Party. This meant that when independence came in 1991, there were hardly any Kyrgyz trained in technology or the bureaucracy, for they had never held privileged positions within the Soviet republic. Stalin's creative map-making has led to particularly acute ethnic problems in Kyrgyzstan; a substantial Russian population in the cities and the north is demanding greater rights whilst the large Uzbek population in Osh and the south complains of discrimination from the ethnic Kyrgyz regime.

In the late-Soviet era, Communist Party politics in Kyrgyzstan had been dominated by three major factions. When the long-running first secretary of the Communist Party of Kyrgyzstan, Turadakun Usubaliev, was dismissed in 1985, he was replaced by Absamat Masalieyev, who was reelected first secretary of the party in April 1990. Almost immediately intense fighting broke out between the factions. Members from Naryn, in the east, representing the most powerful political bloc in the country, supported the former leader Usubaliev. The Talas region in the west backed the soon-to-be-deposed Masalieyev. The powerful economic and business lobby of the Osh region in the south, which was dominated by Uzbeks, resented not being part of the political power structure in Bishkek. They supported a political neutral, Askar Akayev, who had been a researcher at a prestigious institute in St. Petersburg and an associate of the Soviet-era physicist and dissident Andrei Sakharov. In late 1990 the Naryn bloc swung its vote to Akayev as well.

Exacerbating the political tensions were the unprecedented public demonstrations that had been rocking the country for more than a year, weakening the grip of the traditional Communists. In March 1989 young Kyrgyz intellectuals had organized an informal opposition group called Ashar (Solidarity), which occupied empty land in Bishkek to protest the shortage of housing and transport in the city. Then in June 1990 came the violent ethnic fighting between the Kyrgyz and Uzbeks in Osh, which lasted for several days. Officially the government listed the casualties at two hundred killed and some three hundred injured, but unofficial sources put the death toll at more than a thousand. Order was restored only when the Soviet troops from Uzbekistan arrived in Osh. As the Communist regime came under intense public criticism—at a time when it was already being consumed by its own inner rivalries—several political blocs switched their support to Akayev, who became president of the Supreme Soviet of Kyrgyzstan in the October 28 elections. As Kyrgyzstan headed towards independence in the fall of 1991, Akayev, running unopposed, was reelected in full (popular) presidential elections. He is the first—and so far only—non-Communist to be elected president of a Central Asian republic.

But with independence came an end to financial aid from Moscow, and Kyrgyzstan plunged into the worst economic crisis suffered by a Central Asian state. For ten years Akayev has battled to keep the country solvent. It has not been easy. Inflation rose to a staggering 1,200 percent in 1993 as industrial production plummeted and Kyrgyzstan lost its Soviet market for local dairy products. Because the country has few natural resources, Akayev decided to see whether a neutral foreign policy and major economic reforms could bring in Western financial aid. So in 1993 Kyrgyzstan became the first Central Asian state to adopt an IMF program and to privatize state-owned businesses and land.

For a while, Akayev's plan seemed to be working. Western states and Japan backed his reform agenda and the introduction of a new currency, the som, after Russia forced the Central Asian states out of the ruble zone in 1993, hoping that Kyrgyzstan's success would set an example for other Central Asian states to follow. In 1998 Kyrgyzstan became the first Central Asian state to join the World Trade Organization. But Kyrgyzstan still depended on the goodwill of neighbors like Uzbekistan and Kazakhstan for essential supplies of oil, gas, and coal, and the country remained economically weak and vulnerable. Multinational companies were reluctant to invest in such major infrastructure projects as new electricity grids and dams for irrigation water, which Akayev hoped to export to his Central Asian neighbors. Although Kyrgyzstan has mineral resources, few companies have tried to invest in developing them because of the problems involved in transporting them out of the landlocked, mountainous country.

And so gradually Kyrgyzstan built up a mountain of international debt to add to its domestic economic problems. In 1999 this debt amounted to $1.27 billion, the largest debt per population of any Central Asian state. As the economic situation continues to deteriorate, Kyrgyzstan has begun defaulting on its debt repayments.

As joblessness, hunger, and poverty increased, living standards fell, and political opposition grew. In order to keep his grip on power, Akayev became more authoritarian. Kyrgyzstan had held free, multiparty elections until 1995 — the only Central Asian state to do so — and they had ensured a thriving opposition in parliament, with whom Akayev had worked fairly well. But after 1996 parliament and the president were locked in a continual power struggle. Political crises became more frequent, corruption scandals engulfed the government, and Akayev's credibility as a democrat plummeted at home and abroad.

Opposition to Akayev's rule came not just from political parties but from Kyrgyzstan's diverse ethnic groups. The large Russian population (22 percent in 1991) threatened a mass exodus if Akayev did not give in to their demands. Faced with the loss of the most qualified people in the country, Akayev set up a Slavic University in Bishkek to encourage younger Russians to stay; in 1999 he gave the Russian language equal status with Kyrgyz. But every concession to the Russians led to protests and counterdemands from the Kyrgyz nationalists. Meanwhile, in southern Kyrgyzstan, Uzbek-Kyrgyz ethnic tensions continued. The southern towns still seem to consist of two separate communities each, as Kyrgyz and Uzbeks attend separate schools, mosques, and bazaars. The Uzbek population in Osh has been shut out of the political process and remains unrepresented in either the administration or the police.

At the same time, tensions with neighboring Uzbekistan and Kazakhstan multiplied as the two demanded that Akayev end his democratic reforms—which they considered a threat to their own repressive regimes—and clamp down on Islamic fundamentalism in the south, as the regimes had done in their own countries. In order to force Akayev to act, Uzbekistan shut off oil and gas supplies to Kyrgyzstan in the spring of 1999 and again in the winter of 2000. Aircraft were grounded in Bishkek for weeks at a time because there was no fuel to fly them. Akayev gave in to the pressure and began arresting Islamic militants and ordering that all mosques and madrassahs register with the state. Meanwhile, China, which had become a major provider of aid and goods, pressured the government to curb the activities of the Muslim Uighur population, whom China accused of fomenting unrest amongst Chinese Uighurs in Xinjiang Province. Akayev gave in to these demands too, arresting dozens of

Uighurs in Bishkek. Kyrgyzstan, once the leader of the Central Asian states in religious tolerance, has now joined in the repressive policies of its neighbors.

But accommodating his neighbors by arresting Islamic militants has not enabled Akayev to keep Kyrgyzstan out of the line of fire. In the summer of 1999 several hundred IMU militants based in Tajikistan invaded southern Kyrgyzstan, capturing several villages and taking twenty hostages, including four Japanese geologists who were working for a gold-mining company. The militants were seeking passage to the Fergana Valley, where they planned to set up bases against Uzbekistan's President Karimov. The standoff between the weak Kyrgyz army of just eight thousand men and the militants dragged on through the summer before the militants finally retreated. In July 2000 the IMU returned, sparking off renewed clashes in Kyrgyzstan and Uzbekistan.

But the militants have also given Kyrgyzstan more leverage with the international community. For years Akayev had been a leading advocate for greater economic cooperation between Russia and the Central Asian states, but until the IMU threat emerged, Karimov had ignored, even snubbed, his appeals. The IMU threat has brought all the states closer together. At the same time that the IMU was capturing its twenty hostages, Akayev was hosting a summit meeting of the Shanghai Five, who pledged to cooperate in "fighting international . . . terrorism, the illegal drugs trade, arms trafficking, illegal migration, separatism and religious extremism." Kyrgyzstan suddenly began to receive vital military aid from the United States, Russia, and China, and U.S. Secretary of State Madeleine Albright made her first visit to Bishkek in March 2000, where she pledged $3 million to help rearm Kyrgyz border guards.

Nevertheless, these multiple crises have encouraged Akayev to emulate his neighbors, crushing political dissent, arresting opponents, curbing the media, and rigging elections in order to stay in office. A series of referenda has allowed him to bypass the constitution, receive endorsement for his policies, and increase his personal powers.[1] He banned most opposition parties and candidates from the February 2000 parliamentary elections, and the most important opposition leaders were jailed—or fled. Newspapers critical of the regime were either shut down outright or harassed to the point of being forced to close.

Akayev's repressive policies have not had unmixed success. As Western donors condemned the 2000 elections as undemocratic, strikes and protests spread throughout the country. And the opposition is growing. In April 2001 ten political parties formed a coalition called the People's Patriotic Movement to oppose Akayev's centralization of power. Nongovernmental organizations (NGO) that have managed to do a great deal to alleviate poverty and monitor government activity in Kyrgyzstan have formed an umbrella organization, Coalition NGO, made up of a hundred local organizations, to continue the work.

According to the World Bank, 60 percent of the population now lives in poverty. AIDS is becoming a huge problem, which the government acknowledges but cannot do much about. The state budget for 2000 earmarked only $24,000 to deal with AIDS. Politicians, aid workers, and intellectuals have repeatedly warned the government that the growing poverty, unemployment, and disease are responsible for the rise of Islamic radicalism. "A social explosion is entirely feasible. People are disillusioned and they cannot do anything to improve their lot," explained Jypar Jeksheev, chairman of the Democratic Movement Party.[2] There have been protests in Naryn, Jalal Abad, and Bishkek. The increase in poverty in the south has been especially disastrous, providing fertile ground for IMU recruitment. Particularly in the region around Batken, where the IMU has made incursions for two years running, entire villages are suffering acute economic and social deprivation.

The fact that even some Kyrgyz, one of the least Islamicized ethnic groups in Central Asia, are now turning to radical Islam as an answer to their pitiful living conditions demonstrates the desperation of their economic situation. Economically weak, militarily defenseless, and plagued with ethnic problems, Kyrgyzstan has moved from being a potential model for other Central Asian states to follow to being a pawn in the battle for Central Asia.

Turkmenistan: Under the Cult of the Leader

Nothing in Central Asia in the post-Soviet era has been quite so bizarre as the personality cult that President Saparmurad Niyazov has fostered in Turkmenistan. Starting in 1991, when Niyazov erected statues and plastered photographs of himself posing as "Turkmenbashi" (Father of all Turkmens) on walls and squares across the country, the cult has grown to the point where buildings, streets, even entire cities have been named after him. His dead mother has also been elevated to cult status, whilst his birthplace and school have become shrines. Even by the authoritarian standards of the Central Asian regimes, Niyazov's government is unique: the most repressive and dictatorial regime in the region. Political parties are banned, the government controls all media outlets, meetings of all kinds—even academic—are forbidden, and Christian and Hindu sect leaders have been thrown out of the country along with political opposition leaders. (There is no Islamic opposition.)

In January 1994 Niyazov "suggested" that his puppet parliament nominate him to be president until the year 2002; it did so at once. This was followed by a parliamentary vote asking Niyazov to stay on as president for life. However, in February 2001, Niyazov announced that he would step down—in 2010—and at that time more than one candidate would be allowed in presidential elections. In 1996 Amnesty International described the regime as "secretive, repressive and intimidating." Today this appears to be an enormous understatement.

The indiscriminate use of the death penalty, the torture of prisoners in the overflowing prisons (which frequently erupt in riots), and the disappearance of dissenters without a trace all point to a regime that is paranoid about staying in power. In July 2000 the government announced that it would monitor all visiting foreigners, foreign mail, and telephone calls, and strip Internet providers of their licenses. Niyazov banned the teaching of English and other foreign languages in schools to isolate the population from Western trends, and Turkmen students were forbidden to take up scholarships abroad.

In February 2001, Niyazov's orders became positively bizarre. He renamed the streets of the capital with numbers and demanded that all citizens fly the national flag above their homes. Most important, he introduced a new spiritual code of conduct, based on his writings, for the citizens of Turkmenistan. In a three-hour speech he compared the code to the Bible and the Koran.

Yet at independence Turkmenistan had many advantages. It is the most homogeneous of the Central Asian states, with 72 percent of its 4.7 million people belonging to the Turkmen ethnic group. These Turkmen come from more than twenty tribes, of which the two largest—the Tekke and Yomut—provide the country's political leadership. Turkmenistan has thus been spared the ethnic battles that have undermined the other Central Asian republics. In addition, Turkmenistan has proven oil reserves of 546 million barrels and gas reserves of 260 trillion cubic feet, the seventh-largest gas reserves in the world.

The Turkmen originated in the Altai region of eastern Central Asia and migrated to the Caspian region along with the Oghuz Turks. Stateless but with a strict tribal hierarchy, they built a formidable reputation as raiders and warriors in their harsh desert environment, attacking caravans along the Silk Route and raiding Persia, Russia, and Afghanistan to capture slaves, whom they sold to local rulers. They also fought as mercenaries for Persian, Turkic, Afghan, and Central Asian rulers. They decimated an entire Russian army at Geok Tepe in 1881, but a retaliatory Russian force led by General von Kaufmann destroyed them later that year. Von Kaufmann described the Turkmen as the most formidable light cavalry in the world—not surprising as Turkmen horses are revered worldwide, especially the Akhalteke breed. (Alexander the Great rode an Akhalteke horse into battle.) After the Russian Revolution the Turkmen joined the Basmachi rebellion under the leadership of Muhammad Qurban Junaid Khan, a wealthy landlord of the Yomut tribe, and continued to fight until 1927.

Three-quarters of Turkmenistan's 305,000 square miles are covered by the Kara-Kum Desert, and the only arable land is on the banks of the Amu Darya River. The Soviets built canal systems to enable them to grow cotton and forbade the farmers to plant food crops. This canal system has turned the region into an ecological disaster zone, drawing off water headed for the Aral Sea, thereby depleting the sea whilst at the same time creating massive waterlogging and salinity in the soil. But below the desert sands lie enormous reserves of oil and gas. When Turkmenistan became an independent republic Niyazov pledged to turn it into "a new Kuwait." That promise has yet to be fulfilled.

Twice in the past century, in 1929 and 1948, Ashgabat has been devastated by earthquakes. The last one destroyed the entire city, killing 110,000 people, but no one outside Turkmenistan knew about it. Stalin refused to acknowledge that there had been a quake, and the news was never released. Yet many Turkmen relate their intellectual poverty to the fact that the entire educated middle class of the city was wiped out in the 1948 quake. Niyazov himself was orphaned by it; he was subsequently bought up in Communist Party orphanages. Without an educated elite the Turkmen became dependent on Russian cadres, investment, and technical help, and Russians still dominate all levels of the bureaucracy. Because Moscow was not interested in exploiting Turkmenistan's vast gas resources, preferring the Siberian fields that lay within the Russian Soviet Republic, it remained one of the poorest republics in the Soviet Union. At independence Turkmenistan had 18 percent unemployment and an infant mortality rate of fifty-four per thousand births—a figure ten times higher than in Western Europe. Children were forced to work in the cotton fields. Poverty was endemic.

In the past decade Niyazov has made ever more desperate attempts to persuade Western oil companies to build oil and gas pipelines from Turkmenistan that would be independent of Russia. But Moscow has played its brutal game of spoiler, insisting that Turkmen gas be exported to other CIS states and Europe through the Russian pipeline system at prices well below international levels. But even the gas that goes through these pipelines brings less economic relief than it should; CIS customers like Ukraine and Armenia are too poor to pay for their gas, and Turkmenistan has frequently been forced to turn off the tap because of nonpayment. By 2000 Turkmenistan was owed $1.5 billion by CIS members—including Russia—for gas.

Since the early 1990s Niyazov has floated several options for new pipelines for his landlocked country. These include a 950-mile pipeline through Iran to Turkey and Europe, a 1,125-mile pipeline through Afghanistan to Pakistan and India, and a 5,000-mile pipeline to China. The only one that has moved beyond the planning stage is a small (118 miles long) pipeline completed in 1996 by Teheran that provides gas to northern Iran. The Iranians have also built a new railway line linking Meshad, in eastern Iran, with Turkmenistan, thereby providing the first outlet for Central Asia's exports to the Arabian Gulf. But international gamesmanship has stopped even this from providing much relief. Washington refuses to allow U.S. oil companies to build any new pipelines through Iran, whilst Russia has blocked proposed pipelines to Turkey, and the civil war in Afghanistan has prevented a pipeline to Pakistan. Washington is now trying to persuade Niyazov to commit Turkmenistan to the U.S. plan to build an oil and gas pipeline from Baku in Azerbaijan to Ceyhan on Turkey's Mediterranean coast, a move that Russia and Iran are resisting.

Turkmenistan's pipeline woes have resulted in a dramatic drop in

the country's gas production and foreign-exchange revenues. Ashgabat sold 2.8 trillion cubic feet of gas in 1989, but only 480 billion in 1998, although the figure rose to 1.6 trillion in 2000. A few small Western oil companies have invested in Turkmenistan, but the larger ones have shied away because the government refuses to institute a program of economic reforms, privatization, or the international legislation that is necessary to attract foreign investment. When Ashgabat tried to open up 43,000 square miles of its Caspian Sea shelf (where offshore reserves are estimated to be more than 500 million barrels of oil and 101 trillion cubic feet of gas) to Western oil companies for exploration in 1997, international response was weak. The IMF and other multilateral donors have also shied away from Turkmenistan because of its lack of an economic reform process. In April 2000 the European Bank for Reconstruction and Development suspended $209 million in public-sector loans to Turkmenistan in protest against the government's anti-democratic policies. But reforms do not appear likely under Niyazov and his senior government officials, widely believed to be corrupt.

Turkmenistan maintains a foreign policy of neutrality, which has helped distance it from Russia and its own rivals in Central Asia but has also helped further isolate the country. Niyazov has refused to join CIS economic or military pacts, refused to send troops to join the Central Asian peace-keeping force in Tajikistan, and refused to join the other Central Asian states in condemnation of the Taliban in Afghanistan. This last makes some political sense because Turkmenistan thereby enjoys good relations with both the Taliban and the anti-Taliban alliance, and this has prevented Turkmen dissidents and Islamicists from seeking sanctuary in Afghanistan. Most of the Turkmen opposition is actually in exile in Moscow, whilst as yet there are no signs of a strong underground Islamic movement in the country.

Yet despite its policy of neutrality, Turkmenistan maintains close military relations with Moscow. Russian troops guard the Iran-Turkmenistan border, and Russian citizens in Turkmenistan have been

given dual nationality—a measure that stopped the exodus of qualified Russians after independence. Turkmenistan has enormous economic potential, and its strategic location makes it the ideal choice for Central Asian gas exports to the west, east, and south. However, the regime has done little to improve the country's devastating social problems or to introduce economic reforms in order to present itself as a meaningful and legitimate international partner.

Uzbekistan: At the Center of the Storm

The Uzbeks occupy Central Asia's Islamic heartland of Bukhara, Samarkand, and the Fergana Valley and make up the oldest urban civilization in the region. Samarkand, Timur's capital, was founded in the fifth century B.C. by the Sogdian king Afrasiab. The cities of modern-day Uzbekistan have been the capitals of Central Asia's many empires, whilst the fertile Fergana Valley has always been home for the largest concentration of population in the region and the cultural center of both Islamic piety and Islamic rebellion. The Russians followed historical tradition by developing Tashkent into the political, industrial, and trade center of Central Asia. With its population of 2.2 million, broad, tree-lined avenues, bleak but imposing Soviet-style architecture, and huge industrial parks that once turned out Soviet armaments, Tashkent emanates power.

Today Uzbekistan is the largest, most powerful Central Asian Republic, and its 279,375 square miles touch the borders of all the other Central Asian states. Ethnic Uzbeks make up 69 percent of its 25 million people, giving the country a reasonable homogeneity. The most numerous, aggressive, and influential of Central Asia's ethnic groups, Uzbeks also form substantial minorities in Tajikistan (23 percent), Turkmenistan (13 percent), and Kyrgyzstan (13 percent). In addition, some twenty-five thousand Uzbeks live in China's Xinjiang Province, and 2 million in Afghanistan. President Karimov finds these displaced populations extremely useful; they give him enormous influence by

posing a constant threat to ethnic stability of their own countries. After Kabul fell to the Mujahedeen in 1992, Karimov supported the Uzbek warlord Rashid Dostum in his creation of an autonomous Uzbek region based in Mazar-i-Sharif to rival the traditional Pashtun capital, Kabul.

Compared to the nomadic Kazakh and Kyrgyz and the scattered Tajik clans, the Uzbeks have the deepest national roots in Central Asia. The Shaybani Uzbeks founded their empire in A.D. 1500, defeating the Timurids, and establishing the Uzbek language and literature. Mahmud Ibn Wali, a sixteenth-century historian, describes the Uzbeks as "famed for their bad nature, swiftness, audacity and boldness" and writes that they reveled in their outlaw image whilst cultivating a culture of hospitality that was unrivalled in the Muslim world.[3]

After the decline of the Shaybani Empire, the region gradually fell to the Russians, whose forced modernization led to the rise of the urban-based Jadid reform movement, which was largely made up of Uzbek and Tartar Muslims. After the 1917 revolution a few Jadids attempted to combine Islam with communism, but they were crushed by Stalin. Jadid ideas returned in 1991 in the planks of nationalist opposition parties like Birlik and Erk, both of which President Karimov immediately banned. By this move, Karimov ensured that there would be no democratic outlet for the revival of Islam and Islamic nationalism.

The Russians had turned Uzbekistan into an economic powerhouse, and the Soviets continued the work. Tashkent grew into the largest industrial and trading center in Central Asia as thousands of Russian soldiers and bureaucrats arrived to colonize the new frontier. The Soviets developed a huge agricultural base in Uzbekistan and a virtual plantation economy through cotton cultivation. Between 1940 and 1980 cotton production increased fourfold, from 2.4 million tons to 9.9 million tons, making Uzbekistan the third-largest cotton producer in the world. But the ecological effect of forcing cotton agriculture on the region has been devastating. The Aral Sea has lost 55 percent of its original area and 31 percent of its water volume because the rivers that once emptied into the sea have been drawn off for irrigation. The result has been a massive dust bowl, coupled with air and soil pollution. By 1989 cotton production was down to 4.9 million tons, and it has never recovered. But Uzbekistan also has large mineral resources, including gold, estimated gas reserves of 70 trillion cubic feet, and a self-sufficiency of oil, all of which enhance its economic strength.

Uzbeks who rose through the ranks of the Communist Party of Uzbekistan (CPU) after 1920 maintained an ambivalent relationship with Moscow. Obedient Communists, they also constantly resisted Moscow's domination—to which Stalin responded by instigating several ruthless purges. Sharif Rashidov, head of the CPU from 1959 to 1983, perpetrated the Soviet scam of the century: a massive swindle of the Soviet exchequer through falsified cotton production figures. To Uzbeks, who viewed corruption within the CPU as a snub to Moscow, Rashidov was considered a hero—a tradition that continues to this day, creating major problems for the modernization of Uzbekistan's economy. The CPU also had to balance the claims for influence and patronage by party leaders from the various regions of Uzbekistan. This, too, continues to be an issue. Karimov, who hails from Samarkand, must constantly fend off rivals from other elites from Tashkent and the Fergana Valley.

Like the other leaders of Central Asia, Karimov was a first secretary of the ruling Communist Party who parlayed this position into the presidency both before and after independence. Also like them, he has run an authoritarian state ever since, crushing dissent, banning all political parties (except for a brief period of freedom), exerting complete control over the media—even going so far as to have political opponents kidnapped by his fearsome security agencies from neighboring Central Asian states. After he banned the CPU in 1991, he established the People's Democratic Party of Uzbekistan, which had virtually the same structure and membership as the CPU. In presidential elections he allows one other candidate to stand against him to give the impression that voters have a choice, but these candidates have either been denied a chance to air their views or are themselves Karimov loyalists. The 250-member parliament (the Oliy Majlis) is stacked with nominees from local government bureaucracies and state bodies; it meets briefly for a few sessions a year to rubber stamp Karimov's policies. In March 1995 Karimov held a referendum to extend his presidency until 2000, at which time he further extended it through reelection.

A dour, uninspiring, and extremely autocratic figure, Karimov was born to a Tajik mother and an Uzbek father, but he was orphaned as a child. Like Turkmenistan's President Niyazov, Karimov was raised in a state orphanage—a favorite recruiting ground for the Soviets. He later trained as a mechanical engineer. And like all the other Central Asian leaders, he has become increasingly isolated from the public and from political activity over the years, surrounding himself with openly corrupt sycophants. Like them, he has become increasingly unable to find solutions to his country's overwhelming problems because he refuses to recognize their source.

But unlike some other Central Asian leaders, who at least explored the possibility of economic restructuring as a way of reaching out to the international economic community, Karimov has resisted economic reform and privatization from the first. Uzbekistan has therefore had to weather a series of severe economic crises since independence. In 1992 acute food shortages led to riots in Tashkent, which were finally put down by military force. In 1994, after Uzbekistan was forced to introduce its own currency, the Uzbek som (which is different from the Kyrgyz som), inflation rose to 1,500 percent. (The average annual inflation for 1991–95 was 465 percent.)

But Karimov continues to resist IMF pressure to stabilize and reform the Uzbek currency. In April 2001 the IMF closed its office in Tashkent, harshly criticizing the regime's lack of reforms. Rising lev-

els of poverty and unemployment—as high as 80 percent in the Fergana Valley—are now major concerns for the regime, but it appears
to be doing little to tackle the issue. Some four hundred thousand
young people come on the job market every year, and 60 percent of
the population is now under 25 years old. These young people are
jobless, restless, and hungry, and their numbers are growing. The
Uzbek State Planning Agency estimates that by 2115 the population
will rise to 36 million.

Foreign investment has been sporadic. International investors continue to eye Uzbekistan because of the country's strategic location,
abundant natural resources, and trained manpower. But Uzbekistan's
continued refusal to institute economic reforms makes it a risky propo-
sition: before it pulled out of the country altogether, the IMF, along
with the World Bank, suspended loan agreements in 1995 for two years
because of the lack of economic reform. With no international monitoring, corruption, favoritism, and business inefficiency increased rapidly. This has not entirely halted foreign investment. Turkey has invested hundreds of millions of dollars in four hundred joint-venture
projects, whilst the United States is a major investor in mining and energy, and South Korean and German companies are involved in auto-
mobile production. All these deals have been made directly with Karimov and the presidential office because the state has no systematic
foreign-investment process in place.

The United States, initially a sharp critic of Karimov's abysmal
human-rights record, has all but ignored the issue since 1996 and increased investments in the region owing to concerns about Afghanistan, a desire to isolate Iran, and fears about the growing Russian influence in Central Asia. In 1997 U.S. mining companies invested
heavily in Uzbekistan; U.S.-Uzbekistan trade rose to $420 million
from a paltry $50 million in 1996. Uzbekistan has reciprocated by
keeping Moscow at arm's length—although the country's Russia policy seems to rely more on the mood swings of President Karimov than
on reasoned policy initiatives. Uzbekistan was the first Central Asian

state involved in NATO's Partnership for Peace military training program, which Kyrgyzstan and Kazakhstan also joined, and since 1998 Uzbek troops have held joint exercises with U.S. and NATO troops. Yet in spring 2000 Uzbekistan and Russia signed a secret pact for military cooperation (which Karimov rejected in the fall).[4] Karimov also refuses to give Russians living in Uzbekistan dual citizenship, as Turkemistan did.

Karimov's policy shifts, which seem to involve little consultation or debate within the Uzbek bureaucracy, have left the Uzbek elite deeply concerned about the future. "Our leaders cannot face up to reality. They are overwhelmed and paralyzed by the problems they face," a senior Uzbek official told me in Tashkent, adding, "We don't know from one day to the next what the president is going to order us to do in changing foreign or domestic policy. Yesterday's enemies are today's friends, and there is little coherent advice we can give when we are not asked, and policy changes without reason or justification."[5] It was a stinging indictment from a bureaucracy that for ten years had never dared admit the failings of the presidency, even in private.

Karimov's policies have made his neighbor states understandably wary. Karimov seeks to assert Uzbekistan's leading role in Central Asia, strong-arming smaller states like Kyrgyzstan and Tajikistan to support its policies and creating problems for Kazakhstan after it began to receive greater foreign investment from Western oil companies. Uzbekistan periodically cuts off gas supplies to Kazakhstan, Kyrgyzstan, and Tajikistan in order to put pressure on them, even though in 2000 the country earned some $310 million from supplying 1.9 trillion cubic feet of gas to its neighbors. Uzbekistan's assertive foreign policy forays across the region include giving military support to the Tajikistan regime during the Tajik civil war and to Afghan Uzbeks who were resisting the Taliban advance into northern Afghanistan. Such policies have been largely unsuccessful. In Tajikistan, President Rahmonov formed a coalition with Islamicists in 1997 that annoyed Karimov intensely, whilst the Afghan Uzbek leader General Dostum was defeated by the Taliban. Nonetheless Uzbekistan has successfully sold the idea that it is the regional gendarme to both the United States and Russia, and they continue to support the country whilst trying to influence the direction it is taking. The other Central Asian states, meanwhile, remain highly suspicious of Karimov's intentions.

Karimov's real problems lie closer to home. In addition to Uzbekistan's dire economic situation, Karimov faces growing political opposition to his autocratic rule. For a brief period after independence Uzbekistan had the strongest and most sophisticated opposition political parties in the region. The most popular was Birlik (Unity), whose political rallies (which I attended in Tashkent) drew thousands of supporters despite a massive police presence. Birlik was a democratic-nationalist party established in 1988 by Uzbek intellectuals; it was sharply critical of the regime on a variety of issues and was strongly anti-Russian. In April 1990 a splinter group called Erk (Freedom) was formed under the leadership of the poet Salay Madaminov, who is known by his pseudonym Muhammad Solih. Erk was more accommodating towards the regime, and Solih was allowed to run in the presidential elections in December 1991 whilst the Birlik leader Aburahim Polat was not. But in 1992 Karimov banned both parties and forced their leaders into exile. Both parties later established human rights groups; Birlik runs the Human Rights Society of Uzbekistan and Erk the Independent Human Rights Organization of Uzbekistan.

Having crushed the democratic opposition by 1992, Karimov then targeted Islamic fundamentalist groups based in the Fergana Valley. In a series of crackdowns in 1992, 1993, and after 1997, Karimov arrested hundreds of ordinary pious Muslims for alleged links with Islamic fundamentalists, accusing them of being Wahhabis, closing down mosques and madrassahs, and forcing mullahs into jail or exile. The Islamic Renaissance Party (IRP), formed in the Soviet Union as an Islamic political party that would have an inde-

84

pendent branch in each Central Asian state, was never able to register as a legal party in Uzbekistan. In 1998 the government passed the
infamous Law on Freedom of Conscience and Religious Organizations, which established new modes of repression against Muslims.
(Other religious organizations were unaffected by the law.) After unknown Uzbek extremists attempted to assassinate Karimov on February 16, 1999, by exploding six massive car bombs in Tashkent that
killed thirteen and injured more than a hundred, Karimov instituted a massive crackdown. Police arrested several thousand people,
and the government accused both Erk and Islamic militants of the
bombings.

The result of these repressive policies has been the growth of
exactly what Karimov feared: extremist Islamic militancy. The rise of
the IMU, the most powerful militant Islamic group operating in
Central Asia today which carries out yearly incursions in Uzbekistan, Kyrgyzstan, Tajikistan, and elsewhere in the Fergana Valley,
can be directly linked to Karimov's refusal to allow Muslims to practice their religion and his extreme attitude to all religious expression
or political dissent. As the IMU continues to gain adherents throughout Central Asia, its leader Juma Namangani has forged close links
with the Taliban and Osama bin Laden in Afghanistan, strengthening and spreading the power of the militants.

As Karimov has concentrated all power within his government he
has created enemies amongst Uzbekistan's regional elites which
undermines the traditional balance of power amongst them by withholding the jobs, patronage, and influence they are accustomed to.
Many Uzbeks believe that the Tashkent bombings were the work not
of Muslim extremists but of people within the government trying to
get rid of Karimov. In January 2000 Karimov won the presidential
election with 92 percent of the vote. This mandate might have carried more weight had not the only alternative candidate, Abdulhafiz
Jalalov, acknowledged that he himself had voted for Karimov in the
interests of "stability, peace, our nation's independence and the

development of Uzbekistan."[6] Foreign observers declared the election a farce.

The regime has depended on the passivity of the people as well as harsh laws and overwhelming powers of the state security apparatus to retain its hold on power and maintain law and order. "The authoritarian approach has at best postponed, but not defused, a looming economic and political crisis," warns a 2001 report by the International Crisis Group.[7] Others believe that the crisis is already at hand: Uzbekistan has become the center of Islamic resistance and extremism in Central Asia and the weakest link in the arc of instability that is spreading across the region. The population is becoming restive under continued authoritarianism. Although intellectuals may still hope for a peaceful transfer to a more democratic regime, people other than Islamic militants now call for Karimov's overthrow.

Tajikistan: An Opportunity Lost?

More than any other Central Asian state, Tajikistan is a model—of both what can be and what might be. Devastated by a five-year civil war immediately after independence (1992–97), Tajikistan rose from the ashes with a democratically elected coalition government that for the first time in Central Asia accommodated both religious and secular parties. This government has been touted amongst some observers as a model that offers domestic peace and international investment opportunities. Today, however, as its economic crises worsen, militant extremists use its land as a refuge, and Uzbekistan's President Karimov stirs up unrest amongst its substantial Uzbek minority and alternately offers and withholds aid, Tajikistan also stands as a warning of how quickly poverty, repression, and the increasing drug trade from Afghanistan can undermine even the best intentions.

Tajikistan has a small population—just 5.2 million—of whom 60 percent are Tajiks whilst some 23 percent are Uzbeks. One million Tajiks live in Uzbekistan and another two hundred thousand in Xinjiang. There are also 4.5 million Tajiks in Afghanistan, where the majority are opposed to the Taliban. Ahmad Shah Masood, the anti-Taliban resistance leader until he was assassinated on September 9, 2001, was a Tajik from the Panjsher Valley, north of Kabul. Landlocked Tajikistan shares a 650-mile border with Afghanistan and is separated from northern Pakistan by just the thin wedge of Afghanistan's Wakhan Corridor—only 6 miles wide in parts—which was mapped out by Russia and Great Britain in the nineteenth century to ensure that the British and Russian empires were not contiguous. Tajikistan also shares a mountainous 265-mile border with China's Xinjiang Province. Beijing claims some 30 percent of Tajikistan's eastern province of Gorno-Badakhshan, which has large gold and other mineral deposits. The border dispute has remained unsettled for the past decade.

The Pamir Mountains cover 93 percent of Tajikistan, severely limiting communications, industry, and agriculture. Yet despite its difficult terrain the region has always had a remarkable wealth of civilization, for it straddled important routes for trade and conquest, including the famous Silk Route. As the descendants of the ancient Persian Empire, the Tajiks are culturally and linguistically Persian, constituting the major non-Turkic ethnic group in the region. For centuries they dominated trade and business in the Central Asian cities, speaking both Persian and local Turkic dialects and living in relative harmony with Uzbeks and other Turkic ethnic groups as empire followed empire. The remains of these civilizations, which were excavated by the Soviets, but hidden away to prevent the Tajiks from learning about their ethnic history, can be viewed today in the newly opened National Museum in Dushanbe. The Buddhist artifacts from the second-century Kushan Empire are particularly striking. The most famous is the sleeping figure of Buddha, at forty feet in length the largest Buddha in Central Asia. (The huge standing

Buddha statues in Bamiyan were larger, but these were destroyed by the Taliban in 2001.)

In the nineteenth century Tajikistan was the last region in Central Asia to become part of Russia's province of Turkestan. The border between Afghanistan and Tajikistan remained open, however, and tribal leaders and bandits frequently took refuge in one another's territories whilst the Central Asian khans recruited Afghan guards for their palaces. Tajikistan later became a center for the Basmachi rebellion, and these Muslim leaders also took refuge in Afghanistan. Today the resistance that until September 2001 was headed by Ahmad Shah Masood has a supply base in Tajikistan, where arms are funneled from Russia, Iran, and India.

Although regional and clan-based rivalries have always existed in Tajikistan, where valleys surrounded by high mountains cut villages and population centers off from one another, Stalin was largely responsible for their intensification. Through his arbitrary boundary divisions in the 1920s, in which he created republics that had little geographical or ethnic rationale, Stalin weakened the Tajiks at the expense of the Uzbeks, deliberately sowing strife between the two largest ethnic groups in Central Asia. The Tajik cultural centers of Bukhara and Samarkand were handed over to Uzbekistan, leaving the Tajiks without an urban center to offset the disadvantages of a state whose main features were the unproductive Pamir Mountains and a poor agricultural base. In 1925 the capital, Dushanbe, was just a village of six thousand people where a rural market was held every Monday (Dushanbe in Persian). Ignored by Moscow, Tajikistan had the lowest per capita income, the highest unemployment and birth rates, and the fewest industries in the former Soviet Union. Between 1979 and 1989 the population increased 34 percent—one of the highest growth rates in the world.

There were other discrepancies adding to Tajikistan's ethnic difficulties. Whilst the northern city of Khujand (then called Leninabad), with its mixed population of one million Uzbeks and Tajiks, was developed as an industrial center, becoming the main recruiting base for leaders of the Communist Party of Tajikistan (CPTJ), the valleys in the center of the country were neglected. The eastern province of Gorno-Badakhshan, which was inhabited by non-Tajik Pamiri ethnic groups (including Ismaeli Muslims, who are followers of the Aga Khan), remained poverty stricken. The consequence was widespread rivalry not only between the Tajiks, Uzbeks, and Pamiris but amongst the various Tajik clans, a major cause of the later civil war. The Tajik clans in southeastern Kulab had close ties to the former Communist nomenklatura from Khujand, making them bitter rivals of their neighboring clans in Kurgan Tyube, who supported the Islamic insurgents during the civil war. And some of these pro-Islamic clans in Kurgan Tyube originally hailed from Garm; they had been forcefully resettled in the south by the Communists to work the cotton fields. The CPTJ was dominated by Khujandis and ethnic Russian settlers. This ethnic diversity, regionalism, and clanism, allied with poverty, made civil war all but inevitable. When independence came in 1991, the people of Tajikistan had almost no sense of nationhood.

Independence deprived Tajikistan of Soviet subsidies, foodstuffs, and aid. Their loss created an immediate crisis, and there were riots in Dushanbe. Between 1990 and 1992, the leadership in Tajikistan changed three times. Compared with the grip the other Central Asian leaders were able to maintain on their pre-independence power, these changes were a sharp reflection of the ongoing political instability and lack of power of the CPTJ. Rakhmon Nabiev, the former secretary general of the CPTJ and first president of the new republic, was forced to resign in September 1992 after weeks of rioting and protests left hundreds of dead in the streets of Dushanbe. Although Russia had flown in troops, they had not been enough to allow Nabiev to regain control of the country. To date Nabiev is the only Central Asian leader who has resigned as a result of public protest. Seeing the failure of Russia to protect them, two hundred thousand Russians fled Tajikistan in 1992.

The popular opposition of many political groups to the Communists and the Nabiev regime was led by a group of Islamicists under the banner of the newly founded Islamic Renaissance Party, the first populist manifestation of Islamic fundamentalism in Central Asia. Meanwhile, powerful clan-based parties in Khujand and Gorno-Badakhshan threatened to split away from Tajikistan and create their own states. Tajikistan entered a period of chaos after Nabiev's departure. The IRP and several democratic and nationalist groups formed a coalition government, but it was unable to keep peace, and it was bloodily overthrown in December 1992, when neo-Communist forces from Khujand and Kulab invaded Dushanbe and installed Emomali Rahmonov as president. As the IRP retreated to their strongholds in Kurgan Tyube, Gorno-Badakhshan, and the Karategin Valley, the civil war began in earnest. Over the next five years more than fifty thousand (perhaps as many as a hundred thousand) of Tajikistan's 5 million people were killed, whilst two hundred and fifty thousand fled to Afghanistan, Pakistan, Iran, and other CIS states, and half a million more were made homeless.

The IRP, which had formed a broad-based alliance with other nationalist parties called the United Tajik Opposition (UTO), set up bases in the Pamir Mountains and Afghanistan, from which it launched guerrilla attacks against the government. Ahmad Shah Masood, who had fought the Soviets in Afghanistan, gave the IRP military support when they arrived in northern Afghanistan.

Meanwhile, poorly disciplined government militias led by clan warlords rampaged through the countryside, looting villages and murdering civilians. The eight thousand Russian border guards and troops who tried to check the flow of arms (and drugs) through the Afghanistan-Tajikistan border gave the government support inside the country but avoided taking part in major battles. Fearing the spread of the conflict, other Central Asian states sent small contingent troops to back Russian forces. Foreign diplomats fled Dushanbe as the city became the target of bombs and a center for shootouts and assassinations. The economy collapsed, and even food production ground to a halt, forcing the government to mortgage its industrial assets to Moscow to pay for Russian loans, arms, food, and fuel.

Russia, Iran, and the Central Asian states all backed U.N.-sponsored peace talks between the government and the UTO, which were first held in Moscow in April 1994. The talks dragged on for three years whilst heavy fighting continued. They finally concluded in Iran in February 1997. Rahmonov and UTO leader Abdullah Nuri agreed to form a national reconciliation committee and integrate their armed forces into a new, national army. The government issued a general amnesty and pledged to legalize the opposition parties. The accord was signed in Moscow in June, and Nuri returned to Dushanbe under heavy guard in September, but fighting continued as the warlords who had been left out of the agreement continued to mount guerrilla attacks. Final implementation of the agreement did not take place until February 2000, when parliamentary elections were held in which several parties, including the IRP, took part. Rahmonov's People's Democratic Party of Tajikistan won, with 64.5 percent of the vote.

Both sides had given in under pressure. Renegade IRP militants offered pockets of resistance throughout the lengthy peace process, and Rahmonov accepted the agreement only because Russia and the Central Asian states forced him to and because a new threat had appeared—Afghanistan's Taliban. In 1996 the Taliban had captured Kabul and began to move north defeating the alliance of Afghan Uzbeks, Tajiks, and Hazaras then holding all of northern Afghanistan. Containing the Taliban and maintaining a buffer of anti-Taliban forces between Afghanistan and Central Asia became vital security issues for Russia and the Central Asian leaders. Rahmonov gave Masood the use of Kulab air base, where military supplies were shipped to him for the anti-Taliban resistance.

Nevertheless, the peace agreement in Tajikistan represented a landmark. For the first time Central Asia's neo-Communist politicians were forced to share power not only with opposition political groups but with local Islamic forces. Tajikistan's agreement became even more significant as a model for other Central Asian republics like Uzbekistan when the IMU tried to invade the Fergana Valley in the summers of 1999 and 2000 in a bid to topple the regime in Uzbekistan.

The 1997 peace agreement has survived four years of assassinations, social and civil unrest, lack of humanitarian aid, and grinding poverty, which have prevented any significant rehabilitation of the country. But Tajikistan remains the most disadvantaged of the Central Asian nations. The economy is in ruins, the government has no control over large tracts of territory, and the drug smuggling from Afghanistan for onward journey to Europe has become a major factor in the continued destabilization of the country. Though the IMF and the World Bank gave small loans for reconstruction, and the Aga Khan Foundation has launched a highly effective developmental program in Gorno-Badakhshan, Tajikistan receives little other international economic support—support it desperately needs if the coalition government is to succeed and stand as a model of political inclusion for other Central Asian states. In many ways Tajikistan is the key to peace and stability in Central Asia—something the international community must recognize, and soon.

PART II Islamic Movements in Central Asia Since 1991

5   The Islamic Renaissance Party and the Civil War in Tajikistan

THE BLOODY CIVIL WAR in Tajikistan, which had the highest number of casualties proportionate to the population of any civil war in the past fifty years, was Central Asia's first experience of a political coup by a homegrown Islamicist movement. The Tajik Islamicists—heirs to the Basmachis—are unique amongst militant Central Asian Islamic groups. The movement brings together the various strands of Central Asian Islam, a grounding that gives it a legitimacy far beyond that of other extreme radical groups operating in Central Asia today like the IMU, whose Islam derives largely from Saudi Arabia's Wahhabism and the interpretation of Deobandism by the Taliban. Tajik Islamicists include the "unofficial" ulema who were forced underground during the Soviet period, the registered clergy belonging to "official" Islam, the Sufi pirs and their followers in the Pamir Mountains, and a younger generation influenced by the war in Afghanistan and the reassertion of Tajik nationalism following the collapse of the Soviet Union. These groups all joined in the rapid revival of Islam in Tajikistan after 1991—a resurgence that shocked Central Asian rulers. Between 1990 and 1992, a thousand new mosques opened in Tajikistan—

more than one a day—many of them located in homes, schools, and workplaces. After the civil war began, these groups were able to bring many more adherents to their cause.

The Islamic revival was also closely linked to Tajik nationalism. Tajiks had never forgotten the Basmachi rebellion against the Soviets in the 1920s, despite Soviet efforts to portray it in history books as a reactionary movement led by mullahs supported by British imperialism. After independence came many Tajiks sought to rediscover their side of the story as part of an effort to forge a national consensus and identity where none had existed before. Unlike Uzbekistan—where anti-Russian Uzbek nationalism was the first major political movement which developed greater Uzbek national consciousness to arise following independence—Tajikistan had no historical national roots because the Tajiks were scattered across Central Asia and the collectivization of agriculture had fragmented the clan structure. In fact, Uzbeks constituted 23 percent of Tajikistan's own population, dominating parts of the north and southwest; whilst Uzbeks had made up a disproportionate percentage of the Communist Party of Tajikistan before that. Thus many Tajiks saw the Islamic revival as a means to cement a Tajik identity and ensure Tajikistan's development as a unified state.

The extreme poverty of Tajikistan during the Soviet period, its dependence on a forced economy of cotton agriculture, its harsh geography, in which Tajik villages isolated in the high valleys of the Pamir Mountains were cut off from the central regions as well as from their neighbors, all meant that most Tajiks identified with their regions and clans rather than with their country. This lack of nationalism sharply limited political aims on both sides of the civil war, for clan-based warlords repeatedly switched loyalties and perpetrated ever-increasing atrocities in the name of "ethnic cleansing" to "purify" the areas under their control. Thus, when a greater sense of Tajik nationalism began to emerge after the civil war, it took on a distinctly anti-Uzbek rather than anti-Russian cast. The harsh policies of Uzbekistan's President Karimov towards Tajikistan, and his determination to prevent or undermine the Tajik nationalist revival, only increased Tajik resentment against Uzbekistan.

Origins of the Islamic Renaissance Party

Islam was a natural way to encourage Tajik nationalism, for an underground political Islam had thrived in Tajikistan more than in any other Central Asian state during the Soviet period. The most influential underground spiritual leader in the Soviet era was Mullah Muhammad Rustamov Hindustani, who had studied at the madrassah in Deoband, India, before returning home to open a clandestine madrassah in Dushanbe in the 1970s. Hindustani brought the new ideas shaping the Muslim world and the ideology of Islamic fundamentalist movements in India, Pakistan, and the Arab states to Central Asia, spreading his message to both Tajiks and Uzbeks in the Fergana Valley. There is little historical record of this movement, but we do know that in 1982 there were at least twenty-two illegal madrassahs, including Hindustani's, all of which the Soviets shut down, sentencing Hindustani himself to fifteen years' imprisonment in Siberia, where he died in 1989.[1]

One of Hindustani's students was Abdullah Saidov, known as Sayed Abdullah Nuri, who was born in the town of Tavildara in 1947. Along with other clans from the valley, Nuri's family was forcibly moved in 1953 by the Soviet authorities to work the cotton fields in the Vakhsh Valley in the south. By 1974 Nuri had helped form an illegal Islamic educational organization, Nahzar-i-Islami (Islamic Knowledge), whilst training to become a surveying engineer. In March 1987 at Panj, close to the border with Afghanistan, Nuri led the first public demonstration in support of the Afghan Mujahedeen, a few weeks after guerrillas belonging to Gulbuddin Hekmatyar's Hizb-i-Islami (Party of Islam) had launched a rocket attack on the city from the Afghan side of the border. Nuri was arrested along with forty others on charges of circulating illegal Islamic literature and organizing a protest against the Soviet occupation of Afghanistan. Released in 1988, Nuri continued his clandestine political activities, eventually becoming a founding member and leader of the Islamic Renaissance Party (IRP).[2]

Another of Hindustani's students was Muhammad Sharif Himmatzoda, who became a leader of the military wing of the IRP. In December 1991, I met with Himmatzoda in a small house in the back alleys of Dushanbe whilst he was still in hiding. A tall, bearded, good-looking man, he came from a peasant family and had trained as a mechanic. He had fought with the Mujahedeen in Afghanistan, had close links to Afghan and Pakistani Islamicists like Hekmatyar and Qazi Hussein Ahmad (the leader of Pakistan's Jamiat-i-Islami [Islamic Party]), and had spent fifteen years in the Islamic underground avoiding arrest. Some of his colleagues had dubbed him the Gulbuddin Hekmatyar of Central Asia because Hekmatyar was considered the most ruthless and extremist Afghan Mujahedeen leader fighting the Soviets in Afghanistan. "For seventy-five years the Communists tried to wipe out the memory of Allah, but every Tajik today still remembers Allah and prays for the success of the party of Allah," he told me.[3]

Nuri and Himmatzoda were already old friends when they helped found the Tajik branch of the Islamic Renaissance Party. The IRP had been established in June 1990 in Astrakhan, Russia, largely by Tartar intellectuals who sought to organize Muslims within the Soviet Union to campaign for the introduction of sharia (Islamic law) to Russia. At the founding meeting, it was decided to let each Soviet republic set up its own, independent branch of the party. With glasnost in full swing under President Mikhail Gorbachev, the IRP registered as a political party in Russia, but it was banned in the Central Asian republics by their ruling Communist parties. Tajik representatives who had participated in the Astrakhan meeting and returned home determined to set up an IRP in Tajikistan faced an immediate ban.

With support from Nuri's youth organization, however, as well as from clans in the Karategin Valley and Karateginis who had been re-settled in the Vakhsh Valley around the town of Kurgan Tyube, a clandestine branch of the IRP did emerge in Tajikistan. The Tajik-istan IRP's (illegal) inaugural conference was held on October 26, 1991, and it was attended by some 650 delegates, who elected Him-matzoda as the party's first chairman, established an Islamic news-paper, and even approved a coat of arms and a flag. The IRP dedi-cated itself to spreading Islam, promoting a spiritual revival, and working for the political and economic independence of Tajikistan. Himmatzoda reassured the country at a press conference that the party's aim was to establish a democratic state committed to the rule of law, rather than an Islamic state.[4]

The party had already come out into the open in February 1990, after the Dushanbe housing riots, which were incited by fears that Armenian refugees, fleeing the fighting in their republic, would be resettled in the capital. Activists for the IRP managed to include Is-lamic demands amongst those of the masses surrounding the head-quarters of the CPTJ. For several days they staged sit-ins and put up banners demanding that more mosques be opened, that stores sell-ing pork and alcohol be closed, and that Tajik street names replace Russian ones.

As the political situation deteriorated in late 1991 (described in Chapter 3), political infighting broke out within the CPTJ, leading to several leadership replacements. Hard-line Communists in the Tajik parliament eventually forced through the election of 62-year-old Rakhmon Nabiev as president in September. Mass protests at his elec-tion broke out in Dushanbe, as tens of thousands of people camped out in Lenin Square—renamed Azadi (Freedom) Square—in the cen-ter of the city. I was there, and as I walked through the crowds, I saw their enthusiasm, their apparent indifference to the authorities, and their willingness to sit in the square day after day, hungry and thirsty. It was apparent that something very new was happening here, in one of the most politically repressed corners of the world. This was a heady time for the IRP, who fed and cared for the people living in the streets, receiving their first taste of mass mobilization and political agitation in the process. No other Islamic movement in Central Asia has ever been given such a chance at mass contact as Tajikistan's IRP was in those years. When the IRP was registered as a political party by the Tajik authorities in December, just a few days after the collapse of the Soviet Union, it already claimed twenty thousand members.

Meanwhile, Nabiev had been forced to hold a presidential election in the new republic. This took place on November 24, and Nabiev won by only a narrow margin: 58 percent of the vote. Even more shocking to Russian and Central Asian leaders, however, was the fact that Davlat Khudonazarov, the opposition candidate, who was supported by a growing alliance of democrats, nationalists, and Islamicists, won 34 percent of the vote. It was the first evidence in Central Asia of how quickly a well-organized, motivated opposition that included an Islamic party could mobilize popular support. Clearly, the Islamic revival was not limited to cultural reassertion and piety; if it posed a political challenge to the state in Tajikistan it could do the same in all the post-Communist regimes in Central Asia. The controversial election results led to more demonstrations and riots in March 1992, which were followed by a severe government crackdown in which many people were killed. Anarchy broke out in Dushanbe, as assassinations, kidnappings, and random killings became daily events. By now it was clear that a civil war was imminent, and key IRP leaders took to the mountains to set up military bases in the Karategin and Tavildara valleys north of Dushanbe.

The close network of Islamicists working in Dushanbe, related through family, clan, and regional ties, ensured that the IRP radicals were also in touch with the state-sponsored "official" Islam. A key sympathizer was Qazi Akbar Turajonzoda, the grand mufti (qazi) of Tajikistan's Muslims during the last years of the Soviet Union. Born in 1954 near Dushanbe, Turajonzoda studied at the official, Soviet-sponsored madrassah in Bukhara before going to Jordan for further Islamic studies in the 1970s. After his return he worked for a time in the Board of Muslims for Central Asia in Tashkent; he was appointed the first grand mufti of Tajikistan in 1988. In 1990 he was elected to the Supreme Soviet in Moscow, a sure sign that he was trusted by the Russians, and he had his own television show in Dushanbe. A large, rumbustious man, equal parts humor, ruthlessness, and opportunism, Turajonzoda developed extensive grass-roots contacts and encouraged the spate of mosque building that began in the capital in 1990, often blessing mosques on their opening with prayers even though they were outside his official jurisdiction.

When I met him in 1991, he was immensely popular, receiving hundreds of people a day in Dushanbe's main mosque and staying in touch with the IRP clandestinely. He confidently predicted the fall of the Nabiev government and the oncoming struggle between the government and the opposition. "Islam is strong, whilst people mistrust the Communists," he said proudly, even as he attended Nabiev's cabinet meetings.[5] Turajonzoda would later claim that the IRP was not interested in either fighting the government or trying to create an Islamic state but had been pushed into defending itself by the government's severe repression. (Nuri would make the same claim.)

After the civil war began Turajonzoda defected, becoming a prominent leader of the opposition alliance whilst living in exile in Iran. During the civil war he traveled extensively around the world, seeking support for the IRP. His official status, his Islamic learning, and his popularity gave the IRP a legitimacy that was unprecedented in Central Asia—it was as if the pope had left the Vatican to become a guerrilla leader. At the same time, he viewed the IRP with some suspicion, for its hierarchy tried to undercut his own popular status. Turajonzoda's supporters within the IRP argued that a single party could not bring about an Islamic revolution in Tajikistan; instead, society had to be slowly Islamicized from the bottom up. This attitude, which he revived after the civil war ended in 1997, led to his eventual expulsion from the IRP.

As Tajikistan's IRP forged critical alliances amongst other Tajik clans and ethnic groups, IRP parties in other Central Asian republics found it harder to establish a significant presence following independence. In Kazakhstan the IRP was dominated by non-Kazakhs, which made it less attractive to the rest of the country, whilst in Kyrgyzstan the IRP took root only in the south, amongst ethnic Uzbeks. The IRP never took hold in Turkmenistan. Although the IRP spread rapidly in Uzbekistan in the Fergana Valley, it lost force when its leader, Abdullah Utaev, disappeared in 1992, widely believed to have been kidnapped and killed by the Uzbek secret service. Other, more radical, groups emerged in the valley in 1991–92, largely displacing the IRP. These included Tauba (Repentance), Islam Lashkarlary (Fighters for Islam) and Adolat (Justice).

The Fergana Valley became the center of Uzbekistan's Islamic revival, with considerable foreign influence. Saudi, Pakistani, and Turkish missionaries arrived with suitcases full of dollars, trying to find sympathizers who would adhere to their particular Sunni sect or interpretation of militant Islam. Iran tried to muscle into Persian-speaking Tajikistan and create a support base amongst the IRP, but there was little sympathy for Shia Iran amongst the Sunni Tajiks, and despite the cultural and linguistic connections of the two groups, Teheran never had much influence with the Islamicists.

The Civil War

The political struggle in Dushanbe during 1992 created unrest everywhere in Tajikistan, as other regions demanded greater autonomy or threatened to split away from the republic. The Pamiris declared Gorno-Badakhshan an autonomous republic in April, whilst neo-Communist leaders in Khujand in the north and Kulab in the southeast threatened to form independent republics unless President Nabiev crushed the IRP. Armed militias from Kulab began to massacre villagers in the vicinity of Kurgan Tyube who supported the IRP. Tajikistan drifted into chaos, whilst Nabiev became more and more helpless. As violence escalated the president was forced to resign in September—the first time a Central Asian leader had been removed by street violence and public pressure. Karimov wrote to U.N. Secretary General Boutrous Boutrous-Ghali that "the threat of anarchy and chaos looms [over] the entire region."[6] The government claimed that as many as forty thousand people were killed in the first six months of 1992.

Russian troops took control of the Dushanbe airport and the Afghanistan border as tens of thousands of ethnic Russians tried to leave Tajikistan—more than two hundred thousand left in 1992. Fighting intensified in the south, where villages emptied and refugees from all sides fled to Dushanbe, creating the largest population shifts in Central Asia since collectivization, whilst many IRP supporters fled to Afghanistan. After a coup attempt by neo-Communist militias from Kulab in October, the Tajik parliament chose Emomali Rahmonov, a Communist leader from Kulab, to be the new president. Rahmonov swiftly gave control of all government departments and the army to Kulabis, removing any hopes that the government might forge a compromise with the IRP.

The civil war now became a protracted guerrilla struggle as the IRP launched attacks on government forces and the Kulabi militias from its bases in the Karategin and Tavildara valleys, Kurgan Tyube, and Afghanistan. IRP leaders fled to Iran, Pakistan, Russia, and Afghanistan, where they were joined by some eighty thousand refugees. They established bases in Kunduz and Taloqan in the northeast with the permission of the Kabul government, then controlled by Afghan Tajik leaders, President Burhanuddin Rabbani and his defense minister Ahmad Shah Masood. Meanwhile, Tajikistan's secular opposition leaders fled to Moscow, where they set up joint offices with the IRP to publicize their case. The Tajik conflict had now become an international issue and a transnational war: refugees in Afghanistan were trained, armed, and sent back to Tajikistan to fight whilst IRP leaders traveled to Iran, Pakistan, and Saudi Arabia seeking military and financial support. Russia and Uzbekistan threw their weight behind the Tajik government, sending in troops, aircraft, and military supplies, although at the same time they maintained a dialogue with the opposition.

Throughout the conflict the IRP had been flexible enough to forge alliances with other parties. These included the Rastokhez Popular Front, a small intellectual pro-democracy group in Dushanbe; the Democratic Party of Tajikistan; and Lali Badakhshan, the party of the Ismaeli Muslim Pamiris, which now virtually controlled Gorno-Badakhshan. In 1995 these parties, led by the IRP, formed the United Tajik Opposition, headquartered in both Moscow and Taloqan, Afghanistan. But as Tajikistan's economy collapsed and the government became more dependent on Russian aid, the atrocities and massacres continued. The two sides slowly realized that neither was strong enough to overcome the other militarily. A stalemate developed: the UTO launched guerrilla attacks in the summer from Afghanistan, and the government tried to recapture the lost areas in the winter. Gradually, both sides began to move towards peace talks.

In 1996 the regional equation changed dramatically when the Taliban captured Kabul and ousted the Afghan Tajik government. Central Asian leaders were fearful that the Taliban, drawn from the Pashtun ethnic group, would try to spread their harsh interpretation of Islam into Central Asia. Both the governments and the UTO now realized that it was in their common interest to negotiate an end to the civil war. The United Nations sent a special representative to mediate, and several rounds of talks were held between the two sides in Moscow, Teheran, and Islamabad, but it was not until Rahmonov met with Nuri face to face in Khos Deh, Afghanistan, in December that the peace process began to show progress.

Even though their immediate interests were sharply different, the players in the civil war now had concrete motives for seeking a settlement. The IRP knew that Russia and Uzbekistan wanted to isolate the party; and these powers would allow the suffering and poverty in Tajikistan to worsen in order to decrease the popularity of the party and Islam. President Rahmonov realized that he could not control the country with only a small power base of Kulabis, and continuing anarchy could destroy his tenuous hold. Russia and Iran, who supported Masood's continuing war against the Taliban, wanted to limit the role of Saudi Arabia and Pakistan, who were supporting the Taliban. Uzbekistan calculated that despite its military aid to Rahmonov the Tajik government was incapable of protecting the Uzbek minority in Tajikistan or reasserting control over the country. Rabbani and Masood recognized that they needed a secure, stable rear base in Tajikistan, where they could receive military supplies from Russia and Iran. Peace in Tajikistan was essential for this, and the two played a prominent role in the mediations.

Successive U.N. mediators were given a mandate by the Security Council to end the war and draw the armed factions into negotiation. "The success of the peace process depended on U.N. involvement, the support of all the neighboring states—which became guarantors of the peace agreements—and the willingness of the Tajiks to end the war," Ivo Petrov, the secretary general's special representative to Tajikistan, told me in 2001.[7] But the negotiators left out out several important factions, including the Khujandis, led by former prime minister Abdumalik Abdullajanov, and a group of Uzbeks led by renegade army officer Col. Makhmud Khudoyberdiev, who repeatedly tried to disrupt the peace process, even attacking Khujand in November 1998.

Nevertheless, the final peace agreement provided a model for other Central Asian states, even if they only grudgingly accepted it. A general amnesty was declared and prisoner exchanges were carried out, and for the first time in Central Asia a coalition government was established between two warring factions that included an avowedly Islamicist party. IRP rebels were incorporated into the army under U.N. supervision, and Tajik refugees returning from Afghanistan were reintegrated into their villages. The IRP and other parties were legitimized, and parliamentary elections were held in February 2000 in which six parties competed—itself an unprecedented shift away from authoritarianism. International observers criticized the elections as rigged by the government, and there were some local public protests, but Rahmonov's People's Democratic Party of Tajikistan swept the polls, winning 64.5 percent of the vote. The Communists came in second and the IRP a poor third, winning just 7.5 percent of the total vote. Nevertheless, Nuri announced that the results, though controversial, would be accepted and that the peace process was "irreversible." Such a situation of compromise and consensus was unthinkable in Uzbekistan and other Central Asian states, where multiparty polls had never been held except in Kyrgyzstan.

The Decline of the Islamic Renaissance Party

But the peace remained fragile. In 1999 the accords came close to breaking down several times as the UTO demanded quicker implementation of the agreements whilst hard-liners behind Rahmonov resisted. A rash of bombings, assassinations, and kidnappings took place in Dushanbe, whilst fighting between government troops and IRP rebels continued outside the capital. Throughout the violence U.N. mediator Gerd Merrem played a crucial role in maintaining the dialogue between the two sides.

Implementation of the accords was not helped by the dire state of Tajikistan's economy. Agriculture was severely disrupted, factories were shut down, and there was massive unemployment. When the war ended, in 1997, the United Nations had estimated that 60 percent of the under-30 population was unemployed. The reconstruction of the country was essential if both sides were to show their supporters that peace had its benefits. Yet year after year, relief work and the reintegration of the displaced population were hampered by lack of funds and the lack of interest from the international community.

Despite pledges of support the international community did little to aid the reconstruction efforts. The United Nations requested $34.8 million in humanitarian relief aid for Tajikistan for the year 2000, but by the end of the year it had received only half that amount. In 2001 the United Nations asked for $85 million, but six months later only 25 percent of the funds had come in. In Tajikistan living conditions remain dire. Acute electricity, water, and food shortages have led to increased poverty levels, whilst the population rose from 5.2 million in 1991 to 6.5 million in 2001. In 2001 a senior Tajik diplomat earned a salary equivalent to eight dollars a month, and the foreign minister got twenty. A crippling drought in 2000 and 2001 further depleted agricultural production, though the U.N. World Food Program brought in several million tons of wheat to feed the more than 1.2 million destitute people.

With no jobs or security Tajiks sought their livelihoods elsewhere. According to the International Organization of Migration, two hundred thousand men left Tajikistan every year to look for seasonal work in Russia. "It seems that every single family has a relative or friend working abroad, usually in Russia," said IOM official Igor Bose.[8] Others joined the massive drug smuggling organizations operating out of Afghanistan. After the Taliban conquest of northern Afghanistan in 1998, Tajikistan became a major route for exports of Afghan heroin to Russia and Europe. In May 2000 Tajik officials reported that ten times more heroin was arriving in Tajikistan than in the previous year. The money generated by the drug economy led to widespread corruption, a reluctance to carry out badly needed economic reforms, and continuing law-and-order problems, as drug mafias and security forces battled it out. It was a miracle that throughout this period the coalition government survived—or more likely, it was simply a reflection of Tajikistan's war weariness.

Peace brought its own problems to the IRP, where a significant debate was taking place about how the party should secure its political future and the future of Islam in Central Asia. In Tajikistan's disparate ethnic, regional, and clan makeup, the IRP's militant support base had rarely extended beyond either the personal clans of the leaders or regional links. The civil war had quickly became a battle between clans rather than an Islamic jihad. Thus the IRP was strong in some areas and nonexistent in others, where the government easily mobilized warlords from clans opposed to it. The IRP was never able to overcome the problems of regionalization, which increased at the end of the war after it failed to establish a countrywide party. Splits and factionalism dramatically lessened its influence—which was clearly apparent in the 2000 elections.

Qazi Turajonzoda, who had been appointed by Rahmonov first vice prime minister in March 1998, was expelled from the IRP for supporting Rahmonov's candidacy. In February 2000 he escaped an assassination attempt in Dushanbe by gunmen who were later identified as belonging to a hard-line faction of the IRP. IRP leaders opposed Turajonzoda's platform of moderation, in which he argued that Islam could not be institutionalized by a single party but must rather adopt a policy of slowly winning over the population. Some IRP leaders also considered Nuri too soft towards the government, although others accepted Nuri's compromises with Rahmonov. This led to further splits in the party.

In addition, several IRP commanders, along with some rank and file, refused to accept IRP orders to join the government army. Some joined up with the Uzbek leader Juma Namangani, who had also been a military commander with the IRP during the civil war and had decided to reject the peace agreement and continue his crusade, switching his target to the regime of his homeland, Uzbekistan. Namangani established the Islamic Movement of Uzbekistan, which operated out of Afghanistan and the Tavildara Valley in Tajikistan. His sorties in 1999, 2000, and 2001 against Uzbekistan, and the severe embarrassment they caused the Dushanbe government, further deepened the splits within the IRP, allowing Rahmonov to manipulate the party for his benefit. Other IRP rank and file not absorbed into the army became bandits, creating problems for the government through kidnappings and bank robberies. As late as the summer of 2001 one such group of about a hundred men led by a minor IRP commander named Rakhmon Sanginov was still creating mayhem in villages around Dushanbe. The Tajik army finally became involved, and after fighting that lasted more than a month, the rebels were surrounded in August, and Sanginov was killed, along with forty-five of his men.

Within the IRP, moderates led by Nuri advocated that jihad, as espoused originally by the IRP and taken up by the IMU, could not be the only function of Islamic movements in Central Asia. "Jihad cannot be the only criterion as advocated by the IMU. What is needed is a political structure that can further the cause of the Islam," said Moheyuddin Kabir, a deputy leader of the IRP and aide to Nuri, whose views reflect the younger generation of IRP realists. Other IRP leaders, such as Sharif Himmatzoda, the former IRP military commander whom I had met a decade earlier in the Islamicist underground in Dushanbe, had now joined the government. Himmatzoda was a member of parliament. His once-long beard was trimmed short, and he wore a well-cut suit and a tie. "The peace process in Tajikistan can be a model for Central Asia if all parties are willing to build peace just as we were," he insisted. "But governments in the region have to change their attitudes towards Islamic movements to give them a legal, constitutional way to express themselves and play a role in state building. If they don't do so, people will join the extremists."[9] His comments were frighteningly appropriate: by now the IMU and the Uzbek regime had become locked in mortal combat.

As the IRP lost political support, its main faction, led by Nuri, took on the role of parliamentary opposition within the government, in part because the group realized that the IRP—and the country—faced severe challenges from even more extremist Islamic parties and ideologues. The civil war was over, but Tajikistan was still at the center of the continuing instability in Central Asia and Afghanistan, a situation the international community barely recognized. Dushanbe continued to provide a supply base for Masood's resistance to the Taliban—and it became even more critical to Masood in September 2000 after he lost Taloqan, his headquarters in northern Afghanistan, following a month-long siege. The Taliban now controlled a long section of the Afghanistan-Tajikistan border, eyeball to eyeball for the first time with the Russian border guards on the Tajik side.

The regional countries backing Masood quickly realized that if he were to hold the line against the Taliban, he would need greater military support. In a critical meeting in Dushanbe on October 26, 2000, the Russian defense minister, Igor Sergeyev, along with Iran's foreign minister Kamal Kharrazi, and President Rahmonov, met with Masood and pledged to step up their support for him. Masood's anti-Taliban United Front held the line the following summer, preventing the Taliban from capturing Badakhshan, the last northern Afghan province under his control, which also borders Tajikistan. But more than ever before this made Tajikistan a front line against the Taliban, who vowed to destabilize the country. Faced with these external threats and the fear that tens of thousands of Afghan refugees might flood into Tajikistan, the Tajik government was hard pushed to concentrate on economic development.

The Taliban were not the only danger. Tajikistan was also the gateway to the Fergana Valley for the IMU, which continued to maintain a base in the Tavildara Valley and by summer 2001 was recruiting from all the ethnic groups in Central Asia for what was fast becoming a pan–Central Asian Islamic movement. The presence of the IMU on Tajik soil heightened Dushanbe's problems with both Uzbekistan and Kyrgyzstan. It also increased divisions within the IRP because Namangani had the clandestine support of such former IRP commanders as Mirzo Ziyoyev, now a minister in the Tajik government, who saw the IMU as a means to exert pressure on Uzbekistan. Tajikistan also faced a new pan-Islamic movement that had begun to gain popularity throughout the Central Asian Republics—the Hizb ut-Tahrir al-Islami (Party of Islamic Liberation; HT). Unlike the IRP, which had drawn its support mainly from the rural areas, the HT recruited largely amongst the urban educated elite. But even though the HT was nonmilitant, the government refused to tolerate another Islamic movement and so initiated a crackdown against it, a move that ironically was supported by the IRP leaders in the coalition. What Rahmonov saw as a security threat, the IRP saw as a rival for its own Islamic support base. One radical Islamic force was now pitted against another.

Tajikistan remained heavily dependent on Russia for support, but Moscow was unable to provide sufficient economic aid to enable the country to overcome the ravages of the civil war. The West continued to ignore Tajikistan. It was not until 2001—nearly five years after the peace agreement was signed—that the international community began to realize the strategic importance of the coalition government in Dushanbe and the need to provide it with material help. The international community finally seemed to realize that Tajikistan was facing threats from the Taliban, the IMU, and the HT—and that these threats could affect them.

As the United States tried to isolate the Taliban and Osama bin Laden it began to realize the importance of stability in Tajikistan to this process. Gen. Tommy Franks, the head of the U.S. Central Command forces (which cover the Middle East and Central Asia), made his first visit to Dushanbe in May 2001. For the first time, U.S. officials described Tajikistan as "a strategically significant country," which needed to be strengthened to ensure peace and security in Central Asia, and they pledged U.S. military aid to bolster Tajikistan's security.[10] In turn the Tajikistan government agreed to join NATO's Partnership for Peace security program for Central Asia, and the Consultative Group of Countries for Tajikistan, whose main donors are the United States, Japan, and the European Union, pledged $430 million in loans and balance-of-payments support. The aid package was presented to Rahmonov in May in Tokyo, where he had gone to attend the annual meeting of the ten donor countries and fifteen international institutions led by the IMF and the World Bank. This package was nearly twice the amount pledged the previous year, when Tajikistan received only $280 million. By chance I was in Tokyo at the time and met with senior aides to Nabiev who told me that they were delighted that for the first time the world was recognizing the importance of Tajikistan.

The Tajikistan civil war, like the civil war in Afghanistan, convinced many in Central Asia that clan- or region-based Islamic movements that tried to change the status quo were divisive and destructive, and led to a swift economic decline. As I traveled through the Karategin and Tavildara valleys in the spring of 2001, interviewing villagers and local clan leaders who had once been the main support base for the IRP, it was apparent that the IRP's influence and even the Islamicization of the civil war years had declined dramatically. There were few active madrassahs or overt attempts at Islamic education in the valleys, and local mullahs had gone back to their mosques and farms. Compared to Pakistan and Afghanistan, where madrassahs are turning out hundreds of thousands of committed Islamicists, Tajikistan had gone back to being fairly secular. The IRP had been unable to inculcate the madrassah tradition there, and without it, there was nothing to sustain the party into the future. The failure was partly due to the fact that funding for madrassahs largely came from Pakistan and Saudi Arabia, which were inimical to the IRP because it opposed the Taliban and had backed Masood. Neither country exerted much influence in Tajikistan. Also the government had banned external funding of madrassahs in 1993.

Even the local mullahs appeared to have less political influence than they had during the civil war; they could no longer dictate how people would vote or conduct their lives. Young people stopped attending prayers at mosques, which were now filled only with old men, as they had been during the Soviet era. The young had either left home to look for work or spent their free time learning martial arts or watching videos. Education was once again secular rather than Islamic. On the other hand, praying and picnicking at Sufi shrines, which had been looked down upon by hard-liners within the IRP during the civil war, was again immensely popular. There were even village headmen who greeted visitors with vodka or brandy, and when I asked what had happened to Islamic restrictions against alcohol, villagers smiled and answered that there were none now. "When the IRP was here we hid these bottles, but now they have gone, we have taken them out again and drink freely," said a farmer in Tavildara—once the headquarters for the IRP's military.

It was evident that after the losses suffered by the IRP during the civil war its inability to reconstitute itself or to offer an economic or political plan for the country's revival had left the party incapable of institutionalizing political Islam, or even retaining its own appeal. Grass-roots support for the IRP and political activism was lessening, and its influence over the younger generation had become less significant than it had been five years earlier. Instead, regionalism and clan politics had become more firmly entrenched in the valleys as people competed for the scarce developmental resources offered by the government and tried to keep their heads above the flooding waters of poverty. War weariness had destroyed any desire for radical political change. But the attitude throughout the country reflected not so much a changed perception of Islam as a return to the way of life people had known under the Soviets. During the decade of civil war and its aftermath, Tajiks had generally become more committed Muslims, but the radical and political Islamicist overtones of the civil war era were gradually disappearing. People had gone back to their old ways. Whilst they were deeply respectful of Islam, they were not ready for an overt political manifestation of it. Militant

Islam had failed in Tajikistan, but it was not defeated. And in the midst of poverty Tajiks still faced the acute problem of how to create a national consciousness which could unite the clans and usher in greater democracy.

6

The Hizb ut-Tahrir: Reviving the Caliphate

ONE OF THE MOST INTRIGUING questions about Islamic movements in Central Asia today is how a highly secretive, pan-Islamic movement that originated in the Middle East and largely does not even address pertinent issues of public concern in Central Asia has become the most popular, widespread underground movement in Uzbekistan, Kyrgyzstan, and Tajikistan. The challenge that the Hizb ut-Tahrir al-Islami (popularly known as the Hizb ut-Tahrir) poses to the regimes of these countries can be judged by the fact that there are more HT prisoners in Central Asia's prisons than those of any other movement, including the much better known IMU. Government crackdowns against the HT have become fiercer and more widespread, even as the regimes try to figure out how the movement has spread so far, so fast.

The phenomenon is all the more interesting because the HT's aims are probably the most esoteric and anachronistic of all the radical Islamic movements in the world today. The HT has a vision of uniting Central Asia, Xinjiang Province in China, and eventually the entire *umma* (Islamic world community) under a *khilafat* (caliphate) that would reestablish the Khilafat-i-Rashida, which ruled the Arab Muslims for a short time after The Prophet Muhammad's death in 632. Under the Khilafat-i-Rashida, which lasted until 661, the message of Islam spread rapidly across the Middle East and Africa through conquest and conversion. This period is revered by many radical Islamic movements, including the Taliban, as the only time in Islamic history when a true Muslim society existed. But the HT shows unprecedented fervency in its demands for the return of the caliphate. In the scenario envisioned in HT literature, one or more Islamic countries will come under HT control, after which the movement will be able to win over the rest of the Islamic world. HT leaders believe that Central Asia has reached what they call "a boiling point" and is ripe for takeover. As Sheikh Abdul Qadeem Zaloom, the current HT leader and one of its most prolific writers, describes the situation: "The issue of transforming the lands into the Islamic homeland and uniting them with the rest of the Islamic lands is an objective which the Muslims aim to achieve and the method which ought to be undertaken to achieve this objective is that of re-establishing Khilafah."[1]

Origin, Structure, and Beliefs

The HT was founded in Saudi Arabia and Jordan in 1953 by diaspora Palestinians led by Sheikh Taqiuddin an-Nabhani Filastyni (the Palestinian). A graduate of Al Azhar University in Cairo, an-Nabhani was a schoolteacher and a local Islamic judge before he was forced to leave Palestine to make way for the new country of Israel. He settled in Jordan in 1953, and there set up the movement.[2] An-Nabhani wrote many books and leaflets during his lifetime, which form the core belief of the HT. "The minds of the Muslims have been consumed by the present-day situation, and only conceptualize the system of government through the depraved democratic regimes foisted upon Muslim countries. . . . The point at hand is not establishing several states, but one single state over the entire

Muslim world," he wrote in 1962.[3] In his most famous work, *The Is-lamic State*, an-Nabhani interprets the life of The Prophet Muham-mad, describing how The Prophet first spread the message of Islam secretly, then came into the open about His aims, and finally preached the call for jihad. By placing The Prophet Muhammad's life in a modern context and describing the three stages of the spread of Islam under His guidance, an-Nabhani gives his party a blueprint for spreading the HT message and setting up political structures in emulation of the early spread of Islam.

Thus the flight from Mecca to Medina of The Prophet Muham-mad and His followers, a historic journey in Muslim history, is described by an-Nabhani as the moment when "the phase of inviting people to Islam" moved to "the phase of establishing an Islamic soci-ety and state," which in turn was followed by "the phase" of expan-sion through jihad—a process that the HT plans to duplicate in Central Asia. An-Nabhani describes the repression that the early Muslims faced from their non-Muslim opponents as "torture, inter-nal and external propaganda and sanctions"—a virtual replica of what the Central Asian regimes are carrying out against the HT today. In his writings an-Nabhani cleverly uses the history and mes-sage of early Islam as a revolutionary call to arms for the modern era.

But although the HT believes in jihad as a means to mobilize supporters against non-Muslims, it does not advocate a violent over-throw of Muslim regimes as do other extremist groups, such as Osama bin Laden's Al Qaeda. Instead, the HT believes in winning over mass support, believing that one day these supporters will rise up in peaceful demonstrations and overthrow the regimes of Cen-tral Asia. In the repressive climate of Central Asia this—combined with the HT's growing popularity—is enough to ensure government crackdowns against the movement, particularly in Islam Karimov's Uzbekistan.

In *Draft Constitution of the Islamic State*, an-Nabhani confident-ly predicts the party's eventual control over the entire Islamic world and the spread of Islam to the non-Muslim world. An-Nabhani's concept of the future Islamic state envisages a political structure in which a caliph elected by an Islamic shura (council) would have dictatorial powers in a highly centralized system. The caliph would control the army, the political system, the economy, and foreign policy. Sharia (Islamic law) would prevail, Arabic would be the language of the state, and the role of women would be severely restricted. The defense minister, whose title would be amir of jihad, would prepare the people for jihad against the non-Muslim world. Military conscription and training in preparation for this jihad would be mandatory for all Muslim men over 15.

Movement leaders in Central Asia told me that the HT originated in the revivalist Wahhabi movement of Saudi Arabia but that the HT had separated from the Wahhabis on several issues. "We had a united plan with the Wahhabis but we soon developed differences and split. HT wanted to work with people in each country separately and bring about sharia in a peaceful manner, but the Wahhabis were extremists who wanted guerrilla war and the creation of an Islamic army," an HT leader in Uzbekistan, whom I shall call Ali, told me in the autumn of 2000.[4] Although HT beliefs still remain extremely close to Wahhabism, the crude labeling of all Islamic militants Wahhabis by Uzbekistan and other regimes fails to acknowledge the differences between the HT and the IMU, or between radical and nonradical Muslims. However, the HT was also once close to the Ikhwan-ul-Muslimeen, or Muslim Brotherhood, in Egypt. In the 1930s the Brotherhood had been the first to articulate the need for an Islamic struggle against colonialism and for the creation of modern Islamic states. The Ikhwan's message was further developed by the Jamiat-i-Islami in Pakistan, by Ahmad Shah Masood and Gulbuddin Hekmatyar in Afghanistan, and by the IRP in Tajikistan.

After the HT was banned in the Middle East some of the leaders headed to the West, setting up offices in Europe, especially Germany and England. London is now believed to be a major organizational center for the HT. There the HT raises funds and trains recruits to spread the movement in Central Asia. The HT has become extremely popular amongst Muslim students on the campuses of British universities. When it held a conference in the Docklands area of London on August 26, 2001, to debate the political crisis in Pakistan, busloads of supporters arrived from all over Britain. And the facilities at the conference demonstrated how well-organized— and well-funded—the HT is: there were facilities for the disabled and children, an onsite, fully equipped medical team, bookstalls, places for prayer, and a live Web cast on the Internet. The HT is also popular in Turkey, Egypt, and North Africa, and is gaining popularity in Pakistan.

The present leader, Sheikh Zaloom, who is also a Palestinian and former professor at Al Azhar University, has published many books and pamphlets about the movement's philosophy and methods. His present location, probably in Europe, remains a secret. There are no photographs of Central Asian HT leaders and no hint of who the other leaders are, how the chain of command works, or where they are based.

My lengthy interview with "Ali" in Uzbekistan, which was arranged in great secrecy under condition that I not disclose his name or the location of the interview, was the first media interview given by a Central Asian HT leader. I was assured that Ali, a young man with a flowing beard who dressed in traditional Uzbek clothes, was a senior leader of HT cells in several provinces of Uzbekistan. His knowledge of HT history, philosophy, tactics, and political stance with regard to other radical Islamic movements supported this claim.

Ali explained to me that the HT operates secret, decentralized five- to seven–man cells throughout Central Asia, making it extremely difficult for the authorities to penetrate the organization. The cells, called *daira* (circle), are study groups dedicated to the spread of Islam and the HT message. The cell chief, the only person who knows the next level of the party organization, sets out weekly tasks for his members, who are expected to go out and create new cells. The Uzbek police, who have recently had some success in planting agents in a few HT cells and arresting cell members, are still unable to penetrate the chain of command. The biggest success to date was the arrest in Moscow on May 29, 2001, of Nodir Aliyev, believed to be an important Uzbekistan HT leader, by the Russian police. Aliyev was extradited to Uzbekistan.

But the HT has grown phenomenally. At the time of the breakup of the Soviet Union, the movement had not even spread to Central Asia. The party was not even amongst the first flood of Asian and Arab missionaries who came hoping to Islamicize the region and enlist recruits. According to Uzbek officials, the movement was not introduced into Uzbekistan until 1995, by a Jordanian named Salahuddin, who came to Tashkent and set up the first HT cell with the help of two Uzbeks. The first HT pamphlets appeared in the Uzbek underground in 1995–96. Originally the authorities ignored these because they appeared harmless. (For one thing, they were written in Arabic, which few people could read.) But as the movement began setting up its first cells in Tashkent and the Fergana Valley, and from there spread throughout Uzbekistan and to Tajikistan and Kyrgyzstan, government crackdowns began. Ali claimed that the HT now has more than sixty thousand supporters in Tashkent alone and tens of thousands in other cities—a claim that is supported by the large number of arrests of HT members in all three countries between 1999 and 2001. HT literature is now translated into Uzbek, Kyrgyz, and Tajik, and the party magazine *Al-Vai* (Consciousness) and books like *The Islamic State, The Economic System in Islam,* and *How the Khilafah Was Destroyed,* written by an-Nabhani and Zaloom, are available in all three languages and in Russian.

In part, the extraordinary spread of the HT can be explained by technology. Although the HT looks back fourteen centuries for its inspiration, it does not wish to re-create a medieval state. Unlike the

IMU, the HT recognizes the achievements of non-Muslim cultures and societies and wishes to adapt them to its future caliphate. Indeed, the organization relies on modern technology to spread its message. Arrests of HT cell members have revealed computer disks, videos, CDs, the latest printing and photocopying machines, and extensive use of email—all of which are very rare in Central Asia, where people have little access to technology. Much of the HT's equipment was funded and imported from abroad, indicating probable collusion with senior bureaucrats in the customs department. The HT's favorite form of propaganda is the *shabnama* (night letter), which is printed at night and pushed under people's doors like a newspaper. The Afghan Mujahedeen first used this method in Kabul during the Soviet occupation of their cities in the 1980s. Posters are also slapped up on village walls at night—appearing even on the walls of police stations.

The HT makes use of all the methods and technologies of globalization. Indeed, the group's aim to create a single, worldwide Islamic government can best be described as Islamic radicalism's closest equivalent to the Western concept of globalization. But the HT rejects the modern political state, disavowing any interest in nationalism, democracy, capitalism, or socialism, all of which are considered Western concepts, alien to Islam. It also opposes most forms of culture and entertainment and seeks to restrict women's activities to the home, although women are allowed to be educated. In arguments reminiscent of the Taliban and the Wahhabis, the HT claims that the imposition of sharia will resolve all the ethnic, social, and economic problems of the people. The French scholar Olivier Roy calls such movements neofundamentalist because they are "less politically minded than the (earlier) Islamicist movements—less concerned with defining what a true Islamic state should be than with the implementation of Sharia."[5]

Whereas the Ikhwan-based movements seek to seize state power and then transform each country into an Islamic political state, movements such as the Taliban, HT, and even the IMU come from the new Deobandi-Wahhabi tradition, which sees the seizure of power only as a way to impose sharia and transform social behavior. Once that is done, they believe, an Islamic political state will evolve by itself. There appears to be little debate within the HT about how to reconcile the acute economic and social problems of Central Asia with the notion of the caliphate. HT literature places great emphasis on the formation of a jihadi army but tends to ignore the question of how it will be paid for, or how the economy or the social services will be run.

One reason people are attracted to the HT is their reverence for the Ottoman Empire, a caliphate that many believe the HT will revive. The Ottoman caliphate was based in Istanbul and ruled much of the Islamic world in the late Middle Ages including the Middle East and the Balkans. It advocated the unity of all Muslim peoples under Ottoman rule, an idea that appeals to the pan-Turkic views of many Uzbeks. The caliphate was overthrown in 1925 by the Turkish military reformer and modernizer Kemal Ataturk. The HT believes that this was the result of a Western conspiracy with the worldwide Zionist movement. Since that time many movements in Central and South Asia, including the HT, have aimed to revive the caliphate. Interestingly, HT leaders ignore the fact that the Ottoman caliphate allowed many Islamic schools of thought to flourish, and even tolerated non-Muslim communities in such places as the Balkans, all of which is contrary to HT beliefs.

The HT has adopted the idea of Islamic rule, but its beliefs are simplistic and lack historical perspective or a willingness to accommodate Central Asia's own Islamic traditions. The HT is violently opposed to Sufism or any public expression of it, such as prayers at Sufi shrines, both of which have a long history in Central Asia. Although HT leaders maintain that they are influenced by the writings of the Jadids, their beliefs contain none of the modernizing influences of Jadidism. (Their embrace of modern technology does not mean an acceptance of modern ideas about Islam.) Like the

Wahhabis, the HT is virulently opposed to Jews and Israel, and a lot of HT literature portrays Karimov as a Jew, a "stooge" of Israel and the "worldwide Zionist conspiracy." HT leaders ignore the fact that there has been a large Jewish community in Central Asia for more than two thousand years—at the beginning of the twentieth century there were as many as two hundred thousand Jews, who are still called Bukharans, living in Central Asia. "We don't want to kill the Jews, but they must leave Central Asia because they do not belong here," insists Ali.

Also like the Wahhabis, the HT is violently anti-Shia; the group would expel all Shia Muslims from Central Asia if it came to power, a stance that would clearly alienate the Shia communities in southern Uzbekistan and eastern Tajikistan. "We are very much against Shias and Shiaism, which is not the Islamic way," says Ali. These hard-line beliefs, consistent with Wahhabism, have little to do with mainstream Central Asian Islam, which has always been extremely tolerant of other ideas and religious minorities. The HT has imported its beliefs from the Arab world and the debates and conflicts within the Islamic radical camp there. It shows little desire to adapt these ideas to Central Asia. HT pamphlets are far removed from the daily pressures and problems of the people and appear to be written abroad, for global rather than local distribution. They address international problems of the Islamic world such as the Israel-Palestinian conflict or the so-called "Zionist conspiracy against Islam" rather than the concerns of the people of Central Asia: rising prices, unemployment, and the lack of educational facilities.

The HT also has a strong, if bizarre, conviction that although other radical Islamic movements may have preceded them and may even now coexist with them, these will all eventually be proven "wrong," and the HT will be revealed as the only true Islamic movement. "The Koran and hadith [sayings of The Prophet Muhammad] say that when the world ends there will be seventy-three Islamic movements and only one of them will be right. Only Allah knows which movement will be right," explains Ali. The HT bases this claim on a verse from the Koran which reads, "Let there arise from amongst you a group that invites to the good, orders what is right and forbids what is evil and they are those who are successful."[6]

The Hizb ut-Tahrir in the Central Asian States

Yet neither its lack of common regional interests nor its intolerance for other forms of Islam has stopped the HT's growing popularity in Central Asia. One reason may be that the HT is a peaceful movement. It may sympathize with the IMU, but it does not believe in guerrilla tactics. Instead the HT envisages a moment when millions of its supporters will simply rise up and topple the Central Asian governments—particularly the Karimov regime—by sheer force of numbers. Such beliefs resemble those of millenarian Christian movements.

The vagueness of HT aims is offset by the group's undoubted organizational abilities. HT leaders are confident that they are winning support from within Karimov's inner circle, and they do have sympathizers in the army, the intelligence services, and the upper echelons of the bureaucracy—for example, in the customs department—who help promote their program. Unlike the IRP and the IMU, who draw their main support from rural areas and farmers, the HT finds most of its recruits amongst the urban intelligentsia: college students, educated but unemployed youth, factory workers, teachers. Most of the HT members who have been arrested in Central Asia, for example, are educated young men in their twenties from large cities.

In fact, one of the best sources of information about the size and makeup of the HT comes from the arrest records. In Khujand, which is adjacent to the Fergana Valley, there have been large numbers of arrests amongst Tajik college students and ethnic Uzbeks. Yet in villages just a few miles from Khujand, no arrests have been made; peasant farmers have not even heard of the HT, although they all know the IMU. Similarly, in the city of Osh, in Kyrgyzstan, where 40 percent of the population is Uzbek, large numbers of HT activists have been arrested, as opposed to rural Batken, a hotbed of IMU activity farther south, where villagers know nothing about the HT. It is clear that Uzbeks in Uzbekistan and ethnic Uzbeks in other Central Asian states constitute the largest number of HT adherents, although the movement is rapidly gaining popularity amongst all ethnic groups in Central Asia.

In Uzbekistan a massive crackdown against the HT began in May 1998 after Karimov's parliament passed the Law on Freedom of Conscience and Religious Organizations, which severely restricted freedom of worship. Police questioned all men with beards or more than one wife, as well as anyone who was traveling to Pakistan and Afghanistan. Pious Muslims could be refused permission to pray, fathers could be jailed for alleged crimes of their sons, all Muslim organizations and mosques had to be registered with the government, and it was illegal to preach Islam. Women could be arrested for wearing the hijab (head covering). Holly Carter, the director of Human Rights Watch for Central Asia, termed the law one of the most restrictive religious statutes in the world. "The government is painting Muslims with the same brush—those who may have criminal intent and average Muslims who simply wear a beard and go to the mosque," she noted.[7] When the law was being passed Karimov railed in parliament against Islamic fundamentalists. Amnesty International reported that in the first six months of 1999, the courts handed down fifty-five death sentences, and fifteen executions took place—several of them members of the HT.

The HT claims that there are more than a hundred thousand political prisoners in Uzbekistan's jails, a figure that is highly inflated. The U.S. State Department Human Rights Report estimates that between January 1999 and April 2000 some five thousand people were jailed in Uzbekistan. The Independent Human Rights Organization of Uzbekistan has published the most authoritative figures for political prisoners, which show that there were 7,600 political prisoners in the summer of 2001—of which a staggering 5,150 belonged to the HT. Another 1,600 belonged to the IMU or other so-called Wahhabi groups.[8] A new, maximum-security prison has been opened at an army camp at Jaslik, in Karakalpakstan, to house the flood of political prisoners.

The prison, designated penal colony No. KIN 64/74 by the Ministry of the Interior, is known locally as "the place from which no one returns." It is closed to outsiders, including family members of prisoners. Prison conditions are reported to be appalling owing to overcrowding (it currently houses some eight hundred inmates), the heat, lack of facilities, and bad water, which has led to illness and death from hepatitis. Muslims are not allowed to pray or read the Koran, and all prisoners carry out forced labor. Several dozen people are reported to have died in Jaslik from either the poor conditions or torture. The Human Rights Society of Uzbekistan estimates that in 2000 and 2001 fifty people died there.

The deteriorating human-rights situation in Uzbekistan was highlighted by Human Rights Watch's Acacia Shields, who gave chilling testimony to a U.S. congressional panel in September 2000. "Uzbek police and security forces have arrested thousands of pious Muslims. These arrests are illegal and discriminatory, they target people who belong to unregistered Islamic groups, who practice outside state-controlled mosques, or who possess Islamic literature. Police routinely torture and threaten detainees, deny them access to medical treatment and legal counsel, and often hold them incommunicado in basement cells for up to six months. Trials are grossly unfair, as judges systematically punish independent Muslims with lengthy terms in prison for their religious beliefs and affiliations, ignoring allegations of torture and allowing coerced self-incriminating statements as evidence, often the only offered evidence, to convict."[9] According to Human Rights Watch, arrests increased dramatically after the government began to mobilize local mahalla (neighborhood watch committees) to monitor the comings and goings of suspicious-looking people or outsiders. In 2000 it was estimated that the mahalla had identified 10,700 people who were considered enemies of the state and were interrogated by the police.[10]

At the same time, torture is widely used to extract confessions. "Generally people are brutally beaten or killed. But there are other forms of torture, including putting needles into people's nails, or putting plastic bags over people's heads to suffocate them. The most widely used method, however, is brutal beating and in the process of beating many people die," said Mikhail Ardzinov, chairman of the Independent Human Rights Organization of Uzbekistan.[11] Alleged HT member Rustam Norbaev, who was arrested in Tashkent on March 13, 2000, died five days later in a pretrial detention center after being tortured. Amanullah Nosirov, convicted in 1999 of being an HT member, died in prison in Navoi in December 2000. On September 15, 2000, in Tashkent, fifteen alleged members of the HT who were on trial claimed that they had received beatings and electric shocks and been raped by their guards in order to extract confessions. The judge took no notice of their statements, and they were all sentenced to between twelve and sixteen years in prison and sent to Jaslik. "Police routinely plant small amounts of narcotics, weapons, ammunition or Islamic literature on citizens either to justify arrest or to extort bribes. The most frequent victims of this illegal practice have been suspected members of HT," reported Human Rights Watch's Carter.

With little outside information available about the activities of the HT, the trials of alleged HT members provide rare glimpses into the the group's organizational abilities and popularity. On July 20, 2000, a court in Djizak sentenced fifteen alleged HT members to seventeen years in prison. Their leader, Maruf Eshonov, aged 30, was accused of running two HT cells, recruiting two hundred people, and distributing pamphlets. In April 2000 the authorities put out a list of 157 people in the Fergana Valley whom they wished to apprehend for distributing HT pamphlets. That June, in Jalal Abad Province, Kyrgyzstan, 53 alleged HT members were put on trial for subversion. The trial disclosed that the HT ran small neighborhood mosques, distributed pamphlets at night, and ran weekly study groups that discussed Islamic texts, prayed, and read the Koran over tea and snacks. These neighborhood groups, or *ziyofats*, were a Kyrgyz adaption of the Uzbekistan daira.

From its cells in the Fergana Valley the HT movement spread rapidly into adjacent areas of Kyrgyzstan and Tajikistan. More than 150 alleged HT supporters were being held in Kyrgyz jails by the summer of 2001, largely in the Osh region. Throughout 2000 and the following year the central courthouse in Osh was the scene of trials of alleged HT members every few weeks, many of them as young as 18 years old. In May 2000 four HT activists aged 18–25 went on trial whilst the trial of fourteen others was still in progress. "All the accused do not hide their aims and claim that they are ready to make any sacrifice for their sacred goal to create an Islamic state on the territory of the Fergana Valley," said Talant Razzakov, head of public security in Osh.[12] These young men had set up a well-equipped office where they received HT instructions and propaganda material by email, translated it into Kyrgyz, and then photocopied it for distribution. They also used video and audio cassettes. Kyrgyz National Guard commander Lt. Gen. Abdy Chotbaev claimed in June 2000 that three hundred Kyrgyz citizens were training in Afghanistan for underground missionary work for the HT and the IMU.[13] In the first three months of 2001, forty alleged HT activists were arrested and put on trial.

The appeal of the HT in Kyrgyzstan appears to be growing because of the country's increasing poverty and public criticism that the government is incapable of solving the people's problems—and too corrupt to try. The rapid growth in population has magnified the problem of poverty. The census of 2000 showed that Kyrgyzstan has a population of 4.8 million, up 13 percent since 1991. In Osh the population has increased by 23 percent, as out-of-work peasants flood the city. Bishkek now has a population of 1.1 million, and shantytowns have sprung up in the suburbs, even though there are no jobs to be had. In 2001 the World Bank reported that 68 percent of the population lived on less than $7 a month and the average annual salary was just $165; a subsistence-level salary was estimated at $295 a year.[14] Between 1990 and 1996, Kyrgyzstan's gross domestic product was almost halved, falling by 47 percent. Industrial production fell by 61 percent, agricultural output by 35 percent, and capital investment by 56 percent.

In a devastating indictment of the poverty and desperation of many families, the International Organization for Migration reported that in 1999, four thousand Kyrgyz women and girls were illegally sold abroad to work as prostitutes in the United Arab Emirates, China, Turkey, and even Europe.[15] "The trafficking of human beings has become a large industry in Kyrgyzstan now. . . . It has displaced tourism and become the largest industry after drug trafficking," said Ercan Murat, the U.N. head of mission in Kyrgyzstan.[16]

Poverty has also driven many young men to smuggling opium from Afghanistan—a social issue that is highlighted in the Kyrgyz press. In 1999 Kyrgyz border police impounded 17,000 pounds of opium from traffickers; the following year 26,000 pounds of opium were seized. The United Nations Drug Control Program claims that this amount is only a tiny fraction of what is actually being smuggled into Kyrgyzstan and then distributed to Russia and Europe. Heroin addiction has also risen dramatically. Although there are only 4,500 registered heroin addicts in Kyrgyzstan, nongovernmental organizations estimate the number to be at least 50,000. Many of these addicts have contracted AIDS. In March 2001, when a European NGO attempted to control the spread of AIDS in Carasou by encouraging women to use condoms, the HT distributed pamphlets protesting that NGOs were encouraging prostitution.[17]

Kyrgyzstan's President Akayev has admitted that religious extremism is being fueled by the growing poverty of the people, but he appears to be doing little to end corruption within the ruling elite and to address public concerns. "Religious extremists view Kyrgyzstan as a transit country. Their goal is the Fergana Valley, to extend the geographic range of Islam and even to set up a state—an Islamic caliphate. They are reckoning on the support of the local population, being well aware that poverty and social problems exist in both Kyrgyzstan and Tajikistan. It is no accident that country people are following those preaching 'high Islam.' They are being lured by money. Show people a green dollar bill and the people succumb to temptation. We must urgently counter this," Akayev told a Russian newspaper in May 2001.[18]

There is another problem, unique to Kyrgyzstan, which arouses the anger of the Islamicists. Seventeen percent of the population is Christian, and in an effort to stop ethnic Russians leaving the country Akayev has encouraged the Russian Orthodox Church to expand and build new churches. At the same time Kyrgyzstan is the only Central Asian country where a variety of Christian evangelist movements are allowed to proselytize, a concession the HT finds humiliating. Religious and ethnic tensions are intensifying between groups that once lived peaceably together. There have always been severe ethnic tensions between Uzbeks and Kyrgyz in Osh Province, where Uzbeks form 25 percent of the population (40 percent in Osh city). The city of Osh also contains the most important place of pilgrimage in Central Asia—Takht-i-Sulaiman (the Seat of Solomon)—and access to the shrine has become limited because of border restrictions between Uzbekistan and Kyrgyzstan. In the north tensions between the Kyrgyz and the large Russian population now include religious as well as ethnic divisions. "The process of Christianization of the northern part of Kyrgyzstan competes with the Islamicization in the southern part," writes Kyrgyz social scientist Anara Tabyshalieva.[19]

The HT is also slowly gaining popularity in Kazakhstan, where Islamic radicalism has so far not penetrated. In 2001, for the first time, Kazakh police reported the arrest of HT activists in the south of the country, whilst Kyrgyz police have arrested Kazakh HT militants in Kyrgyzstan. On July 6, HT leaflets appeared in thousands of mailboxes in Kazakhstan's largest city, Almaty, shocking the security forces and the population. The day was chosen because it was the official birthday of President Nazarbayev, who only a few weeks earlier had urged his people to resist Islamic radicalism. In a television interview Nazarbayev had asserted, "Some people cherish the hope that the Muslim population of our states will support radicals, that the clergy will take us back to the Middle Ages, put the veil on women's faces and make men grow beards to the waist. This radicalism may start to advance triumphantly in an individual country like Tajikistan or Uzbekistan. But this will be just the beginning."[20]

The HT is becoming extremely popular in northern Tajikistan, despite the war weariness of the people. In 2000 more than a hundred alleged HT members were arrested in Tajikistan and put on trial.[21] By the following year the figure had doubled, according to Western diplomats in Khujand. When I spoke with Ali, he claimed that there were twenty thousand HT supporters in Khujand (now Sughd) Province and with their help the HT was increasing its influence in the southern end of the Fergana Valley. In April 2001, some 7,500 books and 1,500 leaflets were found in a garage in Chkalovsk in Sughd Province, and fifteen alleged members of the HT were arrested. Even the capital, Dushanbe, was not immune to HT activity. Five HT members, aged 26–40, were arrested in Dushanbe on November 16, 2000, for being in possession of 5,000 HT leaflets.[22]

Clearly the Tajik government feels threatened, and in response President Rahmonov has asked the more moderate IRP to begin Islamic preaching and other Islamic educational activities in Sughd Province, even though the IRP has never had a base of support there. Local IRP leaders have urged the public "to refrain from joining illegal parties and movements" and "be vigilant against terrorists," by which they mean the HT.[23] The IRP leaders admit that a new, younger generation of Tajiks are joining the HT, and there is little their party can do about it. "Some of those joining the HT are the older fighters of the IRP who were unwilling to become integrated into the army after the peace settlement, but most are young men who were just children during the civil war and are being introduced to Islamic teachings for the first time through the HT," IRP leader Moheyuddin Kabir told me.

The Hizb ut-Tahrir and Islamic Militancy

The HT is also causing concern in Western capitals, although little is known about the movement. During late 2000 an intense debate took place amongst Clinton administration intelligence experts about whether to officially declare the HT a group that supports terrorism. Washington finally decided against making such a statement because the HT had never participated in guerrilla activity, kidnapped people, or set up armed training camps; in fact, it has always advocated peaceful change. Russia is also concerned about the HT, for it fears that the movement will spread to Muslim regions of Russia. Russian intelligence is now collaborating closely with the Central Asian states to combat the HT. The fear is that young HT militants, who now face the same indiscriminate repression and poverty at home as IMU militants, may soon ignore their elders' advice and turn to guerrilla warfare.

HT leaders deny that they have formal links with other radical movements, such as the Taliban, Al Qaeda, or the IMU. "The IMU is a separate movement, and amongst them there are many tendencies and many conflicts. There are also many smugglers of drugs and weapons with the IMU, which gives them a bad name," explained Ali. "And some elements in the IMU are being used by Russia for its aims in Central Asia. It is impossible to know which party is more popular—the HT or the IMU. The aims of the HT and IMU are for the caliphate in Central Asia, but the ways to achieve it are different, like one doctor uses surgery and the other uses herbs."

The IMU says it is fighting only to overthrow Karimov and bring Islam to Uzbekistan, but that is only the first part of their plan. They have other aims for the whole of Central Asia."

Nonetheless, several hundred HT activists have escaped to northern Afghanistan, where they have been welcomed by the IMU. The HT members live in IMU camps and receive military training from the guerrillas. Kyrgyz officials report that during the IMU offensive in the summer of 2000, they discovered HT literature on the dead bodies of several IMU militants, for example, after an incident on September 12 near Batken, in which seven IMU guerrillas were killed.[24] Clearly there are strong links and cooperation between the rank and file of both groups, especially when the members come from the same village or town.

Ali admitted that the HT is sympathetic to the Taliban but denied receiving aid from them. "The HT supports the Taliban movement in Afghanistan and many HT members have fled to safety in Afghanistan to escape the crackdown in Central Asia. The Taliban have some good ideas; they want a pure Islamic state. But the difference between us is that HT wants a modern life here on earth, to create a heaven on earth and also to prepare people to go to heaven in the afterlife, whilst the Taliban want a life of poverty, and all their preparation is only to go to heaven. The HT want heaven both here and in the afterlife." Although Ali denied that the HT receives support or money from bin Laden, like many HT members he clearly admired him. "We have no special relationship with bin Laden, but he supports all Islamic movements in Central Asia, and he is very famous here for doing so." Diplomats in Kyrgyz and Uzbek dispute these denials, claiming that all the Islamic groups are working closely together. They cite a meeting in Kabul in September 2000 when the Taliban, the IMU, the HT, Chechen separatists, and bin Laden held lengthy talks about future cooperation.

Though the HT has still not taken the path of violence, Ali is not averse to issuing a dire warning: "The HT wants a peaceful jihad, which will be spread by explanation and conversion, not by war. But ultimately there will be war because the repression by the Central Asian regimes is so severe, and we have to prepare for that. If the IMU suddenly appears in the Fergana Valley, HT activists will not sit idly by and allow the security forces to kill them." The HT also warns that the coming crisis in Uzbekistan will give the party its opportunity to seize power. "Karimov is stuck between trying to please the Russians and the Islamic movement. Karimov must choose between the Russians and Islam, and he will have to choose Islam to keep the Russians out. But if Russian troops do come to Uzbekistan, it will be very good for HT because it will expose everybody, force polarization, and the war will begin," says Ali.

Others give similar warnings. "The confrontation between the authoritarian regime and religion creates a worsening situation both in terms of human rights, but also in the social and political climate of the country. Indeed, such a climate could lead to civil war just like we have seen in Afghanistan," warns the Independent Human Rights Organization of Uzbekistan's Ardzinov.[25] One option, which the Central Asian regimes have so far refused to consider, is legalizing the HT and allowing it to operate as an above-ground political party. The HT has never advocated the overthrow of the regimes through violence, and legalization of the party would force the leadership to deal with local problems and articulate concrete economic and political policies rather than rely on vague millenarian promises. And legalizing the HT would make it less likely to forge links with other radical Islamic groups that do advocate violence. But no Central Asian regime except Tajikistan allows any Islamic parties to operate openly. Until this changes the HT will continue to appeal to people, as much for the aura of resistance and defiance that surrounds it as for its program.

Instead, the situation has become worse since the U.S.-led bombing of Afghanistan began in response to the September 11, 2001, attacks in New York and Washington. As Uzbekistan and Tajikistan offered bases which could be used as launching pads for an attack inside Afghanistan by U.S. aircraft and special forces units, both governments intensified their suppression of the HT, clearly hoping that their new-found alliance with the United States would mean less Western criticism of their crackdown on Islamic groups.

In the first week of October a court in Tashkent convicted nine members of the HT of belonging to an illegal party, and the defendants were each given sentences of nine to twelve years. In a significant new step the court also convicted them of belonging to Al Qaeda. The defendants denied their links to bin Laden's organization. "We do not have connections to Osama bin Laden or any other terrorist organizations, as we pursue different methods of struggle. We are fighting for our ideas through peaceful means," explained Nurullo Majidov, the leader of the group.[26]

By linking the HT to bin Laden the authorities were hoping to gain political mileage with the United States. Uzbekistan is keen to establish a link between the HT and the global war against terrorism. This would justify both the harsh laws and the even harsher methods of investigation that Uzbekistan uses against Islamic militants. As the war progresses there is mounting concern amongst human-rights campaigners over the way Uzbekistan is using its acceptability within the Western alliance as a means to intensify repression against its own population.

Meanwhile, the HT's simplistic, one-dimensional ideology, imported from the Arab world, is gaining in popularity because in times of dire stress people grasp at simple straws. Although the HT's program offers no concrete solutions for Central Asia's complex problems, its overriding message is that the coming of the caliphate and an Islamic system will resolve all problems and create an ideal society. For the desperate youth of Central Asia, the HT's single-minded, incorruptible activists, to whom in better times they might not have given a second thought, now appear to be saviors. "Across the region weak economies are nearing collapse and the rule of strongmen has become entrenched. Many parts of the former Soviet Union are seized by a revolution of diminishing expectations. Armed militancy has grown, not as ideology but as a way to express disagreement when other means are unavailable, or have failed," writes the veteran Central Asia watcher Paula Newberg.[27] The fear that the HT will move from an educational to a militant jihad may well become a self-fulfilling prophecy.

7 Namangani and the Islamic Movement of Uzbekistan

THE REVIVAL OF ISLAMIC MILITANCY in Uzbekistan began in a small agricultural town in the heart of the Fergana Valley, a few months before the breakup of the Soviet Union. What started as a relatively peaceful attempt to raise Islamic consciousness in the community had already turned violent by December, when a handful of unemployed young men in Namangan seized the building which housed the headquarters of the Communist Party of Uzbekistan (CPU) after the mayor refused to give them land to build a mosque. That incident set in motion a series of events that have reverberated across Central Asia for the past decade.

The young men were led by 24-year-old Tohir Abdouhalilovitch Yuldeshev, a college drop-out and local mullah from the Islamic underground who was a fiery orator and brilliant organizer. At his side was Jumaboi Ahmadzhanovitch Khojaev, 22, who later adopted the nom de guerre of his home town and became Juma Namangani—a charismatic, action-oriented man whom the younger members of the group hero-worshiped for his daring. Namangani had been conscripted into the Soviet army in 1987 and saw action in

Afghanistan as a paratrooper, eventually making sergeant. There he developed a profound respect for the Afghan Mujahedeen against whom he fought. According to his friends the experience turned him into a "born-again" Muslim. Some of these young men, like Abdul Ahad, 33, had traveled to Saudi Arabia for religious instruction. They had become fluent in Arabic and were influenced by Wahhabism because of their close ties to Saudi Wahhabi foundations, which funded their activities.

With Saudi funds and some five thousand young followers, this group began in 1990 to build a new mosque and a madrassah in Namangan that would house two thousand students. Outside the mosque a sign read, "Long Live the Islamic State." Yuldeshev began to impose strict Islamic practices in Namangan, such as making people say their prayers regularly and insisting that women abandon their colorful Uzbek shifts and cover themselves head to toe in white veils. He also set up neighborhood watch committees to combat crime: vigilantes patrolled the streets maintaining law and order and ensuring that shopkeepers did not raise their prices. Yuldeshev then audaciously demanded that President Karimov impose sharia in Uzbekistan, inviting him to come and debate the issue in Namangan. Karimov arrived in April 1991 to talk to the militants, but the meeting soon turned into a fiery shouting match. Yuldeshev made several impossible demands— for example, that Karimov declare Uzbekistan an Islamic state and open more mosques and madrassahs. A furious and humiliated Karimov promised that parliament would discuss these issues and then walked out. The die was cast.[1] By the end of the year, Yuldeshev and his men had attacked the CPU headquarters and set in motion a movement that they claimed was a jihad to remove Karimov from the government of Uzbekistan.

The Creation of Central Asian Islamic Militancy

Yuldeshev's followers were members of Uzbekistan's recently formed

IRP who had become disillusioned with the party's refusal to demand an Islamic political state. As an alternative they had set up Adolat (Justice), which demanded an Islamic revolution. "The IRP is in the pay of the government; they want to be in parliament. We have no desire to be in parliament. We want an Islamic revolution here and now— we have no time for constitutional games," Ahad told me when I spent a day with him at the Namangan mosque of which he was now imam (prayer leader).[2] Mosques and madrassahs run by Adolat sprang up across the Fergana Valley, in Andijan, Margilan, Kuva, Fergana City, and even Osh, in Kyrgyzstan, undercutting the influence of the IRP. Other underground militant groups, including Tauba (Repentance), Islam Lashkarlary (Fighters for Islam), and Hizb-i-Islami (Party of Islam), also arose in the Fergana Valley.

What differentiated these militant groups from other Islamic revivalist parties and from the IRP was that they had no respect for official Islam, no patience with tradition, and no fear of the political regime, which they overoptimistically considered to be on the verge of disintegration and collapse. And certainly for a time the state apparatus appeared helpless, unable to even mobilize either the police or the state-controlled "official" Islam to confront the radicals. "There were three mosques in Namangan during Communist times, now they are 130 and most of them are controlled by these militants. I don't have the funds to compete with them," mourned a wistful Imam Bilal Khan, the head of the official government mosque in Namangan. These new mosques were full of worshipers, and the madrassas were so packed with young students—both boys and girls— that some ran three shifts a day to teach the Koran and Islamic law and history. "We will ensure that first Fergana, then Uzbekistan and then the whole of Central Asia will become an Islamic state," Ahad told me enthusiastically.

For some months the government accepted Yuldeshev's rule in Namangan. Government ministers in Tashkent told me that originally they had no idea who these militants were or what they wanted—they didn't even know what Wahhabism was.[3] Finally, however, the government cracked down, banning Adolat in March 1992 and arresting twenty-seven members, although many of the mosques continued to operate. Adolat leaders, including Yuldeshev and Namangani, fled to Tajikistan, where they enlisted with the Tajikistan IRP, which was about to plunge into the civil war.

In Dushanbe, Yuldeshev studied for a short time at the madrassah run by Qasi Akbar Turajonzoda, the mufti of Tajikistan and a key member of the Tajikistan IRP. After the war broke out, Yuldeshev left for Afghanistan with the IRP leaders. For a time he helped spread IRP propaganda and newsletters from Taloqan, where the IRP had set up a base in exile. With his heart still set on continuing the Islamic movement in Uzbekistan, Yuldeshev began to travel, first to Pakistan and Saudi Arabia and later to Iran, the United Arab Emirates, and Turkey, trying to learn about Islamic movements and make contact with other Islamic parties.

He also met with intelligence agencies in these countries, from whom he requested material support. Pakistan's Interservices Intelligence, which had run the Afghan war against the Soviets and later supported the Taliban, gave Yuldeshev funds and a sanctuary. From 1995 to 1998 Yuldeshev was based in Peshawar, the center not only of Pakistani and Afghan Islamic activism but also of pan-Islamic jihadi groups. Here he met with the "Arab-Afghans" (Arabs who had gone to fight the Soviets in Afghanistan and stayed to fight for Osama bin Laden), who were later to introduce him to bin Laden and other Afghan groups. Pakistan's Jamiat-i-Ulema Islami, which would later back the Taliban, raised funds for Yuldeshev in Peshawar whilst they enlisted his young Uzbek activists in their madrassahs. In 1996 I visited these madrassahs, which spread from Peshawar to Karachi, and the teachers showed off the special classrooms where hundreds of students from Central Asia were studying Islam with the help of interpreters. The majority of the students were Uzbeks from Adolat and Tajiks from the IRP, although there were also a few Kazakhs, Kyrgyz, and Uighurs from China.[4]

Russian and Uzbek officials claim that Yuldeshev also received funding from the intelligence agencies of Saudi Arabia, Iran, and Turkey and from Islamic charities and organizations in these countries. A significant Uzbek population composed of people who had fled Central Asia during the Basmachi rebellion had settled in Saudi Arabia, where they were now Saudi citizens and committed Wahhabis. Yuldeshev began to receive large donations from this Saudi-Uzbek trade and business community through an influential businessman who had close contacts to some of the Saudi princes, including the head of Saudi intelligence, Prince Turki al-Faisal.[5] Based in Mecca, this Saudi-Uzbek network loathed Karimov because it viewed him as an unreformed Communist, and Saudi contributions to Yuldeshev increased after the creation of the IMU.

Yuldeshev also traveled to the Caucasus, where he met with Chechen rebel commanders during the first Chechen war against Russia (1994–96) and established himself as the spokesman, grand strategist, and spiritual guide for Islamic revolution in Uzbekistan. In Turkey he met with members of the nascent fundamentalist Islamic movements and allegedly received funding from several Islamic groups who saw the Islamic cause in Central Asia as helping to promote an Islamic pan-Turkism. According to some sources, Yuldeshev would often leave Peshawar to make secret forays into Uzbekistan in the late 1990s, using false passports, documents, and money provided by Pakistani religious groups and Saudi Arabian businessmen. During these trips he began to reorganize the underground cells of the Adolat Party in the Fergana Valley and Surkhandarya, in southeastern Uzbekistan close to the Tajikistan border. These cells would play a major role five years later when the IMU launched guerrilla forays into Central Asia.[6]

According to a former Tajik political activist with the IRP now working with a Western NGO in Dushanbe who does not wish to be named, Namangani fled Uzbekistan in 1992 and arrived in Kurgan Tyube, in southern Tajikistan, with some thirty Uzbek militants and a few Arabs, who were acting as liaisons between Saudi Islamic foundations and Adolat. "Within a few months Namangani's force had swelled to some two hundred Uzbeks as more young men fled the crackdown in the Fergana Valley and arrived to join him. More Arabs from Afghanistan, who were fed up with the sickening civil war there, also joined him," says the Tajik source, who first met Namangani in 1992. "As a former Soviet soldier Namangani knew the tactics of the Soviet army and special forces, which was extremely useful to the IRP because they were dealing with the Soviet-trained army of Tajikistan. He knew all about bombs and mine warfare and used them effectively in ambushes. He had money from the Saudis and contacts with the Afghans, so he was not alone."[7]

The IRP attached Tajik guerrillas to Namangani's group and moved him to the Tavildara Valley, which became his base after 1993 and is still the most important IMU base in Central Asia. Namangani captured and lost the town of Tavildara twice during the civil war and fought government troops in the Karategin Valley and Gorno-Badakhshan. In 1993 Namangani fought one of the biggest battles of the civil war at the Haboribot Pass. He constantly attracted outsiders to his cause, such as Arabs at loose ends in Afghanistan who saw the new war in Central Asia as a wider, larger jihad that would take Islamic revolution into the former Soviet heartland. In the process Namangani also got to know the entire IRP political and military hierarchy, many of whom became his close friends and later stood by him when the IMU began its attacks on Uzbekistan.

Several former IRP military commanders—such as Hakim Kalindarov, who led the resistance from Tavildara with Namangani—are now ministers or senior officials in the coalition government in Dushanbe. In 1996 Namangani came under the command of the IRP's army chief of staff Mirzo Ziyoyev, the nephew of Sayed Abdullah Nuri. They struck up a close friendship—Namangani still calls Ziyoyev "Baba" (older brother). Currently minister of emergencies in the coalition government in Dushanbe, Ziyoyev played a crucial role in negotiating between Namangani and the Dushanbe government during Namangani's later forays into Tajikistan from Afghanistan. IRP leaders who knew him at the time said that Namangani commanded loyalty from his troops and was a tough disciplinarian and good speaker who could mobilize people, but he was also erratic, temperamental, and authoritarian. He often flouted orders from IRP political leaders who wanted to coordinate their military strategy to lend force to their political negotiations with the Dushanbe government. Namangani learned Tajik, although he still does not speak it well, and married an Uzbek woman, with whom he has one daughter. During the war he traveled to Afghanistan, where he met with President Rabbani and Ahmad Shah Masood. But he also met with Pashtun commanders in northern Afghanistan loyal to Gulbuddin Hekmatyar who opposed the Kabul government. According to Izatullah Saduloev, who ran the IRP office in Taloqan during the civil war, Namangani frequently visited the IRP headquarters in Taloqan to plan strategy, receive supplies, and meet the IRP political leadership.[8]

None of Namangani's former friends and allies credit him with much understanding of Islam. "He is essentially a guerrilla leader, not an Islamic scholar, and he is easily influenced by those around him, such as today he is influenced by the Taliban and Osama bin Laden," said Moheyuddin Kabir, the principal assistant to IRP leader Nuri who was an adviser on international law during the IRP negotiations with the Dushanbe government. "He is a good person but not a deep person or intellectual in any way, and he has been shaped by his own military and political experiences rather than Islamic ideology, but he hates the Uzbek government—that is what motivates him above all. In a way he is a leader by default because no other leader is willing to take such risks to oppose Karimov."[9]

When the Tajik civil war came to an end, in 1997, Namangani opposed the cease-fire and the peace settlement. "Namangani refused to accept the cease-fire. When the IRP leaders said stop the jihad, Namangani said no. His methods of work and aims were only jihad and he did not have the political flexibility to understand that sometimes compromise is necessary," Kabir told me. "It was very awkward for the IRP because here was a foreigner fighting for the IRP who was not listening to the IRP leaders," said another IRP commander who knew Namangani well. It was left to Ziyoyev to persuade Namangani to come down from the mountains. Eventually, Namangani agreed, dispersing most of his forces but retaining a core group of Uzbeks and maintaining a few guerrillas at his camp in the Tavildara Valley.

Namangani settled in Hoit, a small village north of Garm in the Karategin Valley on the main road to the Kyrgyz border, where he bought a large farm. Here he lived with his wife and daughter, some forty Uzbeks, and a few Arabs. After working some time as a farmer, Namangani went into business with a truck transporter from Garm, quickly becoming the owner of several trucks that carried goods to Dushanbe. Sources say that it was at this time that Namangani became heavily involved in the transport of heroin from Afghanistan to Tajikistan and on to Russia and Europe, in an effort to raise funds to keep his organization going and feed his ever growing entourage at Hoit.

"He was now a businessman and a farmer, but every day there were people coming in from all over Uzbekistan—the Fergana Valley, Tashkent, Samarkand—and telling him about the repression and atrocities that Karimov was committing," said a businessman in Garm, who used to see Namangani once a week whilst he lived in Hoit. "The Uzbeks would come and stay a few days and he would house them and feed them, and they would urge him, 'Act now, do something, the situation at home is terrible and you are sitting comfortably,'" he told me. Another friend of Namangani's at that time who is now a social worker in Garm said that Namangani would tell him, "There is no road for me to go back, I have to go forward, to continue fighting as people are waiting for me in Uzbekistan." Namangani's farm quickly became a center for Islamic radicals, as Uzbeks, Arabs, Chechens, and Tajiks disillusioned with the cease-fire arrived and had to be fed and housed.[10] By the time Namangani left Hoit for Afghanistan, in 1999, there were some two hundred militants living with him, many of them accompanied by their families. Although the majority were Uzbeks, the strong presence of Arabs and members of other ethnic groups from Central Asia and the Caucasus supported Namangani's belief that he was an Islamic internationalist, giving him a sense of power and purpose.

The Birth of the Islamic Movement of Uzbekistan

Meanwhile, Yuldeshev had traveled back to Tajikistan in 1997 to meet with Namangani in Hoit. This was a moment of decision for the two men. Facing a new political situation in a region that now appeared to be against them, they had to decide on their future course of action. The Tajik civil war had ended; they had lost their bases in the mountains, their manpower, and some of their weapons caches, which they had surrendered at the cease-fire. Their IRP allies supported the cease-fire and did not want to appear to be breaking it by continuing to back their small group of Uzbek dissidents. In Afghanistan, Rabbani and Masood had been ousted from Kabul by the Taliban, and Masood, once an IRP ally, was now actively promoting the new government of national reconciliation in Tajikistan. Moreover, back home in Uzbekistan the situation had clearly worsened. Leading Islamicists had disappeared. In August 1995 Andijan's chief prayer leader, Sheikh Abduvoli Mirzoev, disappeared along with his assistant as they were taking a flight from Tashkent to Moscow. In September 1997 another of the sheikh's assistants disappeared. In March 1998, Obidkhon Nazarov, the imam of the Tukhtaboi mosque in Tashkent, disappeared along with his 13-year-old son. All are believed to have been kidnapped and killed by the security forces, although the Uzbek government disclaimed responsibility for their disappearance.[11]

Karimov launched another harsh crackdown against the Islamicists after an Uzbek army captain was beheaded on December 2, 1997, in Namangan and his head displayed outside his office. On December 11 a former chairman of a collective farm and his wife were also beheaded. On December 19 three policemen were killed in a shootout. Nobody claimed responsibility for the killings, but the government reacted swiftly, arresting more than a thousand people in the Fergana Valley. Police questioned any man with a beard. The events in Namangan created a sense of panic within the government, which feared that any breakdown in law and order would spread, further emboldening the Islamicists. When a group of Islamicists arrested in Andijan admitted to having received training from Namangani, Karimov was prompted to make his famous remark to the Uzbek parliament on May 2, 1998, calling for even tougher repression against terrorists. "Such people must be shot in the head. If necessary I will shoot them myself," Karimov promised.[12] The same month parliament passed the repressive Law on Freedom of Conscience and Religious Organizations, banning the use of unregistered mosques and requiring that all Muslim clergy be registered. By then there were some 4,200 mosques in Uzbekistan of which 2,430 were located in the Fergana Valley. Out of these, only 1,566 were ever registered by the government.[13]

The crackdown also targeted the families of the militants. Yuldeshev's mother, Karomat Asqarova, was forced to denounce her son in 1999. "My youngest son was five when his father died. I worked hard in a bakery and brought him up with difficulties. I turned this disobedient Tohir out of the house after he had, for nothing, severely beaten up his younger brother. The years have passed and I have not seen him since. What can I say if this good for nothing, unbelievable evil is my son. . . . May Tohir be swallowed up by the earth, may he and his accomplices rot in their graves. I blush before our President and all the people. May this rebellious Tohir, who made me feel like this, die," she proclaimed at a public meeting.[14]

Namangani's sister Makhbuba Akhmedov and his brother Nasyr Khojaev also publicly disowned Namangani after constant harassment from the police. Later, in March 2000, they traveled to Tavildara to urge their brother to lay down his arms. "We went to tell him face to face about the suffering he was causing his family," explained Akhmedov. Nevertheless, on their return to Tashkent both were arrested, and in June, Khojaev was sentenced to fourteen years in jail, along with a group of ten suspected IMU activists that included four women. Although Namangani's sister is no longer in jail, the police still regularly call her in for questioning. In August, Namangani's mother was summoned to a public meeting at a school auditorium in Namangan, where her neighbors denounced her, and relatives of soldiers killed fighting the IMU blackened her face with paint and condemned her for bringing Juma into the world. She broke down, tearfully apologized, and cursed her son. The government appeared to have no compunction about targeting innocent relatives of known IMU militants or anyone with Islamic connections. Karimov urged young men not to let themselves to be brainwashed by the fundamentalists, warning, "Trying to escape the subordination to authority may result in a personal tragedy."[15]

Although the 1997 events in Namangan probably really were orchestrated by Namangani's followers, the subsequent government crackdown led to a renewed exodus of Uzbek militants from the Fergana Valley. These guerrillas arrived as refugees at Namangani's farm in Hoit and put mounting pressure on Namangani and Yuldeshev to respond to Karimov's repression. The two agreed. But first they needed a new sanctuary. Tajikistan could no longer be considered a reliable base for their operations. The answer clearly lay in Afghanistan. Yuldeshev had been introduced to the Taliban in Kabul in 1997, and the Taliban had every reason to give him refuge:

Uzbekistan was backing the anti-Taliban opposition in Afghanistan, and Karimov himself was belligerently anti-Taliban. Yuldeshev also met with Osama bin Laden, now living with the Taliban leaders in Kandahar, who saw in Yuldeshev an ally for the future in a region where he had few contacts.

Some Uzbek officials and Tajik IRP leaders say that it was bin Laden who encouraged Yuldeshev to set up a distinct Islamic party whose aim would be the liberation of the Fergana Valley and Uzbekistan from Karimov's rule. There is no confirmation of this, but U.S. officials subsequently claimed that bin Laden was a primary contributor of funds to help set up the IMU. With his Wahhabi sympathies, Yuldeshev was comfortable with the Wahhabi Islam and anti-Western rhetoric of bin Laden, as he had already moved closer to the strict Deobandi interpretation of Islam practiced by the Taliban.

In 1998 Yuldeshev settled in Kabul, where the Taliban gave him a house in the diplomatic quarter of Wazir Akbar Khan. He was also given a residence in the southern city of Kandahar, where bin Laden and Taliban leader Mullah Muhammad Omar lived. That summer Yuldeshev conferred with Namangani in Kabul, and together they announced the creation of the IMU, which declared jihad against the Karimov regime. Yuldeshev later set out the IMU's goals in an interview for *Voice of America*, one of the few lengthy interviews he has ever given. "The goals of IMU activities are firstly fighting against oppression within our country, against bribery, against the inequities and also the freeing of our Muslim brothers from prison. . . . Who will avenge those Muslims who have died in the prisons of the regime? Of course we will. We consider it our obligation to avenge them and nobody can take this right away from us. We do not repent our declaration of jihad against the Uzbek government. God willing, we will carry out this jihad to its conclusion."[16]

Yuldeshev pledged to set up an Islamic state: "We declared a jihad in order to create a religious system, a religious government. We want to create a sharia system. We want the model of Islam which has remained from The Prophet, not like the Islam in Afghanistan or Iran or Pakistan or Saudi Arabia—these models are nothing like the Islamic model. . . . Before we build an Islamic state we primarily want to get out from under oppression. We are therefore now shedding blood, and the creation of an Islamic state will be the next problem." Yuldeshev also claimed that "we have a movement of one hundred thousand people. It takes only a spark to burn down a forest, and for that one match is sufficient. We have enough strength to settle the score with Karimov, and God willing there are many more thousands of Mujahedeen who share this dream." In the interview Yuldeshev traced the origins of the IMU back to the Basmachis. Our "roots go back 70–80 years, when our grandfather-Mujahedeen fought against the Communists. We compare ourselves to these ancestors and do not regret that we are continuing their work. . . . We don't need foreign contacts because our roots are deep and are located in our homeland." (In fact, several IMU militants are reportedly descended from the Basmachis. The head of the religious leadership of the IMU, Zubayr Ibn Abdur Raheem, is said to be descended from the Mangyt family of the former rulers of Bukhara, some of whom escaped to Saudi Arabia after the Russian Revolution.)[17]

Karimov, Namangani, and the Struggle for Uzbekistan

Perhaps the most important incident affecting the way Karimov would come to treat Muslims of any kind in Uzbekistan occurred a few months later, starting at noon on February 16, 1999. In the space of an hour six car bombs exploded in the center of Tashkent in an apparent attempt to assassinate the president. The most powerful bomb, set off by two men who jumped from their car and opened fire on police guards before they escaped, exploded at the entrance to the building that housed the office of the cabinet of ministers on Independence Square—one of the most heavily guarded locations in Uzbekistan. Karimov had left his country residence and was on his way to attend a cabinet meeting when his driver was alerted by policemen that explosions were taking place. Although no officials were harmed, 13 people were killed and 128 were injured. Demonstrating his bravado, a furious Karimov arrived at the square a few minutes later to review the damage, even though explosions were still going on in other parts of the city.[18]

Within a few days at least two thousand people had been hauled in for questioning. The government went on a rampage, accusing all opposition groups, including the IMU and exiled secular political groups like Erk and Birlik, of responsibility for the bombs. Karimov initially targeted Muhammad Solih, the leader of Erk who had been in exile in Turkey but had recently moved to Norway. The Uzbek press published photographs of Solih allegedly meeting with IMU leaders in Afghanistan, although many Uzbeks believed that the pictures had been doctored by Uzbek intelligence. The bombings had been well organized and carried out with great efficiency, and they fueled a number of rumors, including the theory that members of the security forces linked to senior politicians jealous of Karimov's power were involved and the contrary idea that Russia had tried to assassinate Karimov in a bid to win greater influence in Uzbekistan. Meanwhile, Karimov continued his rhetorical frenzy as the rumors spread, declaring on April 2 that he would arrest any father whose son joined the IMU. "If my child chose such a path, I myself would rip off his head," Karimov warned.[19]

The most common hypothesis offered by Uzbeks themselves is that the bombing was carried out by clan and political rivals of Karimov within the regime who had not been accommodated in the power structure and were fearful that Karimov's policies were ruining the country. As in Tajikistan, regionalism has become a potent factor in the politics of the elite. Karimov's concentration of power and his favoritism towards his own clan from Samarkand has been a growing cause of resentment. Moreover, Karimov fears that the regional elite of the Fergana Valley may at some future stage endorse

or link up with the IMU. "Why does Karimov resist conflict prevention efforts targeted in Fergana? Because his nightmare is an alliance
of the Fergana regional elites with the Islamicists, as happened in
Tajikistan, and which some Uzbeks think already happened on the
day of the bombing," explains Central Asia scholar Barnett Rubin.[20]

Whoever was responsible, the bombing sent shock waves across
Central Asia. Other leaders feared that assassination would be now
considered a viable option by their own political opposition and
complained that Islamic radicalism was getting out of control. Such
fears were not completely unwarranted; the Kyrgyz government
claimed in May that it had uncovered a terrorist plot to kill President
Akayev. But Karimov had little sympathy with his neighbors, accusing Kyrgyzstan of being too soft towards the radicals and Tajikistan of
harboring the IMU. He also accused the Taliban, Pakistan, Turkey,
and Chechen rebels of training the bombers and giving sanctuary to
IMU militants. Karimov claimed that some of the bombers had
escaped to Pakistan, others to Turkey, and still others to Kazakhstan,
whilst Yuldeshev was alleged to have organized the bombings from
the United Arab Emirates. This last accusation has some support
from Uzbek intelligence.[21]

The situation became even more tense a few months after the
bombings, on April 2 (the same day Karimov fulminated against the
fathers of IMU members), when two shooting incidents left seventeen people dead. First police stormed a bus that had been hijacked
by criminals (rather than Islamic militants), killing nine; then another eight alleged Islamic militants were killed outside Tashkent during a security check on the road. But soon afterwards, in a complete
turnaround—which was to become common in Karimov's erratic
foreign policy—Karimov began making overtures to the Taliban. He
arranged through the Pakistan government to send his foreign minister, Abdulaziz Kamilov, to meet with Mullah Muhammad Omar.
The Uzbeks were anxious to secure Taliban participation in a crucial
U.N.-sponsored meeting in Tashkent designed to get Afghan peace

talks moving. Kamilov was also trying to secure a Taliban reassurance that they would not help the IMU. But when the meeting took place, on June 2 in Kandahar, Omar dashed Kamilov's hopes, telling him that the Taliban would not attend the Tashkent meeting unless Uzbekistan recognized them as the government of Afghanistan. Furthermore, although the Taliban were not supporting the IMU, he claimed, they would not extradite IMU guerrillas either.

Karimov's volatile foreign policy continued on other fronts. In June, Uzbekistan suffered a complete breakdown in relations with Turkey when Ankara temporarily withdrew its ambassador from Tashkent in protest against Uzbekistan's accusations that Turkey was giving shelter to IMU militants. In retaliation Tashkent shut down twenty Turkish-funded schools in Uzbekistan. Also in June twenty-two people allegedly involved in the Tashkent bombings went on trial, and prosecutors charged that the bombings had been planned in Afghanistan, Pakistan, and Turkey whilst Chechen rebels had provided training and materials. According to Human Rights Watch, no good evidence was offered that any of the twenty-two defendants was involved in the bombings. Rather, they were members of the Hizb ut-Tahrir (HT) engaged in Islamic propaganda, not terrorist activity. Nevertheless, six of the accused were sentenced to death, eight received twenty years in prison, and the rest were convicted, although they received lighter sentences.

Throughout the summer Uzbekistan maintained pressure on Tajikistan, accusing the government of harboring Namangani. Although he was clearly there, harboring may not have been the best way of describing the situation: Tajikistan was not in a position to take on the IMU. Nevertheless, Tajik President Rahmonov did exert pressure on IRP leaders in the coalition government to get rid of Namangani, or at the least to send him to Afghanistan. Namangani had now become a liability to the continuing good relations between Rahmonov and the IRP as well as to the future stability of the coalition government.

Fearing that his forces would be disarmed and disbanded, Namangani asserted himself in August 1999. Leaving his Tavildara camp and crossing the border into Kyrgyzstan, he began a wave of kidnappings and killings, following which he left for Afghanistan. On August 25 the IMU issued an official communiqué declaring jihad on the Karimov regime and calling for its overthrow (see the Appendix). The events of the summer of 1999, which were set in motion by the Tashkent bombings, unleashed the IMU as the most potent threat to the Central Asian regimes.

Namangani had now become a major figure throughout the region, even a celebrity, yet he still refused to be interviewed. He even avoided foreign radio stations, which were desperate to talk to him. The only photograph of him was a grubby, undated picture published by the Uzbek security forces in national newspapers. He cultivated an air of mystery that was even more extreme than that of the secretive Mullah Omar. Soon Namangani was being mythologized in the underground of Islamic militancy, not only in Central Asia but also in Pakistan, Afghanistan, and throughout the Arab world. Across the region and as far away as Moscow, Western diplomats, military and intelligence officers, oil company executives, bankers, humanitarian aid workers, and journalists followed his every move, latched onto every rumor about him, and speculated wildly about his plans and intentions. Karimov and the Uzbek government were deeply embarrassed by the speed with which Namangani had become a household name across the region. People did not speak so much of the IMU as of Jumaboi—his nickname—whilst his activities, real and imagined, became an obsession amongst Central Asia watchers.

Apart from the mystery that surrounded the man, there were objective reasons why Namangani would have been turned into a myth, similar perhaps to the legend surrounding Che Guevara after he disappeared into South America for his last revolutionary adventure. Namangani had already fought two wars, in Afghanistan for the Soviet army and in Tajikistan for the IRP, and now he was about to embark upon a third, against the government of Uzbekistan. These wars had given him vast experience in mobilizing and organizing fighters, turning out soldiers who were well trained, flexible in their tactics, and motivated for the higher cause of Islam. He had the charisma and the ability to quietly build up a network of thousands of unarmed "sleepers" in the Fergana Valley and other parts of Central Asia who could rise at a signal or provide his guerrillas with food and guides at need. Although the IMU forces never posed a serious military threat to the armies of Central Asia and Russia, their tactics were infinitely superior, and they created terror amongst the Central Asian regimes.

Moreover, Namangani had the keen political sense to time his offensives to foment conflict within and between the Central Asian republics. Every winter Russia, the United States, and the NATO countries would urge the Central Asian republics to coordinate their military and political strategies. And every summer Namangani would attack, and the governments would hurl a litany of accusations and counteraccusations against one another. In addition, Namangani would change his military tactics for each offensive, often taking the security forces by surprise. "Namangani cannot afford to let the Central Asian states enhance their cooperation, and he calculates every move to create further differences between them. Every year the IMU have used different tactics to gain a foothold in Fergana, because they know that if you control Fergana you control Central Asia," Ivo Petrov, the head of the U.N. mission to Tajikistan, told me in Dushanbe.

Meanwhile, from his base in Kabul, Yuldeshev sent a constant supply of funds, materiel, and volunteers provided by the Taliban, bin Laden, the Uzbek diaspora, Islamic charities in Saudi Arabia and the Gulf states, and Islamic parties in Pakistan. The IMU had extended its control over the heroin trade from Afghanistan through Central Asia to Europe, using its network of militants across the region as couriers. These ever-expanding external links and sources of supplies and funds proved critical to the IMU jihad against Karimov. But even more critical to the IMU's growing strength was the continuing repression by the Uzbek regime and the desperate poverty of the Uzbek people.

8 Namangani and Jihad in Central Asia

JUST A FEW MILES outside Dushanbe, on the road heading north into the Garm Valley, travelers become quickly enveloped by the majestic Pamir Mountains. Across the valley floor the road winds through long vistas of green fields and poverty-stricken villages, punctuated by closed factories and blackened chimney stacks. The land quickly tilts upwards into rocky outcrops and lush green slopes full of grazing animals, heading towards the snow-clad peaks above. For the first part of the drive the valley is broad and open, giving a sense of space and freedom, but higher up it narrows and the road begins to climb dramatically, clinging precariously to the mountainside whilst the Surkhob River thunders below. In villages hanging from the sheer, rock-faced slopes, teahouses with long wooden benches covered with carpets and cushions run by Tajiks dressed in colorful robes beckon the exhausted drivers of donkey and horse caravans and of ancient, exhaust-spewing, Soviet-era trucks, which chug their way down from the Garm district with fruit and vegetables for Dushanbe's markets. Halfway up the valley, at Darband, where the river broadens into a magnificent, primeval vista, a narrow road turns right into the Tavildara Valley, whilst the Garm Valley road continues up to the towns of Garm, Tajikabad, Hoit, and Jirgatal before crossing into Kyrgyzstan and heading for Osh.

The Tavildara Valley road is even narrower than the Garm Valley route—the surface a slush of mud, melting snow, and fallen rocks. The road has been roughly hewn along rockfaces so steep that the mountain peaks above it are not visible. A slight swerve of your steering wheel would send you tumbling hundreds of feet to the roaring river, which is so far below that it looks like a thin brown thread. Even in spring the temperatures go below freezing, and the high passes are often blocked by snow and landslides. At times the valley becomes so narrow that you feel as if you could lean out and touch the mountains on the other side.

The Tavildara Valley road is the main link between Dushanbe and Khorog, the capital of Gorno-Badakhshan in eastern Tajikistan, and for much of the year it is closed by snow. Keeping the road open and under government control is vital to the region, which is why it is littered with the hulks of destroyed tanks, armored personnel vehicles, and trucks belonging to government forces. The Tavildara Valley was one of the strongholds of the IRP during the Tajikistan civil war. Some of the biggest battles of the war were fought here, as government forces made repeated attempts to drive the rebels out. This is ideal guerrilla country, where a handful of men can hold off an army.

Halfway down the valley on the left is a long, narrow gorge, at the end of which, in the village of Sangvor, Juma Namangani has set up a fortified camp, logistics base, and permanent garrison of IMU guerrillas. His men have been here since the early 1990s, first fighting off the Tajik army and later organizing forays against the Uzbek army in the Fergana Valley. Half a dozen men could hold the mouth of the gorge, and attempts to bomb this massive jumble of rocks and overhanging cliffs would be futile. Whenever Namangani arrives from Afghanistan, he holds court at the Sangvor village school, and

Central Asia shivers with expectation. I traveled up here to learn more about him in the spring of 2001, just a few weeks after Namangani had spent three months in the valley with some four hundred men.

"Every day there were lines of people coming to see him— Kazakhs, Tajiks, Uzbeks, Kyrgyz, Arabs, Chechens, Uighurs, Pakistanis, and Afghans—they all wanted to join him and do jihad in Central Asia," a farmer in the village of Tavildara told me. "Every day there were hundreds of people he had to feed and house and give money to," said another. During his stay Namangani had also summoned his many sleepers, who live inconspicuously in the villages of the Fergana Valley, going about their daily business and waiting for his call to arms. They were there to plan strategy for the IMU's summer offensive.

The biggest event during his stay was his second marriage, to a local Tajik beauty, a widow from Gorno-Badakhshan with two sons whose husband had been killed in the Tajik civil war. Hundreds of people fêted Namangani at his wedding feast. Local people said that the bride was one of the most renowned beauties in the Pamirs— and Namangani has an eye for beautiful women. The marriage not only cemented relations with local Tajik clans but also fulfilled a Muslim duty from the time of The Prophet Muhammad: a marriage to the widow of a *shaheed* (martyr in jihad) is doubly blessed. Namangani's first wife, an Uzbek, and their daughter were still in Afghanistan.

The guerrillas regularly bought supplies from local villagers, and they paid well, keeping the local population from being harassed by any of the militants. After five years of civil war, the villagers were interested only in rebuilding their farms, restocking their flocks, and getting on with their lives. "Local people tolerate Namangani's presence because his men are polite and pay for the food and goods they buy," said a farmer. Namangani had pledged to the local population and the Dushanbe government that he would not interfere in Tajikistan's politics or attempt to revive the Islamic movement in Tajik-istan; he asked only that he be left alone in his mountain base and be given transit rights to cross the Tajikistan-Kyrgyzstan border into the Fergana Valley, where he was continuing his war against Uzbek-istan. But by tolerating his presence for so long the Tajik govern-ment was coming under enormous pressure from Uzbekistan.

The Campaign of 1999

When Namangani made up his mind to take up arms again, in the early summer of 1999, he left his farm in Hoit and spent several months in the Sangvor gorge organizing his base. He was building a network of supporters that would stretch from the Tavildara Valley over the mountains into Batken Province in southern Kyrgyzstan, through which he could supply his men inside the Fergana Valley with arms and food. At this point there were few military check-points on the roads, so he was free to use trucks and taxis to trans-port supplies up the Garm Valley road to Jirgatal, where the goods were loaded onto donkey and horse caravans. IMU militants would then trek some four to five days across the mountains and down into the level plain of southern Kyrgyzstan towards Batken and the Sukh and Vorukh enclaves, where the goods would again be unloaded and sent into the nearby foothills that surround the southern edges of the Fergana Valley.

The Sukh Enclave, with a population of 43,000 people and an area the size of the Gaza Strip, is part of Uzbekistan, stranded in and surrounded on all sides by Kyrgyzstan—a result of Stalin's de-structive mapmaking in the 1920s. Mainland Uzbekistan is only twelve miles away, but to reach it you have to cross Kyrgyz territory. The enclave is predominantly populated by Tajiks, who have been ignored by both Uzbekistan and Kyrgyzstan since the breakup of the Soviet Union. The Tajiks of Sukh had been sympathetic to the IRP during the Tajik civil war, and many now transferred their loyalty to

Namangani because of their sense of neglect and their hatred for Tashkent. Yet Sukh is vital to Uzbekistan security: if the IMU were to penetrate the enclave with armed groups, it could claim to have captured Uzbek territory, and the Uzbek army could not respond without invading Kyrgyzstan.

The Sukh Enclave was the cause of a major political controversy in Kyrgyzstan when the Kyrgyz press leaked the news that on February 26, 2001, Prime Minister Kurmanbek Bakiev had signed a secret memorandum with Uzbek Prime Minister Otkir Sultonov granting Uzbekistan a small portion of Kyrgyzstan territory so that Uzbekistan would have a land corridor to Sukh. There was a storm of protest in the Kyrgyz press and parliament, and local officials in Batken prophesied that if the deal were implemented parts of Batken Province would become an Uzbek enclave and endanger Kyrgyz security. The government in Bishkek subsequently backed out of the deal, saying that it had been only a declaration of intent rather than an agreement. But the incident demonstrated the pressure being exerted from Uzbekistan, the weakness of the Kyrgyz state, and the threat that Uzbekistan might some day forcefully occupy Sukh.

The Vorukh Enclave is also situated in Kyrgyzstan, but it is the territory of Tajikistan, populated predominantly by some 25,000 Tajiks. Vorukh has historically been a center of Islamic radicalism—the people of Vorukh fought with the Basmachis against Soviet troops—and mullahs from Vorukh are famous for invoking jihad. Both these enclaves are now hotbeds of IMU support. And both have become critical as Namangani's bid to reach the Fergana Valley has escalated since 1999.[1]

It was confusing enough during the Soviet era to keep track of the borders of the southern fringes of the Fergana Valley where Tajikistan, Uzbekistan, and Kyrgyzstan meet, but now that each state has imposed its own demarcations it is even harder. Since the appearance of the IMU and the tighter security and border patrols that have been imposed, trade between Tajikistan and Kyrgyzstan with the

Fergana Valley and Tashkent, which is the largest market in Central Asia, has come to a virtual halt. The new borders have divided villages, farms, and families. For farmers to visit their relatives in the next village across the border, they now need a passport that costs the equivalent of a hundred dollars and a visa costing ten—amounts that are out of reach for these impoverished peasants. Irrigation channels that criss-crossed the region during Soviet times are now dry, or the flow of water stops at the border, making farming impossible.

Uzbekistan has now mined its borders with Tajikistan and Kyrgyzstan in an attempt to stop the IMU, and local villagers who cross the border illegally are arrested. But the border controls have led only to a thriving business in smuggling, and many of the smugglers give the IMU logistical support. Instead of coordinating their security efforts and cooperating with one another, each state has tried to create its own fortress—and they are far from impregnable. Security efforts have only created more poverty and joblessness, whilst widespread governmental neglect and lack of investment in the very areas these governments should be developing in order to win the support of the people creates ideal conditions for the IMU to sow unrest.

In August 1999, fearing that Uzbekistan's pressure on Tajikistan would force the government to disband his forces, Namangani took the initiative. From Tavildara he sent small, well-armed guerrilla groups down into the Kyrgyz Plain towards the enclaves. On August 9 a twenty-one-man unit kidnapped the mayor and three officials of a small village west of Osh, demanding $1 million in ransom, supplies, and a helicopter to fly them to Afghanistan in exchange for the hostages. The panic-stricken Bishkek government, which was unprepared for such an incursion and had few regular troops to send against the guerrillas, quickly succumbed. On August 13 the hostages were freed after the Kyrgyz government gave the guerrillas safe passage back to Tajikistan. There were persistent reports that the Kyrgyz had also paid $50,000 in ransom. President Karimov reacted furiously, accusing the Kyrgyz president of collusion with the IMU and sending Uzbek bombers to attack the towns of Tavildara and Garm. Predictably, the civilian deaths in Garm sparked protests from Tajikistan and heightened tensions between the two states— exactly the kind of interstate conflict Namangani was aiming for.

More IMU groups moved into the area around Batken, entering three villages and capturing a major general of the Kyrgyz Interior Ministry. On August 23, an IMU group kidnapped seven more hostages, including four Japanese geologists working for a mining company. This incident created headlines around the world, leading to a major international crisis for Bishkek because Japan was an important aid donor and investor in Central Asia. The timing of the kidnapping was even more embarrassing. It occurred whilst President Akayev was opening a summit in Bishkek of the heads of state of the Shanghai Five countries (China, Russia, Tajikistan, Kyrgyzstan, and Kazakhstan). At the summit Akayev denounced what he described as four hundred IMU gunmen who were trying to undermine Central Asia.

In reply the IMU declared from Afghanistan that it had launched a jihad to topple the Karimov regime and capture the Fergana Valley (see the Appendix). As Kyrgyz troops mobilized and Russian military advisers were sent to try to find the Japanese hostages, 3,500 Kyrgyz herdsmen and their families fled the surrounding mountains. They arrived as refugees in Batken, creating an enormous humanitarian crisis. "We hardly had any food ourselves and then these refugees arrived. We had to feed them also because it took weeks before the government could organize relief for them," Aitbu Nasibalieva, a primary-school teacher in the village of Karabakh near Batken, told me later.

The Batken region was not just a refuge and war zone; it was also a recruiting ground for the IMU. Nine young Kyrgyz men from Karabakh left that year to join the IMU, including four sons of a widow. "They just told their mother that they had to follow the path of the Koran and they left. She is still mad with grief and crying," said Nasibalieva. Social worker Gulmira Dovutoka said that a dozen more young men from Batken left to join the IMU in 2000. "It's the same everywhere—the villages are empty of young men—either they have gone to Russia to look for work or they join Namangani because at least he pays them and there is so much poverty here."

Batken is the most undeveloped district in Kyrgyzstan. It was part of Osh Province but became a separate administrative unit in October 1999 after the IMU's first incursion. Schoolteachers and local officials told me that unemployment ranges from 60 to 90 percent, and it has the highest birth rate in the country—3.4 percent. Batken's rich soil has turned to salt because of over-irrigation during the Soviet period and the closing of canals at the Uzbekistan border. Rusting factories have been shut down, electricity is available for only four hours a day, and there are no jobs. The milk plant, the oil mill, and a wine-making factory have been shut since 1991, and the government has made no attempt to revive them.[2] "Poverty is playing into the hands of the extremists. There is nothing like poverty, hunger and not having access to basic services, such as decent housing to create discontent. These are very much conditions that people will grow tired of," noted Ercan Murat, the U.N. head of mission for Kyrgyzstan.[3]

By late August the IMU groups held some twenty hostages, whom they gradually freed as they fought running battles with the Kyrgyz army. But they hung on to the Japanese geologists, creating a political crisis in Japan. Dozens of Japanese secret service agents and diplomats arrived to try to free their countrymen, opening negotiations with neighboring states in an attempt to find a link to the IMU. On September 4 the IMU agreed to free all the hostages in return for a ransom, the release of fifty thousand prisoners being held in Uzbek jails, and safe passage into the Fergana Valley. Kyrgyzstan rejected these demands. Uzbek planes again went into action against IMU-held villages around Batken and Osh, killing twelve Kyrgyz farmers and destroying dozens of houses. The Kyrgyz army launched an offensive, seeking to cut off the guerrilla groups from one another and drive them back into Tajikistan. In the meantime, three senior Kyrgyz military officers began to negotiate with two IMU guerrilla commanders in the village of Sary-Tala, near Batken. Talks and heavy fighting continued until October 25, when the Japanese hostages were finally released. Although both the Japanese and Kyrgyz leaders insisted that no ransom had been paid, Western diplomats reported that Japan had secretly paid 2–6 million dollars to Kyrgyz officials, who then delivered it to the IMU.

With winter fast approaching, when the passes into Tajikistan would once more be closed by snow, the IMU groups retreated to Tavildara. Tajik government ministers from the IRP were already there; they had come to try to convince Namangani to go to Afghanistan. Namangani finally agreed to leave, and in the first week of November, in a bizarre scene that was to be repeated in subsequent years, about six hundred IMU armed militants, along with their wives and children, were flown by Russian army helicopters from Hoit and Tavildara to the Afghanistan border. In Afghanistan they were received by a jubilant Yuldeshev and the Taliban. The IMU militants were housed in the town of Mazar-i-Sharif, whilst the families of the guerrillas were moved into a former U.N. refugee camp outside Mazar that ironically had once housed Tajik refugees escaping the civil war in the mid-1990s. The Taliban allowed the IMU to set up a training camp, open political offices in Kabul, Kandahar, and Mazar, and take in fresh recruits, who soon began to trickle down from the Fergana Valley. Yuldeshev had already struck a deal with the Taliban in which the IMU would be free to carry out their military operations against Uzbekistan. In return the IMU would fight for the Taliban against Masood.

At no point in 1999 had the IMU posed a significant military threat to Central Asia, but the guerrillas had notched up successes beyond their wildest dreams. They had caused consternation amongst the governments of the region, Russia, and abroad, widening the existing rifts between Uzbekistan, Tajikistan, and Kyrgyzstan even as these governments repeatedly pledged cooperation with one another. They had proved that the poorly trained, ill-equipped armies of the region were no match for their hostage taking and pinprick guerrilla attacks and tactics. Most important, they had made a name for themselves, declaring their agenda amid a blaze of publicity that would ensure new recruits. For the first time since the Basmachi revolt, the specter of a military jihad rose across Central Asia.

That winter Namangani and Yuldeshev traveled frequently to Kandahar, where they met with Osama bin Laden and Mullah Omar to plan strategy and negotiate for supplies of arms, ammunition, and money, which would be the key to further expansion. Much of the IMU's financing came from the lucrative opium trade from Afghanistan. According to the U.N. Office for Drug Control and Crime Prevention (ODCCP), opium production in Afghanistan doubled between 1998 and 1999, from 2,750 tons to 5,000 tons. Production was reduced to 3,400 tons in 2000 only because of a severe drought. The Taliban were already using taxes on opium exports to fund their war effort.[4] Namangani was heavily involved in opium smuggling through Tajikistan, and he now used his network of IMU militants in Central Asia and his links with the Chechens to increase his trade.

Ralf Mutschke, assistant director of Interpol's Criminal Intelligence Directorate, reported to the U.S. Congress in 2000 that 60 percent of Afghan opium exports now moved through Central Asia and that "the IMU may be responsible for 70 percent of that heroin and opium transiting through the area." By July 2000, when the Taliban banned poppy cultivation for the first time, the IMU and other drug dealers had built up a stockpile of opium in Mazar and Kunduz that ODCCP officials estimated at more than 240 tons. In the summer of 2001 Tajik officials told me that they believed that Namangani and other drug traffickers had set up laboratories in Tajikistan to refine the heroin, which explained the arrival of large quantities of raw opium from Afghanistan. The record seizure of 2.4 tons of raw opium by Russian border guards on July 2, 2001, appeared to confirm their suspicions. "Probably some laboratories to produce heroin exist here," explained the guards' Colonel Kostyuchenko. "That is why Afghan smugglers would attempt to smuggle raw poppy products, which would seem unprofitable at first glance."[5]

Namangani was receiving funding from even more diverse sources. According to Western diplomats and intelligence officials, bin Laden paid for Namangani to acquire two Mi-8 Russian-built transport helicopters from the Taliban that could seat forty men. Lt. Gen. Boris Mylnikov, head of the CIS antiterrorist center, reported that bin Laden had given Namangani $26 million in early 2000, whilst Namangani's Saudi-Uzbek backers in Saudi Arabia provided another $15 million for hi-tech equipment like sniper rifles, communications equipment, and night-vision goggles, which are believed to have been sent through arms dealers in Pakistan and the Gulf.[6] Claims by the CIA that bin Laden was also trying to acquire nonconventional weapons of mass destruction from the Central Asian states such as the means to conduct biological warfare created suspicions that the IMU was helping bin Laden make contacts in the former Soviet Union. The IMU's growing links with bin Laden offered the Saudi dissident a new base of operations in Central Asia—an area where he had had few contacts previously. In subsequent years there were widespread rumors throughout the region that bin Laden would try to hit U.S. targets in Central Asia: embassies, the offices of oil companies operating in Kazakhstan and Azerbaijan. Although the United States had appointed an ambassador to Tajikistan, he remained in neighboring Kazakhstan and only visited Dushanbe for a few days a month because of threats emanating from bin Laden and the IMU.

Thus the IMU built up a wide, diverse network of fundraising and weapons supply, ranging from Islamic groups in Afghanistan and Pakistan to sponsors in the Gulf states and Saudi Arabia. This was in addition to the income Namangani derived from opium smuggling and hostage taking. Wherever the IMU appeared, it was clear that its fighters were never short of funds, and they were careful to pay for all the supplies they took from local villagers. Namangani reportedly paid his guerrillas monthly salaries of between $100 and $500—in U.S. dollar bills. This rumor alone was enough to ensure that more recruits would join him.

The Campaign of 2000

In July 2000 Namangani returned to the Tavildara Valley from Afghanistan with a force of several hundred well-armed men. He began to move his men, materials, and weapons into Uzbekistan and Kyrgyzstan clandestinely for a new offensive. His forces were now armed with flak jackets, infrared night scopes, sniper rifles, heavy machine guns, and rocket launchers, and his aim was to supply weapons to his sleepers deep inside Uzbekistan. In order to do that, he needed to send well-armed groups into the region whilst creating diversionary attacks that would keep the Central Asian armies away from the routes where supplies were coming in.

In August the IMU launched multipronged attacks from several directions in a well-coordinated offensive, whilst other groups smuggled arms and ammunition into the Fergana Valley. The largest IMU group again descended the mountains opposite Batken, taking Kyrgyz army troops by surprise on several fronts close to Sukh and Vorukh. Another group traveled to Pendzhikent, at the western tip of Tajikistan, and then turned south, crossing the border into the sparse, nearly deserted mountains of Surkhandarya Province in southeastern Uzbekistan. Yet another group traveled to Khujand in northern Tajikistan, crossed secretly into Uzbekistan, and traveled into the mountains north of Tashkent. They then turned and attacked Uzbek forces around Jangiabad and Bostanlyk, a large holiday resort only eighty miles north of Tashkent. No more than an estimated one hundred to two hundred men were involved in all these attacks; Namangani was demonstrating his flair for tactical surprise and his ability to split his opponents' forces by posing a threat on several fronts at the same time. From the countryside around Batken, Surkhandarya, and Bostanlyk thousands of people fled in terror to the safety of the cities. On August 8, President Akayev declared that fifteen hundred IMU guerrillas had crossed over from Afghanistan, and two hundred of them were inside Kyrgyzstan.[7]

Namangani had spent several months quietly infiltrating men into the mountains of Surkhandarya Province, where they built a heavily fortified camp, manned by some 170 IMU guerrillas. The Uzbek army had no idea they were there until fighting broke out. Foreign diplomats in Tashkent recounted to me how in the fighting in Surkhandarya, Uzbek special forces who had been trained by the Russians and had just returned from commando training in the United States were outgunned and outclassed by a handful of guerrillas. "An elite Uzbek unit suffered twelve dead and ten wounded in a single ambush that they should have avoided, and they appeared terrified of anyone with a beard. Morale was extremely low," one diplomat said. "Seven guerrillas were holed up in a defile for a week, and they were running out of ammunition, but they could not be wiped out, even though the army was using helicopter gunships, flame throwers, and heavy artillery," he added.[8] It took more than a month of heavy fire power, including aerial bombardment, before the army was able to storm the fortress. Most of the IMU guerrillas were killed, but none were captured, and a few escaped.

During the operation Uzbek troops had forcibly evacuated more than two thousand people from three villages high up in the mountains. These were Tajik herdsmen, who for centuries had lived in isolation far from any town or government control. Their plight was to become a sorry example of Uzbekistan's ability to alienate and traumatize its own people whilst trying to deal with the IMU. Several months earlier, the herdsmen had been the first to alert the Uzbek army to the fact that IMU guerrillas were in the mountains—reports that the army ignored. Once fighting broke out, the Uzbek authorities accused the herdsmen of providing food to the IMU. "They are very simple and hospitable people. Anyone who comes their way will be invited in, even if he has got a submachine gun hanging around his neck. Also they have no work, so if they had the chance to sell something, they wouldn't refuse," said Zumrat Kurbanova, a resident of Saryassiya in Surkhandarya.[9]

The army first destroyed the herdsmen's flocks, then placed the men in a military camp for two months, where they were given almost nothing to eat. They were next relocated to an even more desolate area, where some died of cold and hunger. When in their naïveté they asked to see President Karimov to describe their plight to him, they were beaten. One herdsman, Khazratul Kodirov, gave an interview to the Uzbek service of the BBC in December describing their miserable conditions. He was tortured and killed by the Uzbek army. When the family received his body, his brother Akhmadul Kodirov reported that his head had been crushed, his arms and legs broken, and at least fifty wounds made on his body by a screwdriver.[10] Subsequently seventy-three herdsmen were charged with subversion, terrorism, and abetting the IMU. In June 2001 a court found them all guilty of terrorism and sentenced them to long prison sentences. A month later, on July 7, Shovriq Ruzimorodov, head of the Human Rights Society of Uzbekistan, who had single-handedly documented and protested the shepherds' plight before he was arrested on June 15, died in police custody. His body was handed over to his tearful family, who accused the security forces of torturing and killing him.

Meanwhile, north of Tashkent the IMU offensive had created even greater panic. Some four thousand holidaymakers and children at summer camps were evacuated from the hills around Bostanlyk and Gazalkent on August 24 after a group of fifteen guerrillas killed two soldiers and took four others hostage. The guerrillas held out for several weeks against repeated assaults by the army, but they finally ran out of ammunition and were wiped out. It was the first time that the fighting had come so close to the capital. Tashkent's citizens could hear helicopter gunships and fighter jets take off from Tashkent military airport for bombing and strafing runs every morning. Rumors flooded the city.

In Batken in early August, the guerrillas launched several assaults against Kyrgyz army posts in the course of which twenty-four soldiers and twenty-five guerrillas were killed. Kyrgyz army officers claimed that the guerrillas were setting up supply dumps and trying to open a corridor to the Fergana Valley. Kyrgyz special forces units—bearing such names as Scorpions and Snow Leopards—who had been trained earlier that year at Fort Campbell, Louisiana, were sent in to eliminate the guerrillas. For the second year in a row, refugees from the mountains flooded into Batken and surrounding villages.

On August 11 an IMU group ambushed and killed twenty-two Kyrgyz soldiers at the Korbakha canyon, at the mouth of the Toro Pass, about four miles from the border with Tajikistan and eighteen miles from Batken. This was one of the largest single massacres of the war. The guerrillas were part of an IMU group of twenty-eight men who had crossed the border from Tajikistan expressly to kidnap foreign tourists and mountain climbers for ransom. After the ambush they split up into two groups, and on August 12 they separately kidnapped twelve foreign mountain climbers and a group of four Americans that included one woman. The other climbers eventually escaped or were abandoned by their captors, but the Americans were held by an IMU group of eight men led by a Commander Sabir from Namangan, who tried to take them back to Tajikistan. On the way Sabir murdered a Kyrgyz soldier whom the IMU group had also kidnapped.[11]

But the IMU group and their hostages were soon surrounded by 130 Kyrgyz special forces troops. After several days of pursuit, the Kyrgyz killed six guerrillas, captured two others, and rescued the climbers. One of the captured guerrillas reported that he was paid $500 a month to fight for the IMU, whilst the other said he was on the run from the law, having been convicted of rape. It is rare for IMU members to be taken prisoner; wounded guerrillas are usually killed by their comrades to keep them from falling into the hands of the army. When Commander Sabir, the last IMU fighter left alive from the group, stumbled into a Kyrgyz army picket less than half a mile from the Tajikistan border and was shot, soldiers discovered a note on his dead body that read, "If you are reading this letter, you have killed me. Please bury my body in accordance with Islamic law."[12]

The American climbers later claimed that they escaped from their captors on August 18 by pushing their IMU guard, a Tajik named Ravshan Sharipov, off a cliff. However, Sharipov was captured unharmed by the Kyrgyz army on August 27. He later told American reporter John Bouchard that he had been drugged (or, more likely, he fell asleep) and awoke to find the Americans gone. The American climbers sold their story to U.S. magazine and book publishers as well as to Hollywood.[13] This one incident had an importance beyond its events: it contributed to the decision made shortly thereafter by the U.S. government to declare the IMU a terrorist group.

The Kyrgyz army had managed to capture a video camera which the guerrillas had been using to film their operations (and which the Kyrgyz army later used to film the bodies of the guerrillas they had killed). The film, which I have viewed, shows a group of well-armed young men, some clearly farmers and herdsmen, others from the city, marching, eating, sleeping, and assembling for prayers and recitation from the Koran. As they cross over the high passes that separate Tajikistan from Kyrgyzstan the group grows to about thirty men before it splits up to carry out kidnappings and other operations. Most obvious is the youth of the fighters—several appear to be teenagers—as well as their enormous ethnic diversity: Uzbeks, Tajiks, Kyrgyz, Chechens, and Caucasians are all represented.

At the end of October, Namangani withdrew his forces and re-treated into Afghanistan—again under the highly suspicious super-vision of Russian border guards. The same month in a Tashkent court the trial began of twelve leaders of the IMU and of Erk, of whom only three were actually in court, behind a barred iron cage. The rest, including both Namangani and Yuldeshev, were on trial in absentia. The Uzbek prosecutor general listed the charges against the accused. "Documents and evidence gathered as a result of ur-gent operations have proved that nineteen murders and thirty-five assaults were carried out between 1991 and 1999 in Tashkent, Samar-kand and Khorezm regions and bomb explosions were carried out in February 1999 in Tashkent. . . . Subversive activities in November 1999 in Yangiabad, and in August 2000 in Surkhandarya and Tash-kent regions were committed by armed groups under the leadership of Tohir Yuldeshev, Juma Namangani and Muhammad Solih." The court charged the twelve men with killing seventy people and injur-ing two hundred.[14] Namangani and Yuldeshev were sentenced to death in absentia, whilst Muhammad Solih, the leader of Erk who was in exile in Norway, received twenty years in jail. The sentences made it clear that there would now be no room for compromise be-tween Karimov and the IMU.

The final official tally for the IMU offensives in 2000 was 24 Uzbek soldiers and 30 IMU guerrillas killed in Uzbekistan and 30 Kyrgyz troops and 120 IMU guerrillas killed in Kyrgyzstan. Indepen-dent sources put the number of deaths in both national armies much higher.[15] The IMU incursions in 2000 prompted a massive interna-tional response. The United States, Russia, China, Turkey, France, and Israel flew in supplies and counterinsurgency equipment to Kyr-gyzstan and Uzbekistan. The Russian government promised $30 million in weapons to Uzbekistan; the arms would include 50 armored personnel carriers, Mi-8 helicopters, and communications equipment. Chinese aircraft airlifted $365,000 in flak jackets, night-vision goggles, and sniper rifles to Tashkent and pledged to help Kyr-

gyzstan boost its defense forces. The United States was already providing $3 million in nonlethal counterinsurgency equipment to Kyrgyzstan and Uzbekistan.

Western nations urged the countries of the region to coordinate their resistance, and Russia took the lead in bringing this about.[16] On August 21 the presidents of Kazakhstan, Kyrgyzstan, Uzbekistan, and Tajikistan met with senior Russian defense officials in Bishkek to coordinate defense plans. But the meetings did little to cool down the heated tensions between Karimov and the other leaders. On August 25, Karimov directly accused Mirzo Ziyoyev, the Tajik minister of emergencies, IRP leader, and former comrade of Namangani, of helping the IMU—a charge Ziyoyev vehemently denied.[17] Such accusations did not make it any easier for these states to coordinate their military strategy. Even though Karimov was the target of the IMU, he blamed everyone for the crisis in Central Asia except himself.

The Clinton administration delivered a bonus to Uzbekistan on September 15 when Washington declared the IMU a terrorist group because of its alleged involvement with bin Laden, the drug trade, kidnapping, and the murder of civilians. The government took this drastic step in part to allow increased counterinsurgency and antiterrorist cooperation and intelligence sharing between Uzbekistan and the CIA and FBI. Officials in Washington told me that the move was prompted by growing evidence that bin Laden's cooperation with the IMU had increased dramatically over the past year and that the IMU had become a virtual partner in Al Qaeda's global jihad against the United States. In addition to drug smuggling, military training, and support for Al Qaeda to extend its cells into Central Asia, the IMU was providing critical intelligence to bin Laden about the movements of senior U.S. officials and diplomats in Central Asian capitals.

Yet the U.S. move seemed to undermine any hope of international or quiet U.S. mediation between Uzbekistan and the IMU, whilst it also made it appear that Washington was condoning Uzbekistan's bru-

tal human-rights record. Some U.S. diplomats had argued against the decision, urging that it was premature; before labeling the IMU a terrorist organization, the United States should extract agreements from Karimov on human-rights and democracy issues, they insisted. But these arguments were countered by the CIA and the FBI, who wanted to share intelligence with the Uzbek government—something they could not do legally unless the United States declared the IMU a terrorist group.[18]

The IMU, now based in Mazar-i-Sharif and Kunduz in northern Afghanistan, was fast becoming a pan-Islamic force. From six hundred fighters with their families, IMU strength had grown steadily, until it now numbered two thousand fighters, drawn from Kyrgyz, Tajik, and Uzbek youth as well as Chechens from the Caucasus and Uighurs from the Muslim province of Xinjiang, China. Fulfilling his bargain with the Taliban, Namangani provided them with six hundred IMU fighters for the forces attacking Masood in northeastern Afghanistan during the late summer of 2000. The Taliban forces encircled Masood's headquarters in Taloqan, which fell on September 5, after a month-long siege. One-third of the Taliban force of roughly twelve to fifteen thousand men was made up of non-Afghans. In addition to the IMU there were four thousand Islamic militants from Pakistan, six hundred fighters from bin Laden's 055 Arab Brigade (part of Al Qaeda), Chechens, and Uighurs. Officers from Pakistan's Interservices Intelligence and Pakistani commandos from its Special Services Group played a major role in coordinating the Taliban attack, providing logistical backup and planning strategy and tactics, particularly in the Taliban's use of armor and artillery. Radio intercepts by Western countries during the siege indicated that the attackers were communicating in three languages: Pushto (for the Afghans and Pakistanis), Russian (for the benefit of the IMU), and Arabic (for the Arab fighters).

The Pakistani contingent fighting for the Taliban included hundreds of adherents of extremist anti-Shia groups, such as the Sipah-i-

Sahaba and Lashkar-i-Jhangvi, who had become notorious for their murders of Shia Muslims in Pakistan. Both groups had been given sanctuary by the Taliban, and along with the Arabs had committed some of the worst massacres of Afghan Shias, in the Hazarajat region of central Afghanistan. Some Sipah and Lashkar fighters had joined up with Namangani as early as 1999, keen to establish for themselves a name as jihadis in Central Asia and thus give themselves a pan-Islamic pedigree, rather than being labeled simply anti-Shia militants. When foreign diplomats tried to contact the IMU during the kidnapping incident with the Japanese geologists in 1999, they were surprised to discover that their contact was a Pakistani from Sipah. These Sipah militants also provided the IMU with supplies, communication facilities, and other help from Pakistan.

The fall of Taloqan caused a major setback for Masood, and for several weeks his supporters Russia and Iran feared that he would be driven out of Afghanistan and be forced to take refuge with his fighters in Tajikistan. Although Masood held the line against further Taliban advance, Taloqan turned out to be a watershed. After the defeat the international community no longer felt able to trust the Taliban. The unprecedented involvement of Islamic militants from so many countries in the offensive, and the continued presence of bin Laden in Afghanistan, prompted Russia and the United States to call for sanctions by the U.N. Security Council that included an arms embargo against the Taliban. The sanctions came into force in January 2001. Meanwhile, Masood continued to receive arms from his supporters.

The siege of Taloqan gave IMU fighters battle experience in a number of techniques, including the integrated use of armor, artillery, and air power. They became more involved in field operations with global jihadi networks like Al Qaeda, to whose members the Taliban had given sanctuary. This was to prove invaluable for the future. In the meantime, the Taliban had discovered that the IMU could provide a useful deniability factor for them. When

China put its close ally Pakistan under pressure to force the Taliban to stop training Uighur Muslims at the Rishkor camp outside Kabul in order to foment Islamic rebellion in Xinjiang Province, the Taliban removed the Uighur fighters from the front lines and sent them up north to join the IMU in Mazar-i-Sharif. At a meeting in Kandahar between the Chinese ambassador to Pakistan and Mullah Omar, the Taliban were then able to deny that Uighurs were part of their armed forces.

Several months later Pakistan's military government asked the Taliban to extradite Sipah and Lashkar leaders, who were wanted on multiple murder charges in Pakistan. The Taliban also sent these guerrillas north to be garrisoned with the IMU. And when Russia exerted pressure demanding the extradition of Chechens from Afghanistan, Chechen fighters on the Kabul front went north to join the IMU. By default the IMU had become a multinational, pan-Islamic force enlisting militants from all over the region, as well as a convenient dumping ground for the foreign militants the Taliban were now finding too embarrassing to keep in their own forces. Even though the IMU continued to insist that its only aim was to topple the Uzbek government, no one now doubted that it aimed to carry its jihad across Central Asia.

In late November 2000, Namangani crossed back into Tajikistan with a multinational force of about three hundred militants. Central Asian leaders refused to admit that he was there, issuing furious denials when a newspaper published the information—and then held a summit conference in Almaty on January 5 to deal with his return. Karimov responded as he had done in previous years. "In 1999 and 2000 we were the objects of aggression, but we must not let this happen again. All the Central Asian states need to take more measures to prevent a repeat of the same scenario in 2001."[19] In fact, Karimov had spent the winter months holding secret talks with the Taliban to persuade them to extradite Namangani. In a bid to reestablish a dialogue between Uzbekistan and the Taliban, Pakistan sponsored talks in Islamabad in October 2000 between the Uzbek and Taliban ambassadors to Pakistan. The Uzbeks brought a list of IMU militants whom they wished extradited from Afghanistan. After three meetings between the ambassadors, the Taliban broke off the talks. Taliban Foreign Minister Wakil Ahmed Muttawakil later told me that the Taliban could never trust the Uzbeks or Karimov; he found the negotiations distasteful and was not prepared to continue them. Muttawakil claimed that "there are only some three hundred and fifty Uzbek families who are seeking shelter from Karimov's repression and whom we have given sanctuary to because of our Islamic duty, but there are no IMU fighters in Mazar."[20]

Namangani's arrival in Tavildara prompted another war of words between the Uzbek and Tajik governments and even greater Uzbek pressure on Tajikistan and Kyrgyzstan to curb all Islamicists. During the harsh winter months Tashkent cut gas supplies to Dushanbe and Bishkek in order to try to force the governments to stamp out the IMU; Uzbekistan also demanded that Kyrgyzstan give Uzbekistan territorial concessions to allow it to establish a corridor to the Sukh Enclave. In addition Uzbekistan stepped up the mining and barbed wiring of its borders with Tajikistan and Kyrgyzstan, further cutting off families, villages, and trade. Western humanitarian workers in Khujand told me in March 2001 that thirty innocent people had been killed and dozens wounded in accidental mine explosions on the border in the past few months. Tashkent then started throwing out Tajikistan refugees who had lived in Uzbekistan for the past six years. These were ethnic Uzbeks who had fled from Tajikistan during the civil war. There were tens of thousands of such people; many feared that if they were all forced back to Tajikistan, the country's fragile economy would be overwhelmed.

Tajikistan's resentment against Karimov was long-standing, but it focused in particular on the fact that Uzbekistan had given sanctuary to several dissidents from Tajikistan, including Col. Makhmud Khudoyberdiev, the leader of an armed incursion into northern

Tajikistan in November 1998 which was supported by Tashkent, and Abdulmalik Abdullajanov, a former prime minister of Tajikistan who was proclaiming himself an alternative leader to President Rahmonov from his refuge in Uzbekistan. Some Tajik IRP ministers argued that as long as Uzbekistan gave sanctuary to these figures, Tajikistan was justified in giving sanctuary to the IMU because this was the only bargaining chip Dushanbe had. Nevertheless, under enormous pressure from Uzbekistan and the international community, Tajik ministers did go to Tavildara to try to persuade Namangani to return to Afghanistan. Namangani refused to talk to anyone but his former comrade in the IRP, Mirzo Ziyoyev, who stayed in Tavildara for a week before a deal was finally struck. Namangani agreed to leave—again under the supervision of Russian border guards. Over seven days in January 2001, Russian transport helicopters airlifted Namangani and more than three hundred men from Tavildara to the Afghan border. A small IMU garrison remained behind in the Sangvor base camp.

In the streets, government ministries, and foreign embassies of Dushanbe, conspiracy theories were rampant. The most intriguing question was who was supporting Namangani. Many Tajik officials—and even poor farmers—believed that the Russians were playing a double game. Whilst Russia officially opposed the IMU, Russian border guards turned a blind eye to his forays from Afghanistan because Moscow was trying to pressure Karimov into accepting Russian troops and greater Russian influence in Uzbekistan. The fact that since 1999 the Russian army had three times helped evacuate IMU guerrillas to Afghanistan was undeniable, and it was a major factor fueling the conspiracy theory. Moscow never bothered to explain the reason for its actions nor why it was helping Namangani escape to Afghanistan rather than arresting him. Other Tajik officials claimed that the IMU was supported by Saudi Arabia and Pakistan, who were backing Islamic movements in Central Asia in order to gain leverage in the region and as part of their support of the Taliban.

These Tajik officials, and even some foreign diplomats, claimed that when Namangani had arrived in Central Asia in November, he had not traveled overland from Afghanistan but had flown with help from Pakistan in a chartered flight from Karachi to Bishkek, wearing a heavy disguise and having shaved off his beard. Namangani then allegedly drove to Osh and on to Tavildara. None of these rumors could be substantiated, and Russian and Pakistani officials dismissed all charges as speculation. Tajik IRP members were more willing to believe them, knowing the realities of fighting a guerrilla war. "When we were in the civil war we took help from anyone who gave it to us. Now Namangani will take help from anyone who is against Uzbekistan," said IRP leader Sharif Himmatzoda.[21]

Namangani's easy access to Tajikistan was only part of the problem. The economic and political situation in Uzbekistan appeared to be getting worse, ensuring ever greater support to the IMU. Despite the heavy hand of the Uzbek police an unprecedented demonstration of some three hundred women took place in the streets of Andijan in the Fergana Valley on April 10, 2001. Carrying placards which read, "2001 will be the year of lonely widows and orphans," they demanded that the authorities free all political prisoners, including their sons and husbands. As the police were arresting one group of demonstrators outside the mayor's office, more busloads were arriving to replace them—a process that was repeated five times during the day.[22] In a sign of international frustration with the Uzbek regime, the International Monetary Fund closed its office in Tashkent in April, explaining that the absence of economic reforms and the failure to introduce a unified exchange rate had stymied all hopes for Uzbekistan's economic development and foreign investment. "It's not a business climate conducive to foreign investment," IMF representative Christoph Rosenberg told reporters before leaving Tashkent.

Uzbekistan's economic crisis was certainly getting worse. According to officials of the Uzbek State Planning Agency, 60 percent of the population was under 25 and most of them were unemployed. The government needed to find four hundred thousand new jobs a year—an impossible task. Inflation was running at 60 percent, which was certainly down from the 465 percent in previous years but still unmanageable for most Uzbeks. In rural areas farmers were still being urged to grow more cotton, but what they received for their crops was meager. The government paid farmers $170 for a metric ton of cotton and then sold that abroad for $1,300. In a throwback to the forced labor of the Soviet era local authorities were urging children to give up school and work in the fields for nothing during the cotton harvest. Many farmers were being paid in goods rather than cash, further deteriorating their buying power.

Such measures led to ever smaller cotton harvests, further decreasing farmers' chances at survival. The tragedy was that the government appeared to recognize that its economic failures were creating new recruits for the IMU, but it was not prepared to undertake the necessary reforms. "It would be fair to recognize that upheavals of religious fanaticism are not originated only and exclusively by religious contradictions in themselves, but predominantly are originated due to unsolved social, political and economic problems," acknowledged Karimov in a government publication.[23]

The Campaign of 2001

As the summer of 2001 approached, governments across the region prepared for another IMU offensive. There seemed to be increasing multiethnic cooperation within the organization. In June reports circulated that the IMU had changed its name to Hizb-i-Islami Turkistan (Islamic Party of Turkistan) and would now seek to bring Islamic revolution to the whole of Central Asia and Xinjiang Province. IMU officials later denied the reports. "We have only one enemy—the Tashkent regime—we have no problems with neighboring countries and our name has not changed," Zubayr Ibn Abdur Raheem, the head of the religious leadership of the IMU, assured listeners of Radio Free Europe in a rare interview. However, Raheem admitted, "Our organization does not only follow Uzbek interests. We are an Islamic group. There are many ethnic groups with us—Kyrgyz, Kazakh, and even Uighurs—but because we are all from Uzbekistan we call ourselves the IMU."[24] Meanwhile, for the second year running, Namangani deployed six hundred IMU fighters in northeastern Afghanistan to join the Taliban's summer offensive against Masood, which began in June and continued until the autumn, when Masood was blown up by two suicide assassins linked to bin Laden who were posing as journalists. Once more fighting alongside the IMU were bin Laden's Arab troops and Pakistani Islamic militants.

But the IMU attacks in Central Asia were not long in coming. The Kyrgyz government reported that "bandits" had attacked two army posts on the Tajikistan-Kyrgyzstan border in the Batken region on the nights of July 24 and 25. Tajikistan hastily—and predictably— denied that guerrillas had crossed its borders and challenged Russian reports that the IMU was massing forces on the Tajik side of the border. On July 31 guerrillas attacked a Kyrgyz television transmitter in the Batken region, and Yuldeshev claimed responsibility. Speaking to Hamid Ismailov of the Uzbek service of the BBC from a base in northern Afghanistan, Yuldeshev announced that the IMU was attacking Kyrgyz targets in the Batken region and that earlier in the summer IMU guerrillas had fought with Uzbek troops in the Surkhandarya region. (The Uzbeks had claimed that the skirmishes were military exercises.) But Yuldeshev was careful to protect his Afghan and Tajik hosts, asserting that IMU fighters had not crossed any borders but were already based in Kyrgyzstan and Uzbekistan.[25]

It is clear that these IMU fighters did not, in fact, come from Tajikistan. Rather, they appeared to be IMU sleepers, already based in Kyrgyz villages, who carried out their attacks and then slipped back into their civilian lives. This was the first sign that Namangani's arms-smuggling efforts during the winter of 2000–2001 in and around the Fergana Valley had succeeded. He now appeared to have permanent guerrilla forces based in Uzbekistan and Kyrgyzstan and a new, independent command structure that could operate without his presence in Tajikistan. Thus Namangani could stop making the hazardous trip from Afghanistan to Tajikistan and keep from annoying the Tajik government by his presence.

When Uzbekistan celebrated the tenth anniversary of its independence on September 1, the economic and political outlook for the country was grim. Facing intense international pressure to reform his human-rights record, Karimov was forced to free some 25,000 of the 64,500 prisoners in Uzbekistan's jails as part of an "anniversary amnesty." The government also reduced the jail terms for another 25,000 prisoners—but the 7,000 political prisoners who had been imprisoned for belonging to Islamic groups were not covered by the amnesty. Then, just ten days afterwards, Uzbekistan's situation vis-à-vis the international community changed dramatically.

The September 11 terrorist attacks in the United States created profound geostrategic changes in Central Asia—one of which was to force the IMU to abandon (temporarily) its late-summer offensive. Within days of the attacks Tashkent was being wooed by Washington, as the United States clamored for military bases and landing rights in Uzbekistan in preparation for an assault on Taliban-controlled Afghanistan. These demands from the United States created a serious dilemma for Russia and Central Asia. For the past decade Central Asia had been Russia's backyard, and Moscow had assiduously tried to block the United States from acquiring a major political or military presence in the region. Moscow now feared that Washington's demands for temporary military bases could lead to a more permanent U.S. military presence in Central Asia once the fighting in Afghanistan was over.

For their part, the Central Asian leaders feared that giving the United States overt help in fighting the Taliban would be a propaganda coup for the IMU and the HT, allowing the groups to depict the regimes as lackeys of the United States. Moreover, such actions could lead to retaliation by both the Taliban and the IMU, who could now justify their guerrilla actions against the Central Asian leadership by claiming that the regimes had not only sold out their states' national interests but also gone against the interests of the wider Islamic world by allowing an infidel force to be based on their soil to conduct a war against Afghan Muslims.

The response to U.S. demands was thus slow in coming. Although Russia's President Vladimir Putin and Central Asia's leaders quickly offered their condolences on the loss of life in New York and Washington, they remained silent about whether they would agree to the demand for bases. Putin disappeared into a Black Sea holiday resort, whence he conferred almost daily by telephone with the Central Asian leaders, trying to convince them that the six of them should present the Americans with a joint policy decision — thus ensuring that Moscow still appeared to be the key policy formulator for Central Asia. But finally, on September 24 and 25, Putin and the Central Asian leaders separately announced that they would give the United States limited military facilities.

Uzbekistan and Tajikistan offered intelligence cooperation, use of their air space, and the use of Khanabad air base, which would not involve the positioning of U.S. ground troops for an invasion of Afghanistan. Kyrgyzstan, Kazakhstan, and Turkmenistan also offered use of their air space, landing rights for U.S. aircraft in trouble, and intelligence sharing. But after a visit to Tashkent by U.S. Defense Secretary Donald Rumsfeld on October 5, Uzbekistan went one step further, granting the United States military bases for American troops and lifting the ban on conducting combat missions from Uzbekistan's soil. More than fifteen hundred U.S. troops from the 10th Mountain Division arrived with attack helicopters at Khanabad, near Termez, close to Uzbekistan's eighty-five-mile border with northern Afghanistan. Uzbekistan also allowed Russia, Iran, and Turkey to use its territory to step up arms supplies to the anti-Taliban

United Front, whose new commander in northern Afghanistan, Gen. Rashid Dostum, was attempting to capture the strategic city of Mazar-i-Sharif.

In return Tashkent sought guarantees from Washington concerning the security of Uzbekistan's territory and the inviolability of its borders, as well as greater technical assistance to its armed forces. The Uzbek government claimed that a classified agreement was signed with the United States on October 7 which established "a qualitatively new relationship based on a long-term commitment to advance security and regional stability." However, many terms of the pact remained secret, as Uzbekistan was anxious not to annoy Russia or provide further provocation to the IMU. Nevertheless, this was a historic agreement which will have far-reaching implications for the future, particularly with regard to a greater U.S. and NATO presence in the region. For the first time, Western forces would be operating from the landlocked heart of Central Asia. As a U.S. official in Tashkent remarked, "This is quite historic — it's the first time something like this has been done with any country that was part of the Soviet Union." It is also clear that the U.S. decision to designate the IMU a terrorist group in 2000 and the increased cooperation this led to between the Uzbek security services and the CIA and FBI had now paid handsome dividends to Tashkent. As Rutam Jumaev, chief spokesman for President Karimov, noted, "Our cooperation with the US began long before the events of September 11."[26] Almost immediately the World Bank announced that it would be sending a delegation to Tashkent to revive its stalled relationship with the government and provide new loans to ensure economic stability — now that Uzbekistan was part of the front line in the war against terrorism.

Despite their concerns about possible IMU retaliation, Russia and the Central Asian states were more than satisfied with the prospect of the demise of the Taliban, which had been harboring the IMU, and they calculated that any U.S.–United Front assault on

Taliban-controlled northern Afghanistan would eliminate the IMU threat forever. Russia was equally keen for the U.S. forces to target Chechen militants fighting for the Taliban. For Russia the only real concern was that the United States not undermine its political influence in Central Asia—whilst Uzbekistan saw a strategic alliance with the United States as a key to greater independence from Russia. The alliance would also provide Tashkent with international support for its own war against the terrorism unleashed by the IMU.

The IMU reacted to these maneuvers predictably, mobilizing its fighters to support the Taliban and resist the U.S. attacks. The IMU deployed fighters to Mazar-i-Sharif, Taloqan, and Kunduz in northern Afghanistan, and Namangani was reported to be commanding all the Taliban forces in Taloqan. In a radio interview on October 9, Yuldeshev said that the IMU was "willing to fight shoulder to shoulder with the Taliban" against their enemies, including Uzbekistan. He described Tashkent's willingness to help the U.S.-led coalition as "an act of treason" which would inevitably lead to revenge attacks by the IMU.[27]

In Tajikistan, the coalition government argued about the extent to which Tajikistan should help the U.S.-led alliance. "If strikes are carried out against ordinary Afghans as well as terrorists, this will look more like American aggression against Afghanistan," said Sayed Abdullah Nuri, the head of the IRP. "I do not rule out that unrest amongst the Muslim believers may occur in Tajikistan."[28] But the United States enlisted the help of the Japanese government to broker greater cooperation from Tajikistan. Japanese envoys in Dushanbe managed to convince the government to allow U.S. special forces to use Tajikistan's air bases to provide the United Front with communications and intelligence.

After the U.S. bombing campaign in Afghanistan began, on October 7, international human-rights groups expressed growing concern that the United States would use its new alliances with the Central Asian states—particularly Uzbekistan—to forestall demands for

greater democracy or respect for human rights. And in fact, Uzbekistan has not hesitated to push ahead with government repression of
all Islamic activism, whether peaceful or violent. Seizing the
moment, the regime now directly links all such activities to Osama
bin Laden, thereby making it more difficult for the Western alliance
to object to the repression. These tactics were successful in the October conviction of nine HT members, who were suddenly charged in
addition with having links to Al Qaeda. The government of Kyrgyzstan is following suit: several dozen Islamic activists were arrested in
early October, accused of belonging to either the IMU or the HT—
but also of having links to Al Qaeda.

With their military alliance with the United States in place, the
Central Asian regimes have stepped up their harassment of Islamic
activism in their own territories. Yet it is clear that the IMU does not
intend to wait for its forces to be wiped out by the bombing in
northern Afghanistan. There is every indication that in the months
ahead the IMU will launch another guerrilla campaign in the countryside around the Fergana Valley, targeting as well civilian and government sites in the major cities of Uzbekistan. Just as Karimov can
now presume that he has full international support for his war
against the IMU, so too can Juma Namangani presume that Uzbekistan's involvement with the U.S. invasion of Afghanistan will give
him local Muslim support for an escalation in his own war to topple
the Karimov regime.

9 The New Great Game?
The United States, Russia, and China

IN ANCIENT TIMES Central Asia, spanning the Eurasian landmass, was considered the center of the world. Its nomadic warrior tribes repeatedly conquered the regions of Russia, Europe, India, China, and Turkey. Chinese emperors built the Great Wall to keep out marauding Central Asian tribes. Russia's early history is largely one of wars waged against Muslim Tartars. (In 1552, when Ivan the Terrible captured the Tartar capital of Kazan, he commemorated the event in Moscow by building St. Basil's Cathedral, topping its towers with onion domes to symbolize the severed heads of the turbaned Tartars.) The great empires in Central Asia—those of the Mongols, the Timurids, and the Shaybani Uzbeks—ruled half the known world and spawned yet more empires: the Moguls in India and the Ottomans in Turkey. As late as the nineteenth century Sir Halford Mackinder, the founding father of modern geopolitics, would describe Central Asia as the political center of the world because it enclosed more frontiers than any other region. Whoever controlled Central Asia would wield enormous power: "It is the greatest natural fortress in the world, defended by polar ice caps, deserts, arid table-land and mountain ranges."[1]

The opening of new sea lanes to Africa, India, China, and the Americas rapidly changed the importance of Central Asia, reducing the traffic on the Silk Route to a trickle. Landlocked Central Asia was now isolated, a tempting pawn in the rivalry between the great powers. In what became known as the Great Game, Russia and Great Britain vied for power, expanding their empires in the Asian landmass. The regions of Central Asia, too weak to stand against the great powers, cut off from their Muslim neighbors to the south, fell one by one to the Russian onslaught. After the Russian Revolution, however, Central Asia became a geostrategic backwater: firmly entrenched in the Soviet Union, it ceased to interest the superpowers. Even the Soviet Union regarded the area as an appendage to its Russian empire.

All this changed after 1991. Russia continued to play a predominant role in Central Asia, but other great powers—the United States and China—also stepped in, forcing rapid geopolitical shifts in the foreign policies of the newly independent Central Asian states. Big power rivalry first emerged with the competition to exploit the oil and gas resources of the Caspian Sea and Central Asia, but it soon extended to other issues of strategic importance, such as how to maintain stability in a vast, fragile region that bordered so many disturbed countries, particularly Afghanistan. Central Asia's situation at the center of a huge landmass remained a major disadvantage, and the great powers have tried to devise policies that would allow them to control its access to sea and trade routes and keep out the competition. But the superpowers are finding things more difficult the second time round, and the game has changed. The leaders of the Central Asian regimes, each of whom has his own game to play, with his own rules, are refusing to be pawns in the superpower game. And the Islamic militants are playing a different game altogether.

The United States: Oil and Arms Trump
Economics and Human Rights

The U.S. oil companies were amongst the first international groups to realize the importance of the region. Even before the United States had established embassies in each of the new republics, major U.S. oil companies had arrived to map out the energy possibilities, spurred on by Chevron's early finds of oil and gas in Kazakhstan. But in the aftermath of the Cold War, as the United States grappled with a new strategic landscape around the world that offered many ill-defined new challenges, Central Asia was not high amongst its priorities. Washington's first task was to figure out its new relationship with non-Communist Russia, and the other states in the former Soviet Union would be of secondary importance until that was achieved.

During President Clinton's terms in office the United States could not even decide how to achieve short-term goals in Central Asia. Although some officials tried to articulate a strategic vision for the region, their ideas were never put into practice. At first the United States viewed Central Asia through the prism of Moscow, as Washington pursued a "Russia first" policy. In the mid-1990s the United States swung to the other extreme, becoming obsessed with the idea of creating a pipeline to carry oil and gas from Baku, Azerbaijan, to Ceyhan, Turkey. Proponents dubbed it the new Silk Route, and they mapped out a provocative course that would avoid both Russian and Iranian territory. And so the much-anticipated new Great Game between the major powers in the Caucasus and Central Asia over the choice of pipeline routes swiftly became a reality. After the IMU's emergence in 1999 the Clinton administration adapted its Central Asian policy to focus on combating terrorism and trying to build up the military capability of the regimes. But the administration failed to make its support contingent on those governments' improving their dismal record in economic and political reform, to say nothing of human rights.

In a major policy speech concerning Central Asia in July 1997 in which he tried to set the tone for the Clinton administration, Deputy Secretary of State Strobe Talbott insisted that the United States was not interested in a replay of the Great Game. "Our goal is to avoid and actively discourage that atavistic outcome," he declared. The Central Asian states "have a chance to put behind them forever the experience of being pawns on a chessboard as big powers vie for wealth and influence at their expense." Talbott went on,

> The consolidation of free societies . . . stretching from the Black Sea to the Pamir Mountains will open up a valuable trade and transport corridor along the old Silk Route between Europe and Asia. But the ominous converse is equally true. If economic and political reform does not succeed, if internal and cross-border conflicts simmer and flare, then the region could become a breeding ground of terrorism, a hotbed of religious and political extremism, and a battleground for outright war. It would matter profoundly to the U.S. if that were to happen in an area that sits on as much as 200 billion barrels of oil. That is another reason why conflict resolution must be job number one for U.S. policy in the region.[2]

Talbott's warnings were prescient, and so were his ideas about future U.S. strategy. The only problem was that Washington failed to follow up on them.

Had the United States been serious about its strategic vision for Central Asia, policymakers should not only have talked about conflict resolution; they should have insisted that it be the number one priority. In particular, the United States should have lent political muscle to the U.N. attempts to end the civil war in Afghanistan, which was posing the key external threat to Central Asia. The United States could have stabilized the economy of Tajikistan with development funds, brought concerted pressure to end the conflict between Azerbaijan and Armenia, worked on its relationship with Iran, and linked pipeline proposals and military aid explicitly to reforms by the leaders of Central Asia's republics. Instead, Washington was clearer about its enemies than its friends, designating two major regional powers—Russia and Iran—its rivals and competitors, whilst failing to identify a single regional power as an ally.

Having declared the IMU a terrorist group early in the game, the United States cut off any chance of playing a mediating role between the IMU and the Uzbek government, whilst the lack of U.S. allies in the region meant that the country had no leverage in Afghanistan either. But Central Asia was too far away, and U.S. influence was too marginal there; Washington could not hope to pursue any kind of regional policies single-handedly. The United States needed allies in the region; without them, even limited U.S. policies were doomed to failure. With the powerful influence of U.S. oil companies in the new Bush administration, Central Asia watchers hoped that Washington would develop a more comprehensive strategic policy, but there were few signs of it as the year wore on and the threats from Afghanistan and the IMU increased.

In the aftermath of the IMU offensives in the spring of 2000, the Central Asian states had been bombarded by visits from top U.S. officials, including Secretary of State Madeleine Albright, CIA director George Tenet, and FBI director Louis Freeh. In June the United States hosted a counterterrorism conference in Washington that was attended by senior officials of the Central Asian states. The Central Asian leaders were treated as honored guests, even receiving tours of CIA and FBI headquarters. The CIA, in fact, had already delivered a chilling verdict on the IMU in February. "We are becoming increasingly concerned about the activities of the IMU, an extremist insurgent and terrorist group whose annual incursions into Uzbekistan have become bloodier and more significant every year. In Central Asia corruption, poverty and other social ills are providing fertile ground for Islamic extremists, terrorist networking and drug and weapons trafficking that will have an impact in Russia, Europe and beyond," Tenet told the U.S. Senate.[3] Although Tenet had defined the problem clearly, the measures taken by the Clinton administration related only to counterterrorism, ignoring "the social ills" that beset the region.

Whilst Albright was in Central Asia, Washington announced the creation of a Central Asian Border Security Initiative, which provided $3 million each to Kyrgyzstan, Uzbekistan, and Kazakhstan to help them improve their counterinsurgency capabilities. In 2001 this nonlethal U.S. aid was extended to Tajikistan and Turkmenistan. Central Asian troops began to train with new U.S. uniforms, helmets, night-vision goggles and scopes, and communications equipment. The U.S. military stepped up joint exercises with Kazakhstan, Kyrgyzstan, and Uzbekistan under the auspices of NATO's Partnership for Peace program, which covered many CIS states. During her visit Albright also spelled out the political and social measures the Central Asian leaders needed to undertake in order to prevent the insurgency from spreading, but U.S. aid was not tied to these reforms. Instead, it was directed entirely at countering terrorism. A few U.S. Congressmen realized that the deepening crisis in Central Asia was being fueled by the regimes rather than the IMU; Congressman Dan Burton noted, for example, that "Kazakhstan is the crown jewel of the region and is thus another likely target of Islamic extremist groups . . . but it is the Nazarbayev regime itself that will likely fuel the growth of Islamic extremism."[4] But such comments had little effect on U.S. policy. The Central Asian leaders did not mind being lectured by the Americans as long as U.S. support was not contingent upon actual reform.

When Gen. Tommy Franks, the head of the U.S. Central Command (Centcom) made his visit to the region at the beginning of 2001, he reiterated the threat that terrorism posed to the region. "I believe it is possible for very small numbers of committed terrorists to bring great instability and a sense of insecurity to the people in the region. The states in Central Asia take this threat very seriously and have un-

dertaken work over the past several years to put themselves in a position to be able to deal with the threat," Franks told a briefing in
Tashkent in May.[5] Franks asserted that the relationship between the
U.S. and Uzbek militaries was excellent, promising that Centcom
would continue to train Uzbek noncommissioned officers and that
U.S. Special Forces would conduct joint exercises with Uzbek
forces—operations that offered a convenient cover to allow U.S. officers to be permanently based in Tashkent in order to train the Uzbek
army.

There was one positive development during the first months of the
Bush administration. With U.S. officers training the Uzbek army
alongside Russian military advisers, and the first extension of U.S. economic and military aid to Tajikistan—a Russian satellite—it became
apparent that the United States and Russia no longer saw themselves
as strategic competitors in the fight against the IMU and the Taliban
but had become at least temporary strategic partners. This was partly
an outcome of a joint working group on counterterrorism that Russia
and the United States had set up in 2000 to oversee policy on every-
thing from the Taliban to the Chechens and the IMU. Franks acknowledged that U.S. and Russian interests no longer conflicted; they
now "intersected" in the region—an admission that would have been
impossible just a few months earlier. After more than a decade of trying to keep Washington's influence out of Central Asia, Russia finally
realized that it needed U.S. support to maintain its own presence in
Central Asia and to provide military aid to the beleaguered regimes.
Whilst Presidents Putin and Bush differed sharply over nuclear non-
proliferation and missile defense, they could finally agree on the need
to combat terrorism and the IMU.

Russia: Drawing Ideological Borders

Since the breakup of the Soviet Union, Russia had been trying to deal
with the trauma of losing an empire and having to live with the new

states of the former Soviet Union. For the 25 million ethnic Russians who lived in what had just become foreign countries, life became unpredictable and threatening, especially in Central Asia. Russians who did not migrate back home looked to Moscow with nostalgia, hoping that Russia would reestablish its preeminent leadership role in the region and offer them security. But in the early 1990s Russian policy oscillated between the liberals around President Boris Yeltsin who wanted closer relations with the West—anchoring Russia's future in Europe at the expense of Central Asia, which they saw as a drain on Russian resources—and hard-line nationalists and former Communists who could not imagine life without the old empire. They renamed the former Soviet states "the near abroad" to differentiate them from the rest of the world.

Russia's dilemma and its policy debates were replicated in Central Asia, where leaders vacillated between wanting to appear independent of Russia in order to placate nationalistic public opinion whilst they developed alternative foreign-policy options and wanting to secure Russian military and economic support. None of the Central Asian regimes wished to live in close embrace with Russia, but none could survive without Russia's help. Throughout the early 1990s both Russia and the Central Asian states swung between these two extremes, cozying up to each other and then turning defiant.

The defining moment for Russia's interests came during the first Chechen war (1994–96), when more than four thousand Russian troops were killed in the attempt to keep Chechnya from breaking away from the Russian union. Russia now clearly articulated that the defense of its territorial borders might stop at the Ural Mountains, but the defense of its ideological borders—especially in countering the so-called Islamic threat—would stretch to Afghanistan. During the war with the Chechens, Russia launched a virtual crusade against Islam, portraying it as an evil beyond redemption or acceptance. Meanwhile, the devastation of the Chechen capital, Grozny, and the killing of tens of thousands of Chechen civilians by the Russian army horrified both the people and the leaders of Central Asia, though for different reasons. Whereas the people sympathized with their Muslim neighbors and admired the courage of the Chechen guerrillas, their leaders realized the power of Russia's military might and recognized that Russia's support would be absolutely necessary if their regimes ever faced a similar threat from their own domestic Islamic forces.

The first Chechen war also demonstrated Moscow's blatant intention of interfering in the domestic concerns of all the states of Central Asia and the Caucasus, whether through direct military support, such as that given to pro-Moscow rebels in Georgia; the manipulation of local governments by stacking them with pro-Russians, as in Tajikistan; or undercover operations, such as those in Azerbaijan and Uzbekistan. Russia insisted that these weak and fragile regimes needed Moscow's support and interference if they were to survive.[6] There were other contributing factors to Russia's belligerence in Central Asia and the Caucasus, as well as to its escalating rivalry with the United States—disputes over oil and gas pipeline routes in the mid-1990s, the battle for influence in the key oil-producing states of Azerbaijan and Kazakhstan, the West's condemnation of Russia's human rights violations in Chechnya, Russia's sale of missile and nuclear materials to Iran and North Korea (which the United States considered "rogue states"), and the expansion of the Taliban in Afghanistan, a growth that the United States supported until 1996.

President Yeltsin's choice of former KGB officer and hard-line nationalist Vladimir Putin to succeed him laid to rest the hopes of Russian liberals for a more neutral foreign policy. Putin would be firmly committed to making sure that Central Asia and the Caucasus remained within Moscow's sphere of influence. However, if the United States were willing to help fight terrorism and Islamic extremism, then cooperation with Washington would also be possible.

The second Chechen war, which began in 1999 and by autumn

2001 had claimed the lives of more than three thousand Russian soldiers, has only intensified Russia's assertiveness in Central Asia. The crusade against Islam has become more shrill; now Moscow does not bother to differentiate between so-called "good" Muslims and "bad" Muslims. From the first, Moscow linked the Chechen resistance and the IMU, although they were separate groups of militants, with global terrorism, Osama bin Laden, the Taliban, and every other Islamic group from Algeria to Indonesia. The United States, on the other hand, has been careful not to jump onto the bandwagon against Islam. The United States has continued to clearly differentiate between Islamic terrorist groups and the rest of the Islamic world. As a new round of violence broke out between Palestinians and Israelis in the Middle East in 2000, Washington became even more careful not to condemn the entire Muslim world for the actions of Muslim terrorists, as the Russians were doing.

Since the breakup of the Soviet Union, Russia has been the key outside player in Central Asia, and there is little doubt that it will continue in that role for the foreseeable future. But Russian policy in Central Asia has been beset by deep suspicion on both sides. Russia's single-minded, clear-cut, monolithic strategy—to bring the Central Asian states within its own orbit of influence and keep out Islamic radicalism—has met with many problems, most notably in Uzbekistan.

The largest state in Central Asia, Uzbekistan has successfully resisted Russian attempts since the mid-1990s to turn it into a vassal state. President Karimov has strongly if erratically maintained Uzbekistan's autonomy, working to keep Russia as an ally whilst avoiding its bear hug. Karimov's dealings with Russia have resulted in extreme swings in policy, which have become ever more unpredictable and poorly defined. Based on Karimov's personal inclinations rather than consultation with the Uzbek elite, these policies have proven extremely damaging to Uzbekistan's long-term interests.

In February 1999 Karimov pulled out of a collective security pact of CIS countries headed by Moscow and joined with Georgia, Ukraine,

Azerbaijan, and Moldova to form the pro-Western GUUAM group of countries, who pledged to promote their common security interests without Russian influence. But by December Karimov was back, signing a new security accord with Moscow whilst refusing to leave GUUAM. Such policy shifts continued the following year. "Uzbekistan is looking for protection. It can't protect itself because those strengths that threaten it have huge resources. Uzbekistan finds this protection in the form of Russia," Karimov suddenly declared in May 2000, taking his own people and his neighbors by complete surprise. The following month Uzbekistan signed a wide-ranging military cooperation agreement with Moscow that virtually handed over Uzbekistan's air space to the Russian Air Force. Yet a few months later, in September, Karimov loudly proclaimed, "Uzbekistan is able to protect itself. We have never invited and are not preparing to invite armed forces from outside Uzbekistan, no matter what country they are from," a clear snub to Russia.[7]

In May 2001, on a visit to Moscow, Karimov hit out even more strongly. He rejected the Moscow-led CIS collective-security treaty in favor of NATO's Partnership for Peace program, declined to join a new Customs Union of CIS countries, condemned his neighbors for allowing Russian troops on their soil, and criticized Moscow's declaration that it was seeking to establish a new military base in Tajikistan. Yet that same month, at a CIS summit in Armenia, Russia had agreed with Kazakhstan, Kyrgyzstan, and Tajikistan to set up a rapid-reaction force for Central Asia that would be based in Bishkek and target such terrorist organizations as the IMU. Karimov refused to have anything to do with the force, even though the IMU was essentially his problem.

These unpredictable swings continued in other spheres of Uzbek policy, causing further problems with Russia. After heaping abuse on the Taliban, Tashkent suddenly opened direct talks with them in October 2000 in a bid to persuade them to extradite the IMU. In his efforts to curry favor with the Taliban, Karimov even accused Moscow of exaggerating the threat posed by Afghanistan. "Those who exaggerate the threat of the Taliban to Central Asia want to cut off from investors the road to our region and frighten them so that capital does not come to Central Asia," he claimed.[8] By spring 2001 the talks had failed—as most analysts had predicted they would—and Karimov went back to condemning the Taliban as the source of terrorism and instability in Central Asia. In a further snub to the Taliban, he met with Dr. Abdullah Abdullah, the foreign minister of the anti-Taliban alliance—the first meeting between a high-ranking Uzbekistan official and an anti-Taliban leader in several years.

Karimov's policies have also affected Russia's relationship with other Central Asian states. At a moment when Kyrgyzstan needs good neighbors and support in countering IMU incursions, Karimov is helping to turn them away. Uzbekistan has long wanted to make Kyrgyzstan a vassal state, and Karimov has not been averse to abusing President Akayev; in February 1999 he announced on Uzbek radio that the situation in Kyrgyzstan was chaotic because its leader could do nothing but smile (a word that was translated in the Kyrgyz press as *irsay*, "grin stupidly"). "Kyrgyzstan is a poor country, and it is not my job to look after the people," proclaimed Karimov.[9] Karimov's main causa belli was his conviction that the perpetrators of the Tashkent car bombings had taken refuge in Kyrgyz territory. In pursuit of them Uzbek security officials crossed the border into Kyrgyzstan without permission to arrest ethnic Uzbeks in Osh who were Kyrgyzstan citizens.

Uzbekistan has also periodically halted critical gas supplies to Bishkek, laid mines and barbed wire on the Uzbekistan-Kyrgyzstan border, and stopped irrigation flow into the Kyrgyz section of the Fergana Valley. The Kyrgyz press and parliament have repeatedly criticized Karimov and accused President Akayev of surrendering to him, but there is little that Akayev can do. Kyrgyzstan is entirely dependent on outside energy sources, and Uzbekistan exports some 15 percent of its annual production of 1.9 trillion cubic feet of gas to

Kyrgyzstan, Kazakhstan, and Tajikistan.[10] Kyrgyzstan was virtually defenseless against Uzbekistan, and turned to Russia for diplomatic support.

That support was not forthcoming. Russia was already annoyed with Akayev for his dependency on the West, and Moscow was not willing to annoy Uzbekistan for the sake of tiny Kyrgyzstan. As a result of these pressures as well as the IMU incursions, Akayev became increasingly authoritarian, both to satisfy his neighbors and to curb political opposition at home. He now spends his meager foreign-currency reserves building up the Kyrgyz army instead of repaying foreign debts and stepping up economic development programs. Kyrgyzstan continues to face the brunt of the IMU offensives, but there is little recognition of that fact from its neighbors or Russia.

Turkmenistan has refused to fall in line with either Russia or the United States. Declaring a foreign policy of neutrality, Turkmenistan has ended up helping both sides in the Afghan civil war. On the one hand it provides fuel to the Taliban and refuses to become involved in Russia's Central Asian anti-Taliban alliance, which has kept Turkmenistan safe (so far) from the IMU, whom the Taliban restrain. But at the same time Turkmenistan has maintained a relationship with the anti-Taliban alliance, and the government took part in the U.N.-sponsored peace talks on Afghanistan. Turkmenistan had hopes that an Afghan peace would mean the construction of gas pipelines from Turkmenistan to Pakistan. But the continuing civil war in Afghanistan and the failure of the Taliban to take control of the entire country or to gain international recognition because they continue to harbor bin Laden have ended hopes for such a project.[11]

Turkmenistan is the only Central Asian state that maintains excellent relations with Pakistan, which in turn has frequently used Turkmen territory to funnel military supplies to the Taliban. At the same time Turkmenistan has been careful not to annoy Russia, allowing Russian troops to remain on Turkmen soil to guard the border with Iran, transporting gas to Europe through Russian pipelines at low prices dictated by Russia, and preventing the large-scale migration of ethnic Russians from Turkmenistan by offering them dual Russian and Turkmen citizenship. But Turkmenistan remains a deeply isolated country as a result of the myopic and whimsical political decisions of President Saparmurad Niyazov. In a region beset with authoritarianism, Niyazov heads the most dictatorial regime in Central Asia, and his personality cult casts even that of Stalin in the shade. The lack of economic and political reforms during the past decade has reduced foreign investment to a trickle, even in Turkmenistan's lucrative gas fields.

It is difficult to see how long Niyazov can keep his state isolated from the Islamic radicalism around him, or how long the IMU and the HT will keep their distance before they try to mobilize Turkmenistan's crushed and impoverished people into their wider Islamic causes. Already both the Taliban and the IMU have forged routes through Turkmenistan to help smuggle Afghan heroin to the West with the help of corrupt Turkmen officials. Turkmenistan has become one of the most significant transit corridors for the drug trade in Central Asia, and Interpol maintains a long secret list of senior Turkmen officials involved in it. For several years Chechen rebels and Arab militants from the Gulf States have also used Turkmenistan as a corridor to travel to Afghanistan and Pakistan, an accommodation that annoys Russia intensely. Niyazov brooks no opposition to his rule, but the underground Islamic movements in the region are ideally placed to whip up antigovernment sentiment. If the Niyazov regime begins to look shaky, Russia is almost certain to instigate a coup and bring in a new Turkmen leadership that will be more amenable to Russian demands that Turkmenistan join the anti-Islam crusade in Central Asia.

Kazakhstan, with its enormous territory spanning two continents and its oil and gas wealth, has had considerable leverage with both Russia and the United States. It has been able to court both superpowers even as it keeps them at a distance whenever President Nursultan Nazarbayev feels the need. Thus Nazarbayev invites U.S. investment in the oil and gas sectors and has attempted to introduce the economic reforms demanded by foreign investors, but he has also snubbed Washington repeatedly on issues of reducing authoritarianism and corruption or increasing democracy and political reforms. Kazakhstan's heavily rigged presidential elections have become models for the other Central Asian leaders.

Nazarbayev employs similar tactics with Russia. Although he faces constant political challenges from the large ethnic Russian population in northern Kazakhstan, he has managed to keep peace in his country by placating them only to the extent that such actions do not annoy ethnic Kazakhs. Until new pipelines are built by Western oil consortiums, Kazakhstan must rely on Russian-owned pipelines to export its oil and gas to Europe, and it also needs Russian military support as it starts to feel threatened by the IMU. Kazakhstan has joined the Moscow-led attempt to create a rapid-deployment force for Central Asia, but it has also accepted U.S. military aid and training for its officers. Since 2000 Kazakhstan has stepped up its spending on the military to meet the IMU threat. Kazakhstan's problems with Russia will increase, however, when pipelines that are independent of Russia are built and routed either to Turkey or Iran or to the huge, lucrative markets in China.

China: An Old Player Returns to Central Asia

China's role in Central Asia remains the most unpredictable of the three superpowers, but Beijing may be the most important player in the future. Since 1991 China has built close bilateral trade and investment ties with all the Central Asian states, but until recently it avoided becoming involved in military and security pacts and tried to distance itself from the U.S.-Russia rivalry in the region. That is now swiftly coming to an end as the IMU and the Taliban recruit

Uighur Islamic militants and separatists from China's only Muslim majority province, Xinjiang, and create growing political unrest through their guerrilla attacks against Chinese security forces. Throughout the 1990s China's main strategic aim was to ensure that the Central Asian governments kept a tight lid on Uighur political activities on their soil, stopping the Uighur minorities from helping the Uighurs in Xinjiang Province. The Central Asian states obliged China by shutting down Uighur publications and offices, arresting Uighurs who criticized Chinese policies, and keeping their borders with China open for trade whilst guarding against the export of arms, propaganda, or funds for Uighur separatists in Xinjiang.

China's other major strategic interests have been to end the tension on its long borders with Central Asia and Russia, reduce the vast numbers of Chinese troops stationed on these borders, and settle the multiple claims and counterclaims on one another's territories that were inherited from tsarist times and continued to plague relations between China and the Soviet Union. Starting in the mid-1990s China set up joint border commissions with Russia, Kazakhstan, and Kyrgyzstan that over the years have resolved most of the hundreds of border disputes. Territorial disputes with Tajikistan remain unresolved, however. Beijing claims some 30 percent of Tajikistan's territory along their common border in Gorno-Badakhshan, where there are huge gold deposits. It was with the aim of settling these disputes that China took its most significant step in Central Asia, calling a summit meeting in Shanghai in 1996 between the five states that shared common borders: China, Russia, Tajikistan, Kazakhstan, and Kyrgyzstan. The summit resulted in a process of demilitarization and demarcation of the borders. An eighty-mile-wide transparency zone was created, with joint military patrols. The most significant outcome of the summit was the creation of the Shanghai Five, a permanent group pledged to annual summit meetings.

The Shanghai Five has steadily become a wide-ranging military, security, and economic pact. When leaders of the five countries met in August 1999 in Bishkek, the IMU had just launched its first attacks in Kyrgyzstan and taken the four Japanese geologists hostage, creating a huge embarrassment to the summit host, Kyrgyz President Akayev. The summit became a forum to discuss the threat of Islamic fundamentalism, drugs, and weapons spreading from war-torn Afghanistan and destabilizing Central Asia. At the end of the summit the five leaders signed a declaration to enhance cooperation in "fighting international terrorism, the illegal drugs trade, arms trafficking, illegal migration, separatism and religious extremism." They also pledged to create a "multi-polar world"—a Russian-inspired formula that basically meant opposition to U.S. hegemony. Russian President Boris Yeltsin and Chinese President Jiang Zemin held a breakfast meeting in which they discussed ways to broaden "their strategic partnership." The message was clear—Russia, China, and Central Asia now saw radical Islam as a threat to them all, and they were prepared to set aside their differences to combat it more strongly. For the first time the Central Asian states began to look to China for military help.[12]

The following year (2000) in Dushanbe the Shanghai Five became the Shanghai Forum as Uzbekistan was given observer status even though it shared no borders with China. The summit agreed to add a military dimension for the first time—the creation of a joint counter-terrorism center in Bishkek in order to meet the threat from the IMU and the Taliban. By now the Forum had become the most important geo-strategic alliance in the region, developing joint programs for security as well as economic, political, and other agendas. Countries such as India, Pakistan, Mongolia, South Korea, and Iran clamored to join, whilst Uzbekistan insisted on full membership. At the summit in Shanghai in mid-June 2001, Uzbekistan became a full member, although the other countries were kept out. The Forum again changed its name, to the Shanghai Cooperation Organization (SCO). The leaders signed a new security cooperation pact and pledged to increase trade and investment between their countries.

The main concern of the leaders remained the same. "The Shanghai Convention lays a legal foundation for the joint efforts to combat the forces of separatism, terrorism and extremism," said President Jiang after the new pact was signed. Added Kazakh President Nazarbayev, "The cradle of terrorism, separatism and extremism is the instability in Afghanistan."[13] The leaders pledged to speed up development of the still-dormant counterterrorism center in Bishkek. By now China was providing military aid to the Central Asian regimes to counter the IMU. In 2000 and 2001 China gave Uzbekistan and Kyrgyzstan $1.3 million each in technical and military assistance. This included sniper rifles and material aid to their border guards. China later agreed to fund the building of bunkers and housing for Kyrgyz border guards.

For China the threat from the IMU was now palpable as Uighurs from both Central Asia and China were being recruited and trained at IMU camps in northern Afghanistan. "The Uighurs in Xinjiang are waging their own jihad against Beijing and China sees that there is a trans-national threat that cannot be stopped just from Xinjiang. The Chinese understand that if the IMU is successful, more Uighurs will find support and sanctuary with Namangani," explained Moheyuddin Kabir of the Tajikistan IRP. In fact, militant Uighurs had been deeply involved in the Islamic jihads around the region since the 1980s, when they first traveled south to Pakistan to join the Afghan Mujahedeen parties. Hundreds of Uighurs began to study in Pakistani madrassahs and honed their battle skills in Afghanistan, first with the Hizb-i-Islami Party and later with the Taliban. Masood captured several Uighur guerrillas from the Taliban frontlines, whom he proudly displayed to the foreign press.[14] Under pressure from China and its ally Pakistan, the Taliban moved their Uighur fighters in 2000 from the Kabul frontline to northern Afghanistan, where they were encouraged to join up with the IMU to allow the Taliban to deny that they were directly hosting Uighur fighters.

Changing the Game

China, Russia, and the United States are likely to remain rivals in Central Asia, but the Great Game has changed. In the nineteenth century, Russia and Great Britain used the Central Asian states as pawns; today the superpowers are finding themselves at the mercy of forces they helped unleash but that are now beyond their control. The threats from Afghanistan—the Taliban, Osama bin Laden, and the IMU—have highlighted the weakness of the three great powers and forced them together in bilateral agreements. The big powers now share a common interest in undermining the Taliban and the IMU and bolstering the military capacities of the Central Asian states, even as they remain rivals over pipeline routes and the best way to exploit Central Asia's energy resources.

The events of September 11 underscored dramatically how the game has changed. As Russia and China pledged to cooperate with the United States in its bid to eliminate the Taliban and Al Qaeda, the three big powers suddenly found themselves united in the fight against terrorism and Islamic extremism in Afghanistan and Central Asia. The three could now hope not only that the Taliban would be defeated and a new broad-based, multiethnic government established in Kabul but that the IMU would be neutralized as a threat to both Central Asia and Xinjiang Province. In addition, China believed that the U.S.-led attacks would weaken the links between the Uighur separatists and Islamic radical movements in Pakistan and Afghanistan. As U.S. forces arrived in the region, China carried out a massive military exercise in Xinjiang Province to display its military might, moved in extra troops to patrol China's borders with Afghanistan and Pakistan, and banned the entry of visitors from Afghanistan and Pakistan. As long as the alliance continued to battle the Taliban and Al Qaeda, there was no doubt that the three big powers would find themselves united—but what was not so certain was how the relationship would evolve once the shooting was over.

If, as Russia fears, the United States is seeking a permanent military presence in Central Asia, there will almost certainly be a new round in the Great Game rivalry.

Russia and China have forged a close relationship on a wide range of issues, particularly the desirability of keeping the United States from emerging as a unilateral global power. But although Russia and China share a common concern over security issues in Central Asia, Russia will always be leery of encouraging a Chinese military role in its own backyard, just as most of the Central Asian states are wary of an overt Chinese military presence. For their part the Central Asian states have their own Uighur minorities to worry about; if they cozy up to Beijing, they will annoy those Uighurs. Thus the Central Asian states maintain a difficult balancing act, encouraging Chinese support for their armies but discouraging an overt Chinese military presence or influence in Central Asia.

China and the United States still have to find common ground in Central Asia. In addition to enlisting China's support of the U.S.-led alliance, Washington is now believed to be sharing intelligence with Beijing about the involvement of Uighur militants with the Taliban and the IMU. The United States and China remain rivals in most other areas, however. Once the military threat declines, if the Central Asian states prove able to improve upon their economic and political performance, the three-way rivalry will increase. Central Asia's own interests lie in bringing the three big powers onto a common platform that will not just deal with threats to their own security but involve them in an equitable exploitation of Central Asia's energy resources. This in turn could speed up economic development and political liberalization in Central Asia.

Yet there is still hope. For the first time the three big powers have joined in Central Asia in defense of the territorial integrity of the region and in a common bid to eliminate terrorism there. Perhaps in the future they will be willing to cooperate on oil and gas pipelines from Central Asia to the outside world, help to develop the economies of the deprived Central Asian states, and stabilize the political and economic situation in Afghanistan sufficiently so it once again can become part of the international community. The terrible war that began on October 7, 2001, with the U.S. bombing of Afghanistan could result in cooperation rather than competition between the big powers for the first time in the history of the region.

10 Central Asia and Its Neighbors

CENTRAL ASIA'S MUSLIM NEIGHBORS to the south represent a plethora of competing interests and rivalries, which the Central Asian leaders have been trying to juggle for a decade. Even as these neighbors—Pakistan, Iran, and Turkey—rhetorically pledge cooperation with Central Asia in such multilateral organizations as the Economic Cooperation Organization, the Organization of the Islamic Conference, and the United Nations, their inherent rivalries and individual agendas have proved to be destabilizing factors. Farther afield, parties and individuals in the Arab Gulf states have provided funds and backing to the IMU, whilst the wider Muslim world has made only marginal efforts to bring Central Asia into the world community.

The most pressing issues for Central Asia are the continuing civil war in Afghanistan and the Taliban's role in giving sanctuary to the IMU and other militant Islamic groups. The tragedy is that like Russia and the United States, Central Asia's Muslim neighbors have fed this civil war, arming and funding one side or the other and drawing in the republics regardless of their own desires.

The Threat from Afghanistan

The crisis in Afghanistan is the single most important external factor in the growing instability in Central Asia. Afghanistan has long been linked to Central Asia, historically and culturally. Over the centuries the two regions have been joined in various empires, and ethnic groups in northern Afghanistan come from the same stock as Central Asian Uzbeks, Tajiks, and Turkmen. The ethnic, social, cultural, and political ties between Afghanistan and Central Asia are thus deeply rooted, and the give and take between the two regions today cannot be seen as an aberration of history but rather as a continuation of the historical process that was briefly interrupted by the seventy-four years of the Soviet Union.

In a historical sense, when the IMU retreats to Taliban-controlled Afghanistan, it is only continuing an ancient tradition of demanding and receiving hospitality and sanctuary. In the twentieth century, guests in Afghanistan have included the rulers of Bukhara, Khiva, and Kokand after the Russian Revolution; Basmachis who were escaping the Bolsheviks; and members of the Tajikistan IRP who took refuge during Tajikistan's civil war. And like the IMU, both the Basmachis and the IRP continued fighting their Central Asian wars from bases in Afghanistan. For their part Afghans have also taken refuge in Central Asia, particularly since the fighting began in 1979.

But neither tradition nor the proverbial Muslim hospitality can account completely for the Taliban's willingness to give sanctuary to the IMU. Before the events of September 11, the Taliban played host to most of the extremist Islamic groups in the Muslim world, and their motives have clearly been militant. In Afghanistan these groups fight for the Taliban, and in return they receive military training, battle experience, weapons, funding, access to the drug trade, and contacts with the whole world of Islamic radicalism.

Centuries of history also do not explain why Afghanistan should become the host for the world's Islamic extremists. That answer lies in more current events; in the efforts during the 1980s by the United States to foment rebellion against the Soviet Union. When the CIA funneled arms to the Afghan Mujahedeen via Pakistan's Interservices Intelligence (ISI), the ISI gave preference to the radical Afghan Islamic parties—which could more easily be turned into an engine of anti-Soviet jihad—and pushed aside moderate Afghan nationalist and Islamic parties. At that time the CIA made no objections to this policy. The Taliban are the heirs of that war and that favoritism, although their harsh interpretation of Deobandi Islam and their desire to transform Afghanistan to fit their interpretation of sharia are foreign to Afghan's Islamic traditions.

The Taliban reflect none of the major Islamicist trends that were earlier prevalent in Afghanistan or that emerged during the jihad of the 1980s. They are not inspired by the Ikhwan-ul-Muslimeen (Muslim Brotherhood)—the earliest Islamic radicals in the twentieth century—they do not follow the path of the mystical Sufis. They do not base their Islam on the ulema. All these strands of Islam either have historical roots in Afghanistan or arose during the jihad. Nor do the Taliban have a secure tribal base or tribal legitimacy amongst their own majority ethnic group, the Pashtuns, the largest ethnic group in Afghanistan. Many of the Pashtun tribal elite refuse to recognize the Taliban and have fled to Pakistan. In fact, they fit nowhere in the Islamic or nationalist spectrum of ideas and movements that emerged in Afghanistan between 1979 and 1994. Instead, their ideology of Deobandi Islam is largely imported from Pakistan. Their initial popularity in 1994–96 was due not merely to their Islamic zeal but to other factors operating in Afghanistan—the revival of Pashtun nationalism in the face of Tajik control of Kabul and the need to restore law and order, reopen the roads, and end rapacious warlordism—that the Taliban made part of their early agenda, before they began to host foreign militant groups in 1996.

But the Taliban had no international Islamic agenda until they met up with Osama bin Laden and other non-Afghan Islamic groups after they captured Kabul in 1996. A few Taliban leaders had earlier dreamed of "liberating" the holy Muslim cities of Bukhara and Samarkand, but most had no idea where Bukhara and Samarkand even were. The tens of thousands of Pakistani militants, and the thousands of Central Asians, Arabs, Africans, and East Asians who have fought for the Taliban since that time, have bought with them a global perspective of Islamic radicalism that the Taliban have adopted as their own. Most recently, bin Laden and his Arab followers have become part of the decision-making process within the Taliban leadership, pushing the Taliban to expand their goals beyond Afghanistan into Central Asia.[1] I have explored this issue more fully in my recent book on the Taliban; here suffice it to say that the Taliban now depend on these foreign fighters to expand their ideology as much as the foreign groups depend on the Taliban for sanctuary.[2]

Until Afghanistan is at peace—or at least until the present Taliban leaders are removed from power, most likely as a result of the U.S.-led military campaign aimed at Osama bin Laden—it is highly unlikely that the Taliban will change their policies. Lacking any desire to build a modern political state, the Taliban see the continuation of the present war against the anti-Taliban United Front as the only means of securing the loyalty of their fighters. Thus even if the United Front were defeated and forced to retreat into Tajikistan, the present Taliban leaders would probably become even more aggressive against the Central Asian regimes. Conjuring up new enemies is the best way to fuel the permanent state of jihad, the only thing that keeps the army united and motivated. The first enemy to be singled out would probably be Tajikistan because of the Russian forces based there; later would come Uzbekistan. The Taliban's tragedy is that their leaders fear that peace will destroy the movement because they have no agenda for the reconstruction of the country. Thus they are unwilling to change their policies.

Although the start of the U.S. bombing campaign against the Taliban on October 7 has now made it virtually certain that the Taliban leadership will be eliminated from Afghanistan, once the war is over there will be an intense tussle between the ethnic groups, warlords, and remaining Taliban defectors as to who will form the new government. Afghanistan's best bet is for Afghans to rally around the former king Zahir Shah, who has set out to build a broad-based, multiethnic coalition to oppose the Taliban. This coalition could be the basis of a new, internationally accepted government in Kabul. However, such efforts will be successful only if the West remains in Afghanistan after the shooting stops. Not only will U.N. peace-keeping forces need to stay for a while to stabilize the region, but massive funds must be available for the reconstruction of the country. The reconstruction of the region will require a determined and prolonged international effort to help Afghanistan back into the global community.

Pakistan: Educating Islam's Militants

Pakistan did not create the Taliban, but the Taliban could not have survived amongst Afghanistan's warring factions without the support of Islamabad. Indeed, fear of Pakistan's influence in the region has been a critical factor in the mobilization of the Central Asian states (with the exception of Turkmenistan) against the Taliban. Central Asian leaders also believe (correctly) that the ISI has until recently been supporting the IMU and other radical Islamic groups in their countries. These men do not forget that in the 1980s, when they held power under the Soviet Union, the military regime of Pakistan's President Muhammad Zia ul Haq encouraged the Afghan Mujahedeen to attack Central Asia and that the CIA supplied arms to the Mujahedeen for this purpose through the ISI. In fact, the aversion of these leaders to even the most peaceful Islamic practice or piety arose in part as a result of the Afghan war, when Pakistan was on the other side. Pakistan's subsequent support for the Taliban and the Pashtuns, and President Pervez Musharraf's rejection in the summer of 2001 of non-Pashtun ethnic groups in Afghanistan as irrelevant to Pakistan's interests, has further antagonized the leaders of Central Asia.[3] Musharraf's myopic foreign policy since he seized power in a military coup in 1999 did much to further alienate Pakistan's northern neighbors.

Although successive Pakistani governments have repeatedly promised the Central Asian leaders that they would curb the support given by the ISI to Pakistan's Islamic parties, the Taliban, and other militant groups in Central Asia, and forbid Central Asian militants to study in Pakistani madrassahs, Islamabad has failed to implement these measures out of self-interest and the fear of an Islamic backlash within Pakistan. In fact, in recent years Central Asian and Uighur militants have been pouring into the country to study in the huge network of Deobandi madrassahs. The IMU, the HT, and the Chechen rebels have sent many of their young men to study in Pakistan, whilst Pakistani Islamic parties continue to show off their Central Asian students as proof of their influence in the region. Even more than the battlefields of Afghanistan, this madrassah education and the culture of jihad it inspires is turning out ideologically committed Islamic radicals for future fighting in Central Asia.

Pakistan's policies have been driven in part by the mutual animosity between India and Pakistan and Islamabad's fears of Indian hegemony in South Asia. India's earlier influence in Kabul has significantly affected Pakistan's relationship with Afghanistan, which is why Pakistan has wanted to see a friendly Pashtun government there since the 1950s. And since the 1980s Pakistan has seen Afghanistan as a source of what President Zia ul Haq called "strategic depth" in the event of war with India. Determined to deny India any influence in Afghanistan, Pakistan in 1989 helped fuel what was originally an indigenous popular uprising in Indian Kashmir. When India and the United States accused Pakistan of training and arming Kashmiri and Pakistani militants on its soil to fight in Kashmir—thereby sponsoring terrorism—the Taliban provided a convenient deniability factor. Just as when the Taliban send Pakistani or Chinese militants to join the IMU so they can deny that they support them, so Pakistan has sent many of its Kashmiri fighters to train in Afghanistan with the Taliban. Several Pakistani groups now make it a matter of policy to let their young guerrillas fight first for the Taliban before they are moved to the more arduous guerrilla fronts in Kashmir.

After the 1991 collapse of the Soviet Union, Zia ul Haq's references to the need for strategic depth in Central Asia as well as Afghanistan took on a greater significance. For a time it appeared to some Pakistanis that the Islamic revival in Central Asia and the civil war in Tajikistan would blow away the present generation of Soviet-trained Central Asian leaders. Thus Pakistan's military stepped up its efforts to create a client Pashtun government in Kabul, in the hope that such a government would give Pakistan easy, exclusive access to Central Asia. Moderates who argued in 1991 that Islamabad should instead support a quick end to the Afghan civil war in the hope that whichever government came to power in Kabul would provide trade routes to Pakistan were quickly silenced. The military extended the idea of strategic depth to Central Asia as a natural corollary to their policies in Afghanistan, even as Pakistan's civilian governments tried to follow more positive policies and build economic ties with Central Asia.

In 1991 the elected government of Prime Minister Nawaz Sharif sought a new relationship with Central Asia built on trade, pipeline routes, investment, and joint economic development. This made eminent good sense. Karachi is the nearest port city for the Central Asian states, and Islamabad is closer to Tashkent than it is to Karachi. The distance from Dushanbe to Karachi by road is only 1,700 miles compared to 2,125 miles to the Iranian port of Bandar Abbas, 2,625 miles to Rostov-on-Don in western Russia, and 5,940 miles to Vladivostok in eastern Russia. All that was needed to realize these opportunities was peace in Afghanistan. But the ISI consistently blocked this outcome. The attempts by Sharif and his minister for economic affairs Sardar Asif Ali were also undercut by the arrival in Central Asia of Pakistani Islamic parties, who viewed the region as virgin territory, ripe for recruitment to their particular brand of Islam. Qazi Hussein Ahmad, the chief of the powerful Jamiat-i-Islami party, urged Sharif "to provide Central Asia with Islamic guidance rather than economic aid."[4] At the same time several Pakistani and Arab groups sympathetic to Wahhabism were being funded by Saudi Arabia to make inroads into Central Asia. The Pakistani extremist groups Lashkar-i-Jhangvi and Sipah-i-Sahaba, initially funded by Saudi Arabia, have militants fighting with the IMU.

By 1994, when the Taliban emerged, Pakistan's hopes of forging new productive links with Central Asia had virtually collapsed, apart from a blossoming relationship with neutral Turkmenistan. Ironically, it was not the ISI but Prime Minister Benazir Bhutto, the most liberal, secular leader in Pakistan's recent history, who delivered the coup de grâce to a new relationship with Central Asia. Rather than support a wider peace process in Afghanistan that would have opened up the natural north-south trade routes between Central Asia and Pakistan through Afghanistan, Bhutto backed the Taliban, in a rash and presumptuous policy to create a new western-orientated trade and pipeline route from Turkmenistan through southern Afghanistan to Pakistan, for which the Taliban would provide security. The ISI soon supported this policy because its Afghan protégé Gulbuddin Hekmatyar had made no headway in capturing Kabul, and the Taliban appeared to be strong enough to do so. The idea that Pakistan would ignore the rest of Central Asia in favor of Turkmenistan whilst backing the Taliban in Afghanistan created even greater suspicion amongst Central Asia's leaders about Pakistan's intentions.

In turn Pakistan became more anxious as the Central Asian leaders gravitated back towards Islamabad's two long-standing enemies, Russia and India, whilst rivals Iran and Turkey began to make inroads into the region. The military, which has always been the key formulator of Pakistan's foreign policy, saw little hope of persuading the Central Asian leaders to change their strategic intentions and befriend Islamabad. As Pakistan became more wedded to the Taliban, more hostile to the anti-Taliban alliance, and more embroiled in the conflict in Kashmir—which escalated dramatically in 1999 because of Pakistan's military incursion in Kargil—Islamabad's antagonism to the Central Asian leaders increased. These feelings were reciprocated by the Central Asian leaders, who blamed every significant northward advance of the Taliban on Pakistani military support or collusion.

It is widely believed that the ISI's discreet support of the IMU, which included giving refuge to Yuldeshev in the 1990s and allowing Namangani's frequent clandestine visits to Pakistan, has remained fairly consistent. The ISI sees the IMU as a force that may not be strong enough to seize power in Uzbekistan but that can nonetheless be a catalyst in the shake-up of Central Asia's leadership. Yet Pakistan's military regime is hedging its bets; it also predicts that it can win back the friendship of Central Asia by acting as a mediator between the regimes and the IMU. Thus Pakistan does not necessarily intend to support the ideological Islamic views of the IMU or help bring it to power but rather intends to use the IMU as leverage within Central Asia. At the same time senior ISI officers are convinced that the IMU has close intelligence links to Russia that would explain the group's freedom of action on the Afghanistan-Tajikistan border. These ties make the IMU an unreliable long-term partner, compared to, say, the anti-Russian Taliban. The ISI does not trust the IMU, believing that Pakistan is locked in a covert power struggle with Russia for influence over it but at the same time it wishes to keep the IMU on its payroll for tactical reasons.

Despite Pakistan's persistent denials that it supports the IMU, until September 11 the military regime appeared set on a course where it followed a state policy of friendly relations with the Central

Asian governments but at the same time backed dissident groups such as the IMU in order to win more leverage over these regimes. Islamabad believes that the present generation of Central Asian leaders must be replaced by more Islamic-orientated leaders who would look to Pakistan, rather than India and Russia, for support. Thus a vicious cycle of suspicion, accusation, and counteraccusation now mars Pakistan's relationship with the Central Asian regimes.

At the same time Pakistan's frequent internal crises have weakened state power, increasing the influence of nonstate actors. These include extremist Islamic parties, with their madrassah culture and jihadi strategy; Arab terrorist groups such as Al Qaeda; the truck and transport smuggling mafias; and drug traffickers—all of whom have close links to the Taliban and the IMU quite independent of the ISI and its policies. The result has been an explosion of self-interest groups in Pakistan, both Islamic and non-Islamic, who have benefited from the Afghan civil war and Islamic insurgency in Central Asia. These groups see no need for peace. The weakening of state authority, not just in Pakistan but across the entire region, would enable their business interests and Islamic agendas to flourish.

But the events of September 11 have forced the military regime of President Musharraf to make a dramatic U turn. U.S. president George W. Bush's ultimatum—that states must be either with the United States or against it—left Pakistan with little choice but to cease its support for the Taliban and help the U.S. effort to defeat both it and Al Qaeda. Musharraf's move has proved deeply controversial inside Pakistan as the militant Islamic parties oppose his decision to side with the Western alliance and have staged protests in the streets of Pakistan. The majority of Pakistan's population, however, has supported the decision. Pakistan now has a chance to change its policies towards the entire region and set its own house in order.

If Pakistan goes along with the elimination of the Taliban and the IMU, and supports a new, internationally accepted government in

Kabul, it can win back the trust of the Central Asian states. The move would give Pakistan renewed opportunities to be involved in new oil and gas pipelines from Central Asia that would cross Afghanistan and Pakistan to the Gulf. Eventually, the military regime's policy reversal on Afghanistan will also necessitate a reconsideration of Pakistan's support for the Kashmiri separatists, forcing the country to build better relations with India. Lastly, the regime will need to clamp down on the madrassah culture that has spawned so much unrest in the region. This moment of opportunity for Pakistan—a chance to reestablish its international credibility, end its diplomatic isolation in the region, and become a partner rather than a rival of Central Asia—will require that the military and the ISI relinquish their strategic vision of the past fifty years and adopt a strategy which makes friends rather than enemies in Central Asia.

Iran: Shias Amongst the Sunnis

Iran, despite its Islamic rhetoric, has played the most cautious and prudent role in Central Asia. Iran moved swiftly into the region as the Soviet Union hovered on the verge of breakup. In November 1991 Foreign Minister Ali Akbar Velayati traveled to all five republics, reaping the most benefits in Persian-speaking Tajikistan, which was trying to counter Uzbek-Turkish influence, and Turkmenistan, which borders Iran and needed to find a sea outlet for its gas exports. Iran intervened briefly in the Tajik civil war, siding with the IRP, but quickly realized that it had to stay out of the conflict if it wanted to keep Russia as an ally. Subsequently, Iran played a major role in helping to end the war, even though many of the IRP leaders were based in Teheran. Iran also funded the construction of a railway and a gas pipeline from Turkmenistan to Meshad, in eastern Iran, that allowed Turkmenistan to export goods and gas to Iran and abroad from Iranian ports.

Iran's major asset in Central Asia in the early 1990s was its close friendship with Russia. Between 1989 and 1993 Iran purchased $10 billion in Russian weapons to reequip its armed forces after the devastating war with Iraq. Iran also began to buy Russian nuclear and missile technology—over U.S. objections—and to institute extensive trade and energy relations with Moscow. Central Asian leaders felt comfortable dealing with Iran because of these ties and because Iran was clearly not involved in exporting Islamic radicalism. In fact, Iran and Russia were joined in considering the Taliban and U.S. influence the two greatest dangers to regional stability. Russia and Iran were also united in their determination not to allow the United States to dominate energy exploration in Central Asia. For its part the United States vowed to undercut any attempt by Iran to present itself as the natural export route for Central Asia's oil and gas—even though Iran's large ports on the Caspian and Arabian seas and its enormous infrastructure of pipelines and engineering facilities for its own oil industry do, in fact, make it the natural exit point for those oil and gas pipelines.

Although U.S. energy companies are barred by U.S. sanctions from doing business in Iran, European and Asian oil companies are setting up offices in Tehran seeking not only to invest in Iran's oil and gas fields but also to consider options for export routes from Central Asia. Washington, meanwhile, has been putting pressure on both Western companies and the Central Asian leaders to keep Iran from setting up a major pipeline route that would run south through Kazakhstan and Turkmenistan to Iranian ports on the Gulf. But the pipeline could be just a matter of time; the costs involved in building longer pipelines to Turkey or China make the Iranian option ever more desirable. In the meantime Iran has managed to arrange for oil swaps: Central Asian oil comes to Iranian ports on the Caspian Sea to be used in the Iranian industry, and in return Iran gives the Central Asian states Iranian oil located near ports on the Gulf to sell on the international market. Just as the United States has blocked Iran's attempts to build pipelines in Central Asia, so Iran has kept U.S. companies out of the region, as when it blocked the projected gas pipeline from Turkmenistan to Pakistan of the U.S. company Unocal.

Iran's caution in Central Asia is not only due to economics. The pragmatic Iranian mullahs realized early on that their Shia ideology would be unwelcome in Sunni Central Asia. Teheran has perforce limited its ideological agenda in the region, preferring to build state-to-state relations and trade ties rather than send Iran's Revolutionary Guards to promote Islamic revolution. Nowhere in Central Asia does Iran emphasize the particularities or the benefits of the Shia faith or Islamic revolution, the way it does in the Middle East. In fact, Iran's other major strategic aim, which also matches Russia's, has been to curb the growth of Sunni Islamic radicalism, whether manifested in the Taliban in Afghanistan, the IMU in Uzbekistan, or Sunni extremists in Pakistan.

Modern Sunni radicals refuse even to acknowledge Shiaism as a legitimate branch of Islam; they denounce Shias as *kafirs*, nonbelievers. In the new Sunni jihadi worldview fostered by Wahhabism and Deobandism, Iran is only slightly less evil than the United States or Russia. Whilst refraining from proselytizing, Iran nonetheless feels obliged to respond to such attacks, for it sees itself as the protector of Shias worldwide. Thus Iran has responded strongly to the frequent massacres of Shias in Pakistan by Sunni extremist groups and in Afghanistan by the Taliban, condemning Pakistan and at times closing its border with Taliban-ruled Afghanistan. And Russia has benefited enormously from having a staunch, unthreatening ally within the fold of radical Islam, even if it belongs to the minority, Shia faction.

Iran's relations with Uzbekistan are central to its overall position in Central Asia and have undergone massive fluctuations. President Karimov will cut off ties with Teheran one day and reestablish them the next. Karimov mistrusts Iran, but he doesn't like Turkey and Pakistan any better, and he can't afford to have so many potential enemies along Uzbekistan's southern rim at one time. Iran, on its side, is constantly baiting Uzbekistan, broadcasting interviews with IMU leaders on its Persian and Uzbek radio services. In the mid-1990s Iranian intelligence agents met with Yuldeshev in the hope that they could play on the IMU's Uzbek ethnic origins to enlist it in Iran's anti-Taliban and anti-Pakistan agenda—perhaps even make the IMU a future surrogate for Iran in Central Asia. Although some Uzbekistan officials believe that the IMU accepted financial aid from the Iranian intelligence service, the organization subsequently linked itself with the Taliban, Sunni extremism, and anti-Shiaism. Iran is presently the major supplier of arms and ammunition to the anti-Taliban alliance, and Teheran's willingness to stand up to the Taliban has won it greater appreciation in Central Asian capitals.

Turkey: Forging Pan-Turkic Alliances

Turkey has had an equally complicated relationship with Central Asia. In 1991 Turkey had high hopes of becoming the most influential player in the region because the Turks were linked both ethnically and linguistically to the people of Central Asia. Turkish internationalists dreamed of a contiguous Turkic-speaking bloc stretching from the Mediterranean to China. The old dream of pan-Turkism was resurrected for the first time since Kemal Ataturk abolished the Ottoman Empire in 1924 and made Turkey a secular state that looked towards Europe rather than the East. Turkey was also encouraged by the United States and NATO, who wished to see Central Asia follow the Turkish model of pro-Westernism, capitalism, and secularism. U.S. diplomats urged the Central Asian leaders to emulate Turkey, suggesting that they travel to Turkey to see how a modern secular Muslim nation flourished. Meanwhile they urged American companies to find Turkish business partners to help them enter the Central Asian markets.

And for a time Central Asia's leaders seemed to accept Turkey as a model. Turkey managed to be rich, Westernized, and secular without losing its Islamic and Turkic identity. Improving relations with Turkey seemed like a natural way to keep peace at home, where there was a growing public fascination with Turkey, and Turkish television channels were broadcast by satellite. Thousands of Central Asians arrived in Turkey on Turkish scholarships and training programs. By December 1992—just one year after independence—Central Asia had been the recipient of $1.2 billion in Turkish loans, trade credits, and joint ventures with Turkey's private sector. Turkish Muslim leaders began building state-supported madrassahs and schools in Central Asia that taught Turkish Islam and rejected Islamic radicalism. But soon Turkey became convulsed by a series of political and economic crises, and radical political Islam began to grow even within Turkish society. Notions of pan-Turkism now took on radical Islamic overtones, which frightened Central Asia's leaders.

However, Turkey has always played both sides in Central Asia. Turkish intelligence has kept in close touch with the Central Asian opposition movements, giving refuge to leaders who have been driven out of Turkmenistan or Uzbekistan. In 1999 the Uzbek government shut down a chain of Turkish schools run by the Sufi cleric Fetullah Gulen, accusing him of supporting radical Islamic groups and the banned opposition party Erk. IMU leaders had in fact traveled to Turkey in the mid-1990s in search of funding, and they had received some. As Turkey was also funding the Afghan Uzbek leader Rashid Dostum in his fight against the Taliban, the IMU appealed in a spirit of pan-Turkism rather than Islamic fundamentalism. Turkey initially supported the IMU both to cover its options and to keep tabs on the IMU's activities, but Turkish support stopped after the IMU linked itself to the Taliban and bin Laden. There have been reports that Turkish Islamicists have recently appeared in Afghanistan.

Turkey now sees the IMU as a threat to Central Asia and seeks to rebuild relations with Uzbekistan, providing military aid and offering training to Uzbek and Kyrgyz officers in Turkish military schools. However, Turkey has also been hurt by the lack of political and economic reforms in the Central Asian republics and the repressiveness of their leaders. The Turkish private sector has cut back its investments in Central Asia not simply because of the economic crisis in Turkey but also because the lack of reforms and transparency in business dealings and allocation of contracts makes investment unsafe.

Turkey's role in Central Asia has diminished in recent years because of the economic and political crisis in Turkey itself, the unwillingness of Central Asian leaders to adopt reforms, and the mutual rivalries amongst the six countries. Turkey was keen to establish a common economic market and joint security treaties amongst the Central Asian states but the competition and rivalry between the leaders have made this impossible. Nevertheless Turkey remains an important player in Central Asia because of the close affinity between its people and those of Central Asia and because it offers a political example for secular and democratic groups in Central Asia. It also enjoys the support of the United States, NATO, and Israel, which encourage Turkey to have a greater role in the region. But until a new generation of leaders arises in Central Asia who see the Turkish model more positively—perhaps even try to emulate it— Turkey will not be able to help bring stability to the region.

Saudi Arabia: Spreading Wahhabism

Saudi Arabia has neglected state-to-state relations with Central Asia, instead allowing Saudi Islamic charities and groups that promote Wahhabism to pursue a policy of funding Islamic groups, mosques, and madrassahs, and sponsoring people coming to Mecca for the annual hajj (pilgrimage). Saudi Islamic charities have provided Central Asia with missionaries, scholarships, and Islamic literature, including millions of copies of the Koran translated into native languages. But Saudi generosity has come at a price, as the Saudis seek to turn Central Asians towards their own radical Wahhabism. Moreover, Saudi Arabia has provided little real investment in the region despite its considerable oil wealth, although some minor Saudi-owned oil companies were involved in the proposed pipeline project across Afghanistan. Initially the Saudis saw their mission in Central Asia as winning back the people to Islam (preferably Wahhabism), rather than cultivating trade, economic, or political ties. Such policies have proven shortsighted, even dangerous for Saudi Arabia: the groups the Saudis have been funding have now linked themselves to bin Laden, the enemy of the Saudi royal family, whilst the Central Asian governments have become deeply critical of Saudi Arabia, regarding the Saudis as a threat to future stability rather than an ally.

Saudi Arabia has consistently backed the most extremist Islamic groups in the region, beginning in the 1980s with the funding of Hekmatyar's Hizb-i-Islami party in Afghanistan. They also backed the Taliban until 1996, when they fell out over the issue of bin Laden. The Saudis provided funds to the IRP during the civil war in Tajikistan to keep them from joining with Iran, and the Saudi regime has made no attempt to stop the lavish funding of the IMU from the Saudi-Uzbek diaspora in Mecca and Medina (outlined in Chapters 7 and 8). Many of the large, wealthy Islamic charities in the forefront of the funds transfers are controlled by the Wahhabi ulema, and the royal family is reluctant to interfere because of its sensitivity to criticism from that ulema.

Saudi Arabia's diplomacy has traditionally depended on the country being able simply to buy out potential opponents, as it did with the more extreme Palestinian groups in the Middle East and other Islamic groups in Sudan and the Gulf. In the 1980s the government encouraged Saudi dissidents to go fight in far distant places like Afghanistan, thus keeping them from stirring up trouble at home. But today the several thousand Saudis fighting for the Taliban, the IMU, and the Chechen rebels pose a grave threat to Saudi national security. These radicalized Saudis are now determined to overthrow the royal family and have gravitated to bin Laden. Saudi Arabia is in danger of becoming another Algeria, where hundreds of militants who fought in Afghanistan in the 1980s returned to fight the civil war in the 1990s.

Saudi foreign policy tends to be run on the basis of personal relationships and the patronage of domestic groups like the ulema, making it almost impossible to frame a coherent national-security policy. The Saudis have never developed a clear foreign policy towards Afghanistan and Central Asia, an omission the United States and other Western nations find deeply frustrating. But because they depend on Saudi oil, arms contracts, and goodwill, the Western nations, and in particular the United States, have refused to exert real pressure on Saudi Arabia to change its policies. Thus even as the United States shores up Central Asia's armies, its most important ally in the Muslim world, Saudi Arabia, continues to allow funds from Saudi citizens to reach the IMU.

All this dramatically changed after September 11. Fifteen of the nineteen suicide bombers who flew planes into the World Trade Center and the Pentagon, and highjacked the plane that crashed in Pennsylvania, were Saudi citizens. Although Saudi Arabia immediately announced its support to the U.S.-led alliance against terrorism, the Saudis were reluctant to provide bases for U.S. forces or cooperate with the FBI to discover the source of the Saudi terrorists. U.S. politicians and media became increasingly hostile to Saudi Arabia, with officials denouncing the Saudi government's refusal to control the funding of the Taliban and even Al Qaeda by Saudi Islamic charities. Since the United States began releasing lists of terrorist organizations and charities which had funded bin Laden—some of Saudi origin— the Saudi regime has been forced to scrutinize the actions of these charities and other businessmen funding the IMU. This may yet lead to government crackdowns on these sources of supply.

A New Muslim Partnership?

The Gulf Arab states have also tried to buy off radical Islamic groups, allowing private funding to reach them or giving them facilities in their ports and cities. The Taliban, bin Laden, and the IMU have used these cities as hubs for drug trafficking, smuggling of consumer goods, arms trading, money laundering, and other criminal activities. The free port of Dubai, in the United Arab Emirates, has become the center for all these activities; Western intelligence agencies identify Dubai as the main banking and money-laundering center for Islamic extremist groups around the world.[5] But neither the United Nations nor the Western countries have tried to monitor the situation in Dubai, even though the U.N. Security Council imposed sanctions and an arms embargo on the Taliban in January 2001 and the United States has a strong troop presence there. Dubai, rather than Peshawar or Karachi, has now become the center for fund-raising and arms purchase by the Taliban and the IMU.

Multilateral Islamic organizations have also failed to play a more positive role in Central Asia. The most important Islamic multilateral organization, the Organization of the Islamic Conference, which has the support of fifty-three Muslim countries, has done little to try to ease tensions in Central Asia or mediate between the Uzbek government and the IMU, just as it has failed to mediate between the warring parties in Afghanistan. Heavily dominated by the Gulf Arab states and divided by rivalries within the Muslim world, the OIC has proved useless in the areas where it is most badly needed.

In fact, Central Asia's Muslim neighbors have always had competing foreign policy aims or aims set by Islamic radicals at home that have kept them from taking constructive action in the region. Unless the Islamic world becomes actively involved in trying to help Central Asia end its conflicts and begins increasing investment in and economic development of the region, Central Asia and Afghanistan will continue to nurture radical Islamicists who will in time turn their attention to the Muslim regimes at home. If the Central

Asian regimes have failed to understand the need to incorporate their own Islamic organizations into their states, the wider Muslim world has failed to understand the needs of Central Asia and the vital necessity of helping stabilize the region. In the new era that has been promised after the war in Afghanistan is over and the Taliban is eliminated, those who hope for peace in the region can only hope that the Muslim world and Central Asia will address these shortcomings.

11 An Uncertain Future

THE GROWING POPULARITY of militant Islam in Central Asia is primarily due to the repressiveness of the Central Asian regimes. These governments refuse to broaden their political base, institute even the mildest of democratic reforms, or allow any kind of political opposition. Whilst poverty and unemployment increase—and economic opportunities decrease—Central Asia's debt-ridden societies are ripe for any organization or party that offers hope for a better life. The regimes respond with increased repression, viewing not just Islamic militancy but all Islamic practice as a threat to their grip on power. Such shortsightedness has only fueled the support for the more radical Islamic groups.

If the biggest threat to Central Asian stability comes from the ongoing civil war in Afghanistan, the problems in the region have also been exacerbated by the growth of Islamic extremism and terrorism associated with Osama bin Laden and his Arab-Afghans, who have considerable influence with the Taliban, the IMU, and Islamic jihadi groups in Pakistan. Bin Laden has encouraged the Taliban leaders to embrace a pan-Islamic ideology; for example, he played a key role in persuading the Taliban to give sanctuary to the IMU in 1999. In addition to funding IMU operations, he has enlisted other Central Asian militants into his own group, Al Qaeda. Al Qaeda's global network—which, according to U.S. intelligence has operatives and cells in thirty-four countries—links the Central Asian radicals to the politics of global radical Islam, providing financial and military support for the groups and helping them to travel in and out of their respective states clandestinely.

All these groups have profited from the drug trade from Afghanistan, in which bin Laden is heavily involved. In the 1980s the drug export routes ran solely through Pakistan; now they extend through Iran, China, the Central Asian states, and the Arabian Gulf and are controlled by Pakistani, Afghan, Arab, Chechen, and Central Asian crime organizations. Drugs fund political activism, and drugs pay for weapons. They are now the financial mainstay of the IMU and other radical Islamic movements.

Meanwhile, the regional conflicts have created economic havoc in Central Asia as extremist groups and organized crime feed off war itself. Their armies depend on military bases, sanctuaries, and criminal economic activities that may be far from their own countries but that undermine those countries nevertheless. "The weakening of borders and administrative capacity combined with the mobilization of transnational networks and the organization of transnational armed groups creates ideal conditions for the growth of a contraband war economy based on looting, smuggling, or trafficking in drugs, arms, or even human beings. These economic activities create interests in perpetuating the network of weak states and conflicts that create opportunities for profit," noted Barnett Rubin.[1] Poverty, organized crime, and the drug trade are also creating previously unforeseen problems. The International Committee for Combating AIDS reports that the five Central Asian republics now have an estimated three hundred thousand people infected with the AIDS virus and that the likelihood of a major epidemic in the region increases with the rise in needle sharing and drug use.[2]

As the summer of 2001 faded and Central Asia awaited another IMU offensive, for the first time the international community seemed to appreciate the global danger of the crisis in Central Asia, which was spilling over into the entire region. In the corridors of NATO, the European Union, the Bush White House, Beijing, and Tokyo statements were made, reports issued, and warnings given that the conflicts in Central Asia and Afghanistan and the threat of international terrorism posed a risk to global security and stability. Anthony Lake, the former national security adviser to President Clinton, published a study about six hotspots that threaten the world in which he labeled the Fergana Valley one of the world's three "hottest danger zones" for the future. "Religious zealots based in Afghanistan have started to spread throughout Central Asia and the Caucasus, hoping that economic hardship will make radical appeals more popular," he warned. The European-based International Crisis Group was similarly ominous: "The situation [in Central Asia] is so dire for the vast majority of the population that patience is beginning to evaporate and unrest to grow sharply. . . . The likelihood is that dire poverty—combined with despair and outrage over rampant corruption, repressive policies and government's failure to address local needs—could lead to outbreaks of localized unrest with the potential to spread into a wider regional conflict."[3]

And in the first recognition of the crisis by the mainstream U.S. media, the *New York Times* warned in August 2001 that "the governments [of Central Asia] claim that they are a steadying force, but their repression is creating instability. Uzbekistan is leading a region wide crackdown on all forms of Islam that are not state-controlled—repression that is driving entire villages into opposition and forcing religion underground. . . . If a Taliban style threat arises in central Asia, it will be because the dictatorships inadvertently helped to create it."[4]

Yet before September 11 the region's authoritarian rulers found it easy to manipulate the international community by exaggerating the threat they faced or playing off the various conflicts against one another, just as Pakistan, Uzbekistan, and Russia have done. Even as Uzbekistan begged for more arms to beef up national security, it denied that the IMU was either a political or a military threat, and the government remained unwilling to tackle the economic root causes of the conflict. Whilst Pakistan pretended to act as a mediator between the Taliban, the IMU, and the international community, it also clandestinely supported these armed factions as part of a power play with India and Iran. Saudi Arabia would tell the international community that it was not involved with the Central Asian conflict and did not want to be whilst urging its extremist Wahhabi ulema to continue funding the Taliban and the IMU. Moscow's role has been even more pernicious; Russia acted as a responsible superpower at one level, helping to control militant incursions, whilst feeding the conflicts with arms and encouraging localized state repression to continue. Moscow is also suspected of having maintained a clandestine intelligence relationship with the IMU.

This complex regional scenario has been replicated in even greater complexity in each of the republics. Thus in Tajikistan, IRP ministers in the coalition government continued their relations with the IMU, and even funneled support to it, in order to maintain their own power base within the coalition. Meanwhile, President Rahmonov's faction supported the anti-Taliban alliance in its war with the Taliban in order to retain leverage and military aid from Moscow. Thus both sides backed external forces that were irrelevant—even damaging—to the economic development of Tajikistan because they were critical to the fragile power structure in Dushanbe.

The situation has been equally complicated in Uzbekistan. The peace settlement in Tajikistan excluded key political actors from northern Tajikistan who were predominantly of Uzbek ethnic origin, and President Karimov exploited this issue by giving these

Tajiks sanctuary and support bases in Uzbekistan. Even after he began sending these refugees home, in early 2001, he found them a useful means to foment trouble in Tajikistan, where they would clash with the majority Tajiks and their numbers would overwhelm the country's fragile economy. And by maintaining the ethnic Uzbek commander Makhmud Khudoyberdiev and his men in Tashkent, Karimov was able to exert pressure on Tajikistan and Russia, both of which were believed to be clandestinely supporting the IMU. "The Karimov regime's abusive behavior is now directly undermining regional stability by fuelling support for armed Islamic extremism and producing severe economic dislocation and growing tensions with neighboring states," noted the International Crisis Group. Chinese president Jiang Zemin advised his neighbors, "No country can develop its own security by harming the fundamental security interests of others."[5] But Jiang was worried that this was precisely what was happening on China's western frontiers as both the Taliban and the IMU trained Uighurs to foment rebellion in Xianjiang Province. China has perforce had to become a major player in Central Asia.

If the Central Asian regimes, China, and Russia have lacked a comprehensive strategy to deal with these problems, so have the United States and the Western nations. The Clinton administration policy of helping Central Asia's repressive governments combat terrorism whilst mildly lecturing them on their human-rights violations did not constitute a strategic vision for the region. Such a vision demanded that military aid be coupled with economic aid and incentives. Concerted pressure had to be placed on these regimes to liberalize their economies and political systems, whilst international support needed to be mobilized to end the war in Afghanistan. The West needed a strategy that considered the region as a whole rather than as a series of local problems.

For example, the West could not join the fight against the IMU without acknowledging the worsening situation in Afghanistan and the fact that thousands of Kashmiri and Pakistani militants have trained in Kabul along with the IMU. To the untrained Western eye the region may have appeared to be a patchwork of different states, ethnic groups, and interests, but the conflicts showed a growing unity amongst the dissidents and a common sense of purpose. The various militants fed off one another, supported one another, and became increasingly intertwined both militarily and ideologically. Pakistani anti-Shia groups joined the Taliban and the IMU to give themselves "jihadi" credentials, whilst the IMU fought for the Taliban, and bin Laden's Arabs fought for everyone.

Instead of working to create a strategic vision, Western policymakers have largely concentrated on two elements that they hoped would shore up stability in the region, to the exclusion of other important factors: the building up of Central Asia's armies to help them fight insurgency and the exploitation of energy resources—including the creation of new pipelines—to provide economic incentives for the regimes to improve social conditions at home. Of the two, the military aid took precedence, and it soon became a major international venture.

The Central Asian republics, like the other CIS countries and even Russia, saw a dramatic deterioration in their military capability as their economies soured. In Central Asia, aircraft, tanks, and artillery inherited from the Soviet Union were already in a state of disrepair, and a large percentage of the heavy weapons nonoperational, when the IMU first struck in 1999. Military officers, many of them ethnic Russians, were untrained for counterinsurgency, whilst morale was abysmal because of the low pay, corruption, poor housing, and lack of promotion opportunities. The armies of all of the republics are based on conscription rather than volunteers. Levels of training, motivation, and professionalism are low and desertion rates high, as soldiers endure hazing, forced labor, poor food, and disease. Recently, Russia and the United States stepped in to offer large-scale retraining of officers and men, and the United States helped create special commando units in the Uzbek and Kyrgyz armies modeled on the U.S. Army Special Forces—but army morale and preparedness cannot be increased overnight.

Uzbekistan had the largest army in the region, with fifty thousand men and an equal number of reserves. These forces included eighteen thousand Interior Ministry troops and a thousand men belonging to the National Guard.[6] Yet Uzbek forces were found sorely wanting during the IMU offensives in 2000, when they easily fell into IMU ambushes. Moreover, Uzbekistan's long borders (with all the Central Asian republics as well as Afghanistan) gave the Uzbek forces a mammoth task. Sealing off its borders, as Uzbekistan attempted to do in the Fergana Valley, was no solution; the IMU has repeatedly outwitted and outflanked the Uzbek border guards. As history has proved many times over, large armies are virtually useless in counterinsurgency.

Kyrgyzstan neglected its armed forces until the 1999 IMU incursion, when the government was forced to call for volunteers because the level of training and the commitment of the conscripts were so low. The soldiers they acquired included nomad hunters and trackers, who at least knew how to handle a weapon. Between 1999 and 2001 the Kyrgyz government raised its defense budget from $14 million to $29 million—8 percent of its gross domestic product. By 2001 Kyrgyzstan had raised twenty thousand troops; twelve thousand were in the regular army and the rest were divided between the ministries of Interior and Defense, and the National Guard. Kyrgyzstan's air force consists of about fifty aircraft from the Soviet era that remain nonoperational to this day owing to a lack of spare parts and maintenance, although the air force is now building a small helicopter fleet. The Russian army maintains a headquarters in Kyrgyzstan that operates from a Russian transportation battalion base in Osh. It fields more than a hundred Russian military advisers attached to Kyrgyz counterinsurgency units. Ironically in early 2001, hotels in Osh were also filled with Green Berets, U.S. Army Special Forces operatives who were rushing Kyrgyz troops through commando courses.

After the civil war in Tajikistan, a thousand IRP guerrillas were inducted into the regular army, yet by 2001 Tajikistan's armed forces, beset by a lack of funds, still numbered only nine thousand men. The key to Tajikistan's security was the Russian forces stationed in the country. These included the 8,200 men of the Russian army's 201 Motorized Rifle Division, known as the Gatchinskaya Division, who were deployed in five bases around the country, and the 14,500 Russian guards on the Afghanistan-Tajikistan border, who were mainly Tajik conscripts officered by Russians. Russian officers and men received a 50 percent higher salary than the Tajiks to entice them to stay on. These border guards were notoriously corrupt, and some senior officers were involved in the drug trade.

In 2001, seeking to protect its oil fields from IMU attacks, Kazakhstan more than doubled its defense budget, to $171 million, or 1 percent of its gross domestic product. Officers and soldiers were given a 30 percent salary increase. Over twelve days in July 2001, Kazakhstan held its largest military exercises ever in three southern districts, and with U.S. help began to train commando units for counterinsurgency. Ancient Soviet equipment was rapidly overhauled, whilst the United States supplied new communications and mountain warfare equipment. Kazakhstan also completely restructured its defense strategy, creating four new military districts, which were allotted mobile counterinsurgency units. The Kazakh forces now number some sixty thousand men.

In January 2001 Russia announced that it would join with Kazakhstan, Kyrgyzstan, and Tajikistan to create a rapid-deployment force of three thousand men based in Tajikistan at a new military base, which Russia would lease from Dushanbe. In spite of the announcement, only Tajikistan appears willing to accept such a force operating on its soil under Russian command. It is unlikely that the rapid-deployment force will become operational in the near future, except as a convenient cover to allow Russia's 201 Motorized Rifle Division to remain in Dushanbe as a newly dubbed rapid-deployment force.

A parallel attempt by the Shanghai Five is also under way. In 2000 the group proposed setting up a new counterterrorism center in Bishkek, which would coordinate intelligence gathering, troop deployment, and military operations. But to date none of the countries has contributed the necessary funds or officers for its creation. Each state still prefers to maintain and control its own armed forces, and despite the national rhetoric, actual military cooperation is still a long way off.

As I outlined in Chapter 8, foreign military aid has poured into the region. Up until September 11 the United States, China, Israel, and the NATO countries through NATO's Partnership for Peace program all provided military aid to help rebuild the Central Asian armies. Although the West largely provided nonlethal aid, such as training and funds, China and Russia supplied arms. Building up the depreciated military capacity of Central Asia's armies and training them in the modern techniques of counterinsurgency is clearly important, but this international aid has not come with significant economic and political riders. The Central Asian regimes have not been forced to reform their state systems. Military aid has also not been accompanied by large-scale economic incentives—promises to write off the governments' foreign debts, for example, or comprehensive funding for economic development—that would have prodded the regimes into developing not just a military strategy but also a socioeconomic strategy.

Historically, socioeconomic aid has proved to be the critical factor in counterinsurgency. A well-fed, well-housed, and fully employed population would not provide recruits for the IMU—or any other terrorist organization. Such an opportunity now exists. The

Western alliance has asked for and received bases in Central Asia for its war against the Taliban and Al Qaeda. Although the United States may be reluctant to place additional pressures on the Central Asian regimes during the war, once the fighting is over, it will almost certainly be in a position of strong influence and can push the regimes towards reform, if it so chooses. The other major Western strategy that could help deal with the crisis in Central Asia would be to exploit the energy resources of Kazakhstan, Turkmenistan, and Azerbaijan, laying new pipelines that would be independent of Russia and Iran, secure Central Asia's oil and gas exports to the West, and bring foreign exchange to the regions, where theoretically it would be spent on the people. But so far no money from investments by Western oil companies in Central Asia has trickled down to the masses. The most corrupt regimes in the region—those of Azerbaijan, Kazakhstan, and Turkmenistan—belong to the most oil-rich nations. The leaders of these countries have received fat bonuses from U.S. oil companies, as well as trips abroad and expensive gifts. All these states lag behind in providing regular salaries and pensions to the workforce despite their foreign-exchange earnings.

In fact, Western oil company investments, by creating an extremely wealthy, corrupt minority class, are breeding even greater social discontent. The evidence of the economic disparity and the corruption is visible every day to the people of Central Asia—the Mercedes and BMWs on the streets of Baku and Almaty, the expensively kept mistresses of the ruling elite who frequent five-star hotels clad in designer clothes and gaudy jewelry, and maintain large dachas and lavish lifestyles, and the Swiss bank accounts of the leaders and their entourages. The pattern has appeared in other oil-rich Third World countries like Indonesia and Nigeria, where money has suddenly poured in: the minuscule elite becomes richer, whilst the overwhelming majority of the population grow poorer and more angry and frustrated.

It would be apt here to remember how the American Communist John Reed described America's obsession for oil to Central
Asia's Bolsheviks eighty years ago.

Do you know how "Baku" is pronounced in American? It is
pronounced "oil." And American capitalism is striving to establish a world monopoly of oil. On account of oil, blood is
being shed. On account of oil, a struggle is being waged in
which the American bankers and the American capitalists attempt everywhere to conquer the places and enslave the peoples where oil is found. . . . You the peoples of the East, the
peoples of Asia have not yet experienced for yourselves the
rule of America.[7]

The presumptuous, failed attempt by Unocal to build a gas pipeline
through Afghanistan in the midst of civil war is an example of how
U.S. oil companies continue to use conflict as a lever to extract maximum benefits.

Yet it would be an exaggeration to compare today's mighty but
more socially conscious U.S. oil companies with the crass capitalism
of the past that Reed describes. Today the major oil companies often
build schools, hospitals, and roads, and implement environmental
protection programs in the areas where they drill for oil, as Chevron
is doing in Kazakhstan. But the oil companies do not seem to feel
any obligation to use their wealth and influence to convince the governments of these regions to create a more comprehensive strategy
built on conflict resolution and problem solving, rather than simply
raising new regiments of soldiers. Developing Central Asia's oil
resources and building pipelines that will cross every country—even
those that have no oil—is the most important tool the United States
and other Western countries have to force the regimes to initiate
social and political reform. It is an instrument that has never been
strongly enough applied. If the oil companies think that they can

simply lay pipelines through a country beset by war, misery, and conflict, or that they can maintain those pipelines without attending to the social ills of the people, then they are being both irresponsible and politically shortsighted.

Oil offers the greatest hope for regional cooperation. The present competition between the big powers—Russia, China, and the United States—to exploit the energy resources of the region and build pipelines there needs to be converted into cooperation. Russia should not expect U.S. cooperation on counterterrorism if it is blocking U.S. oil companies from developing the region and preventing Central Asian states from choosing the routes they want to use to export their energy. China, whose energy needs will be stupendous in the next decade, needs to join with the United States and Russia to create oil company consortiums that would not just offer new energy sources but would show the Central Asian regimes that they can no longer exploit differences between the big powers to avoid desperately needed reforms at home.

The best hope for the region is that after the war in Afghanistan is over, and a stable coalition government is in place in Kabul, the United Nations -backed by the big powers, the regional governments, the World Bank, and even the oil companies—will be able to begin economic reconstruction in the country. Pipelines from Central Asia that traversed Afghanistan to the Gulf would bring revenue, jobs, training, and education to both the Afghans and the peoples of Central Asia. They would link Afghanistan to the outside world and improve the chances of greater regional cooperation. "Pipelines for Peace" could be the new slogan of the oil companies.

Any comprehensive strategy for the region has to look particularly at the Fergana Valley, which remains divided between Uzbekistan, Kyrgyzstan, and Tajikistan. The United Nations Development Program's Fergana Valley Development Program, the Soros Foundation's Fergana Project, and the U.S.-based Fergana Valley Working Group, run by the Center for Preventive Action, have spelled out in extensive reports that the acute problems of the valley can be addressed only when it ceases to be partitioned into separate zones of influence and political and economic control. There need to be cross-border institutions that "promote economic development and interethnic cooperation and . . . monitor potential conflict."[8] The three states must allow direct foreign investment in the valley by international aid agencies that would capitalize on the geographical reality that Fergana is a single valley and would work to rehabilitate agriculture and industry as a single unit. This cannot take place—and the ten million inhabitants cannot become gainfully employed—unless the regimes recognize that border controls, minefields, barbed wire, and the shutting down of roads and irrigation channels that cross the valley and borders are inconducive to economic, agricultural, or any other kind of development.

When Juma Namangani dreams of capturing the valley, he sees it as a single contiguous block, paying no attention to the artificial partitions set up by the states. Namangani may well succeed in his quest if the regimes continue to see the valley as three separate entities ruled by three sovereign states. Uzbekistan is the major culprit in fostering this attitude. The government has refused to allow aid agencies like the United Nations, the Soros Foundation, ACTED, and the Aga Khan Foundation to undertake cross-valley developmental work. Currently all these agencies are forced to set up separate units in the Tajikistan and Kyrgyzstan portions of the valley, whilst they are forbidden to enter the Uzbekistan section. Tashkent claims publicly that there are no economic problems in the valley so aid agencies are not needed.

But in the sectors where they are allowed, these aid agencies are creating elementary yet beneficial development programs, such as microcredit schemes, which allow the people to subsist on employment rather than charity. Moreover, their efforts have proved that huge sums of money are not required for a comprehensive plan to develop the Fergana Valley. With a total budget of just $100,000, ACTED has helped tens of thousands of farmers in the Batken and Fergana regions of Kyrgyzstan through a microcredit scheme that provides funds for planting new crops, animal husbandry work, and rebuilding irrigation networks.

The lack of an integrated approach to economic development amongst the Central Asian republics is also increasing the danger of a water war in the near future. During the Soviet era huge reservoirs and a complex irrigation system were built to carry melting snow-water from the mountain ranges of Tajikistan and Kyrgyzstan to irrigate the vast cotton plantations of Central Asia. These irrigation systems were fully integrated from the Chinese border to the Ural Mountains, but the creation of new states and border controls has disrupted the flow of water. Both Kyrgyzstan and Tajikistan have used water as a weapon to forestall punitive actions by their neighbors, for example, when Uzbekistan cut off gas supplies to Bishkek and the Kyrgyz threatened to cut off water supplies to Uzbekistan's irrigation canals. Moreover, the World Bank reports that the volume of irrigation water has been reduced by 50 percent across Central Asia because of water shortages, the breakdown of the irrigation system, and the blackmailing politics of the states. Since 1991, 20–30 percent of the total arable irrigated land in Central Asia has been put out of use because of water shortages. In Tajikistan, where only 7 percent of the territory is arable, some 50 percent of irrigated farmland no longer receives water because the irrigation systems were destroyed in the civil war.[9]

A comprehensive strategy for peace in the region has to focus on Tajikistan, for if there is any country that could conceivably stand as a political model for the future of the region, it is Tajikistan. Here a brutal civil war ended with the creation of a coalition government that included Islamicists, neo-Communists, and clan leaders. Islamicists have lost elections, but they were *represented* in the elections, and they accepted their loss. Central Asian regimes that currently seek to repress their Muslim population should follow Tajikistan's lead—and support the idea of more inclusive governments where different factions, political parties, and ideas are represented.

But Tajikistan is immersed in grinding poverty. In 2000 Tajikistan experienced its worst drought in seventy-four years. Cereal production fell by 47 percent, leaving 1.2 million people—a fifth of the population—facing hunger and malnutrition. "It would be wrong, even dangerous, to view food insecurity crisis as purely a drought driven natural disaster. It is an emergency with complex political and economic root causes," said a report by the International Committee of the Red Cross (ICRC). By August 2001 the ICRC was reporting that the year's harvest would be 15 percent lower than the catastrophic 2000 harvest and that one million people faced starvation, unless Western donor aid was forthcoming. "People have sold the doors and windows of their houses to buy food and they have nothing left to sell," said ICRC official Roger Bracke. "We have seen children digging among rat holes in wheat fields, searching for grain hoarded by the rodents for the winter." Sixty-five thousand children in southern Tajikistan were unable to go to school because they had no shoes or clothes.[10]

The coalition government has proved unable to deal with these economic hardships. Tajikistan's weak state institutions cannot even claim to control the entire country, forcing it to play host to the IMU, which at least pays the farmers and feeds the people who join the guerrillas. And because the West has ignored it in the past, Tajikistan has become a satellite of Russia, depending on Moscow for security and economic survival. Generous Western economic aid and support in rebuilding the state apparatus, rehabilitating agriculture, and reconstructing the economy could pay huge dividends not only in stabilizing Tajikistan but in showing its neighbors the advantages of joining the global community and adhering to international standards of behavior and nation building. Until the Central Asian states start to implement some of these policies with the help of the international community, Central Asia will continue to be a major source of instability across the region. Terrorism, Islamic militancy, drug trafficking, AIDS, and ethnic unrest will multiply. According to officials from the United Nations Drug Control Program, some 30–50 percent of the Tajikistan economy comes from the drug trade from Afghanistan.

Neither the IMU nor the HT has the power, the popularity, or the military force to emerge as a victor in the region. Their present success is due primarily to the repression of the Central Asian states, which turns them into martyrs, and the incompetence with which they carry out this repression. It is also the result of external sources of instability like the war in Afghanistan. The IMU has a different ideology, organization, and social base from that of either the Taliban or the HT, but its military capability has been increased with help from the Taliban, and its ideology has been affected by the Afghan-Pakistani-Arab network that helps advise and run the Taliban.

Although the IMU's Islamic ideology is not pure Wahhabi, as Karimov claims, its idea of a universal jihad is strongly rooted in the Deobandi-Wahhabi teachings imported from Pakistan and Saudi Arabia—teachings that have little to do with the traditional Islam of Central Asia. The IMU's inability to include the history and traditions of the people it purports to represent within its extremist Islamic ideology should limit its public support beyond the volatile Fergana Valley. The HT, too, draws its ideology from external sources alien to Central Asian traditions, whilst its jihadi literature is written for a global audience and does not reflect the real problems of Central Asia and its people. Moreover, the leadership and political hierarchies of both groups are kept secret; these leaders cannot pose as alternatives to Presidents Karimov and Akayev without first disclosing themselves and then spelling out what they have to offer to the people of Central Asia. The best way for the Central Asian regimes to destroy the influence of these groups would be to bring them out into the open; to allow Islamic practice in their countries and to institute reforms that would leave the movements with only their alien ideologies to sell.

Under better economic and social circumstances, such movements would have had little public appeal or impact and would have remained on the fringe of the Central Asian Islamic world, just as the HT remains marginalized in many other Muslim countries. It is the particular circumstances of the crisis in Central Asia that have pushed the IMU and the HT to center stage and provided young people with alien role models. Yet as the threat increases, the Central Asian regimes have become more intransigent and less willing to address the pressing needs of their people. As the public becomes more angry and frustrated, the ruling elites continue to ignore the need for change. "A failed state is not a dying state, although it can be that too. A failed state is one in which failure of policies is never considered sufficient reason to reconsider them," warns Pakistani diplomat and scholar Ashraf Jehangir Qazi. Qazi could be talking about any state from Pakistan to Afghanistan to the Central Asian republics.[11]

The crisis that has blown up since the September 11 attacks is fraught with danger, but it also offers an enormous opportunity for change. By joining the Western alliance against Al Qaeda, the Central Asian states have made a commitment to the international community's war against terrorism and Islamic extremism. In so doing, they cannot afford to ignore the long-term consequences of their actions. If the U.S.-led alliance succeeds in removing the threat of the IMU, the international community will be in a position to insist that the Central Asian regimes conduct themselves in line with international standards of democracy building, economic development, and social responsibility. The Central Asian regimes are at a critical crossroads. They can ignore the lessons from Afghanistan and the collapse of the Afghan state and watch terrorism, instability, and famine increase in their countries as it did in Afghanistan. Or they can take advantage of the global community's new engagement with the region to rebuild their countries. The real crisis in Central Asia lies with the state, not with the insurgents. As the international community finally begins to recognize this, the prospects for real peace in Central Asia have never looked brighter.

APPENDIX:
THE CALL TO JIHAD BY THE
ISLAMIC MOVEMENT OF UZBEKISTAN

The following document was issued in August 1999 by the Islamic Movement of Uzbekistan as a declaration of jihad against the government of Uzbekistan. Originally written in Uzbek, it has appeared on the Internet in English.

In the Name of Allah the Most Compassionate the Most Merciful

A Message from the General Command
of the Islamic Movement Uzbekistan

"And fight them until there is no more fitnah and
the religion is all for Allah"
Al Anfaal: 39

The Amir (commander) of the Harakatul Islamiyyah (Islamic Movement) of Uzbekistan, Muhammad Tahir Farooq, has announced the start of the Jihad against the tyrannical government of Uzbekistan and the puppet Islam Karimov and his henchmen. The leadership of the Islamic Movement confirm the following points in the declaration:

This declaration comes after agreement by the major ulema and the leadership of the Islamic Movement.

This agreement comes based on clear evidence on the obligation of Jihad against the *tawagheet* as well as to liberate the land and the people.

The primary objective for this declaration of Jihad is the establishment of an Islamic state with the application of the Sharia, founded upon the Koran and the Noble Prophetic sunnah.

Also from amongst the goals of the declaration of Jihad is:

The defense of our religion of Islam in our land against those who oppose Islam.

The defense of the Muslims in our land from those who humiliate them and spill their blood.

The defense of the scholars and Muslim youth who are being assassinated, imprisoned and tortured in extreme manners—with no rights given them at all.

And the Almighty says:

"And they had no fault except that they believed in Allah, the All Mighty, Worthy of all praise!" Al Buruj: 8

Also to secure the release of the weak and oppressed who number some 5,000 in prison, held by the transgressors. The Almighty says:

"And what is the matter with you that you do not fight in the way of Allah and the weak and oppressed amongst men, women and children" An Nisaa: 75

And to reopen the thousands of mosques and Islamic schools that have been closed by the evil government.

The Mujahedeen of the Islamic Movement, after their experience in warfare, have completed their training and are ready to establish the blessed Jihad.

The Islamic Movement warns the Uzbek government in Tashkent from propping up or supporting the fight against the Muslims.

The Islamic Movement warns tourists coming to this land that they should keep away, lest they be struck down by the Mujahedeen.

The reason for the start of the Jihad in Kyrgyzstan is due to the stance of the ruler Askar Akayev Bishkek, in arresting thousands of Muslim Uzbeks who had migrated as refugees to Kyrgyzstan and were handed over to Karimov's henchmen (i.e., Uzbek regime).

The Most High says:

"**Verily the oppressors are friends and protectors to one another.**"

The Islamic Movement shall, by the will of Allah, make Jihad in the cause of Allah to reach all its aims and objectives.

It is with regret that Foreign Mujahedeen (Al Ansaar) as of yet have not entered our ranks.

The Islamic Movement invites the ruling government and Karimov leadership in Tashkent to remove itself from office—unconditionally, before the country enters into a state of war and destruction of the land and the people. The responsibility for this will lie totally on the shoulders of the government, for which it shall be punished.

Allah is Great and the Honor is for Islam.

Head of the Religious Leadership of the Islamic Movement of
  Uzbekistan
Az Zuhayr Ibn 'Abdur Raheem
4th Jumadi Al Awwal (ah)
25 August 1999

NOTES

All dollar figures are in U.S. dollars, and all measurements are in U.S. measures.

SOURCES

In addition to the sources listed below, I consulted the following media and international agency services.

Agence France Presse (AFP)
Amnesty International reports
Associated Press (AP)
BBC World Service
BBC Uzbek Language Service
Central Asia Analyst (Washington, D.C.)
Daily Telegraph (London)
Dawn (Karachi)
The Economist (London)
Energy Information Administration Web site (eia.doe.gov)
Eurasia Insight (Web site news service based in New York, located at
  Eurasianet.org)
Far Eastern Economic Review (Hong Kong)
Herald (Karachi)
The Nation (Lahore)

The News (Lahore)
Human Rights Society of Uzbekistan reports
Human Rights Watch reports
The Independent (London)
Institute of War and Peace Reporting (London)
Interfax (Russian wire service based in Moscow)
International Crisis Group reports (Brussels)
International Herald Tribune (Paris)
Itar Tass (Russian news service based in Moscow)
Jamestown (Virginia) *Monitor*
Los Angeles Times
Le Monde (Paris)
New York Times
Nezayisimaya Gazeta (Moscow)
Radio Free Europe (Prague)
Rossiyskaya Gazeta (Moscow)
Turkistan Newsletter (Web site news service, located at
   euronet.nl/users/sota/turkistan)
United Nations Integrated Regional Information Network (IRIN, Islamabad)
U.S. State Department Human Rights reports
Uzbekistan Ovozi (Tashkent)
Wall Street Journal (New York)
Washington Post

CHAPTER 1 Introduction
1. Barbara Metcalf, *Islamic Revival in British India, 1860–1900* (Islamabad:
   Royal Book Company, 1982).

CHAPTER 2 Conquerors and Saints
1. Marco Polo, *The Travels of Marco Polo* (New York: Dell, 1961).
2. The most recent and most authoritative work on the Fergana Valley is
   Council of Foreign Relations, Ferghana Valley Working Group Report,
   *Calming the Ferghana Valley: Development and Dialogue in the Heart of
   Central Asia* (New York: Century Foundation Press, 1999).
3. The sources for this brief history can be gathered from my earlier book *The
   Resurgence of Central Asia: Islam or Nationalism?* (London: Zed Press, 1994).
4. Julian Baldick, *Mystical Islam: An Introduction to Sufism* (London: Tauris,
   1989).
5. Bruce Lawrence, "The Eastward Journey of Muslim Kingship," in John

Esposito, ed., *The Oxford History of Islam* (Oxford: Oxford University Press, 1999).
6. Fernand Braudel, *A History of Civilizations* (Harmondsworth, U.K.: Penguin, 1993).

CHAPTER 3 Islam Underground in the Soviet Union

1. F. M. Bailey, *Mission to Tashkent* (1946; Oxford: Oxford University Press, 1992).
2. See Alexandre Bennigsen and S. Enders Wimbush, *Muslim Nationalism in the Soviet Union: A Revolutionary Strategy for the Colonial World* (Chicago: University of Chicago Press, 1979).
3. Robert Conquest, *Harvest of Sorrow* (London: Arrow, 1988).
4. Gustav Krist, *Alone Through the Forbidden Land: Journeys in Disguise Through Soviet Central Asia* (1938; Cambridge: Ian Falkner, 1992).
5. Yaacov Roi, *Islam in the Soviet Union from the Second World War to Gorbachev* (London: Hurst, 2000).
6. Ibid.
7. This process is outlined in greater detail in my book *Taliban: Militant Islam, Oil and Fundamentalism in Central Asia* (New Haven: Yale University Press, 2000).
8. Aide to Deputy Prime Minister Yegor Gaidar of Russia, interview with the author, Moscow, November 24, 1991; Alexander Solzhenitsyn, *Rebuilding Russia* (London: Harvill, 1991).

CHAPTER 4 The First Decade of Independence

1. The referenda were held in October 1994, February 1996, and October 1998.
2. World Bank, *Kyrgyzstan Data* (Washington, D.C.: December 2000); International Crisis Group, *Kyrgyzstan at Ten: Trouble in the Island of Democracy* (Brussels: August 2001).
3. Quoted in Edward A. Allworth, *The Modern Uzbeks from the Fourteenth Century to the Present: A Cultural History* (Stanford, Calif.: Hoover Institution Press, 1990).
4. AFP, "Uzbekistan Asks Russia for Protection Against Terrorism," May 19, 2000; AFP, "Uzbek President Hits Out at Russia," September 22, 2000.
5. Quoted in Ahmed Rashid, "Asking for Holy War," *Far Eastern Economic Review*, Tashkent, November 9, 2000.
6. International Crisis Group, *Uzbekistan at Ten: Repression and Instability* (Brussels: August 2001).
7. Ibid.

CHAPTER 5 The Islamic Renaissance Party

1. Olivier Roy, *The New Central Asia: The Creation of Nations* (London: Tauris, 2000).

2. Kamoludin Abdullaev and Catherine Barnes, *Politics of Compromise: The Tajikistan Peace Process* (London: Conciliation Resources, 2001).

3. Muhammad Sharif Himmatzoda, interview with Ahmed Rashid, in "The Crescent of Islam Rises in Tajikistan," *The Nation*, December 25, 1991.

4. S. Olimova, "Islam and the Tajik conflict," in Roald Sagdeev and Susan Eisenhower, eds., *Islam and Central Asia* (Washington, D.C.: Center for Political and Strategic Studies, 2000).

5. Qazi Akbar Turajonzoda, interview with Ahmed Rashid, in "Crescent of Islam Rises in Tajikistan."

6. Reuters, "No Policy Change Following Nabiev's Ouster," September 8, 1992.

7. Ivo Petrov, interview with the author, Dushanbe, March 15, 2001.

8. IRIN, "IOM Meets over Overflow of Itinerant Workers," Dushanbe, December 22, 2000.

9. Moheyuddin Kabir and Muhammad Sharif Himmatzoda, interviews with the author, Dushanbe, March 16 and 17, 2001.

10. Gen. Tommy Franks, quoted in Ahmed Rashid, "Western Powers Bolster Tajikistan," *Central Asia Analyst* (Tokyo), May 23, 2001.

CHAPTER 6 The Hizb ut-Tahrir

1. Abdul Qadeem Zaloom, *How the Khilafah Was Destroyed* (Lahore: HT publication, 1998). Zaloom followed Nabhani as the leader of the HT.

2. Personal communication by HT member, August 2, 2001.

3. Taqiuddin an-Nabhani, *The Islamic State* (1962; Lahore: HT publication, 1998).

4. "Ali" (HT leader), interview with author, Uzbekistan, October 2000.

5. Olivier Roy, "Changing Patterns Among Radical Islamic Movements," *Brown Journal of World Affairs* (Winter– Spring 1999).

6. An-Nabhani, *Islamic State*.

7. Human Rights Watch statement to press by Holly Carter, January 25, 2000.

8. U.S. State Department, *Uzbekistan: Human Rights Practices 2000* (Washington, D.C.: February 2001); Independent Human Rights Organization of Uzbekistan, *About Political Prisoners in Uzbekistan* (July 2001). According to the organization, in addition to the 5,150 prisoners belonging to the

HT and the 1,600 from the IMU and other Wahhabi organizations, 650 were practicing Muslims with no political affiliation, 200 were people from social organizations, and 6 were human-rights defenders.

9. Acacia Shields, statement to the U.S. House of Representatives Committee for International Relations, September 7, 2000.

10. State Department, *Uzbekistan: Human Rights Practices 2000*.

11. IRIN, "Uzbekistan: Interview with Human Rights Activist," May 31, 2001.

12. AFP, "Islamic Extremists Charged in Kyrgyzstan," Bishkek, May 1, 2000.

13. Daily briefing on post-Soviet states, *Jamestown Monitor*, June 28, 2000.

14. U.S. State Department, *Kyrgyzstan: Human Rights Practices, 2000* (Washington, D.C.: February 2001).

15. AFP, "4000 Kyrgyz Women, Kids Sold to Slavery," Bishkek, December 20, 2000.

16. IRIN, "Interview with UN Chief in Kyrgyzstan," Bishkek, August 28, 2001.

17. "Bishkek Fighting Islamicists as Best as It Can," *Nezavisimaya Gazeta*, April 14, 2001.

18. "Kyrgyz President Pledges to Fight Religious Extremism," *Rossiyskaya Gazeta*, May 16, 2001.

19. Anara Tabyshalieva, "The Kyrgyz and the Spiritual Dimensions of Daily Life," in Roald Sagdeev and Susan Eisenhower, eds., *Islam and Central Asia* (Washington, D.C.: Center for Political Strategic Studies, 2000)

20. Reuters, "Neighbors Asked to Resist Radicalism," Almaty, June 19, 2001.

21. U.S. State Department, *Tajikistan: Human Rights Practices, 2000* (Washington, D.C.: February 2001).

22. AFP, "Islamic Militants Held in Tajik Capital," November 16, 2000.

23. "Crackdown on Terrorist Groups in Central Asia," *Jamestown Monitor*, October 2, 2000.

24. Igor Rotar, "The Hizb ut-Tahrir Party in Central Asia: A Fault Line?" *Jamestown Monitor*, May 1, 2001.

25. IRIN, "Uzbekistan: Interview with Human Rights Activist," May 31, 2001.

26. "Tashkent Cracks Down on Islamists," Institute of War and Peace Reporting, October 12, 2001.

27. Paula Newberg, "Central Asia and Democracy," *Los Angeles Times*, November 19, 2000.

CHAPTER 7 Namangani and the Islamic Movement of Uzbekistan

1. Yuldeshev is reported to have made the following demands: "We set five conditions which must be fulfilled by the authorities. First Islam Karimov must come here. Second, he must swear his faithfulness to Islam on the

Koran and here and now proclaim an Islamic state. Third, visiting mosques must become compulsory for all Muslims including leaders of the state who must pray together with the people. Fourth, Friday should be announced as a day off and fifth to open religious schools immediately" (Oleg Yakubov, *The Pack of Wolves: The Blood Trail of Terror* [Moscow: Veche, 2000]). The book is a propaganda treatise published by the Uzbek government, but it reprints some interesting speeches.

2. Abdul Ahad, quoted in Ahmed Rashid, "Caught in a Cleft: Economic, Religious Pressures Threaten Uzbekistan," *Far Eastern Economic Review*, November 19, 1992.

3. I wrote a series of three articles for *The Nation* in November 1992 that described these new militant groups for the first time. See, in particular, Ahmed Rashid, "Karimov Faces New Threats," *The Nation*, November 13, 1992. All the young men I interviewed were proud to claim that their funds came from Saudi Arabia.

4. I discuss Pakistan's role in Central Asia and the reasons for its support to the IMU in Chapter 10. Both Pakistani intelligence officials and Uzbek diplomats claimed that Yuldeshev received funds from a variety of sources.

5. This information comes from interviews with Western and Asian diplomats, IRP leaders, and individuals close to the IMU in Dushanbe during February 2001. I was given several names of Uzbek-Saudi businessmen who funded the IMU, including the name of the influential businessman Haji Jamshed, but I cannot independently confirm their dealings with the IMU.

6. This information comes from interviews with several IRP leaders and activists who know Yuldeshev well in Dushanbe, during March 2001. In October 2000 Uzbek officials in Tashkent told me that Yuldeshev travels extensively on false passports, which have been provided by Pakistan, Turkey, Saudi Arabia, and Iran. Both Yuldeshev and Namangani were to become masters of disguise, often posing as Pakistani, Gulf Arab, or Tajik businessmen.

7. Former IRP activist, interview with the author, Dushanbe, March 14, 2001.

8. Izatullah Saduloev, interview with the author, Dushanbe, March 16, 2001.

9. Moheyuddin Kabir, interview with author, Dushanbe, March 16, 2001.

10. This information comes from interviews by the author conducted in Garm between March 18 and 21, 2001, with businessmen and others in Garm who knew Namangani during this period. They all wished to remain anonymous.

11. Amnesty International reported in 2001 that Mirzoev had been held in an underground cell in Tashkent for several years, where he was constantly

tortured and refused permission to pray or read the Koran.

12. Council on Foreign Relations, Ferghana Valley Working Group Report, *Calming the Ferghana Valley: Development and Dialogue in the Heart of Central Asia* (New York: Century Foundation Press, 1999). Karimov made his speech on May 2, 1998.

13. A. Ilkhamov, "Political Islam in Uzbekistan: Imported Ideology or Grass-Root Movement?" (Center for Social Research, Uzbekistan, 2001.)

14. Karomat Asqarova, quoted in Uzbekistan Ovozi. I am grateful to John Bouchard for supplying this newspaper clipping, for which I do not have a date.

15. G. Bukharvaeva, "Uzbek Terror Suspects Targeted," Institute of War and Peace Reporting, July 7, 2000; U.S. State Department, *Uzbekistan: Human Rights Practices, 2000* (Washington, D.C.: February 2001); Islam Karimov, *Uzbekistan on the Threshold of the Twenty-first Century* (Tashkent: Uzbek Government Press, 1997).

16. Tohir Yuldeshev, interview on Voice of America, October 6, 2000.

17. Raheem is the signatory of the IMU's Declaration of Jehad in Appendix 1.

18. Yakubov, *Pack of Wolves.*

19. Islam Karimov, quoted in Amnesty International, *Human Rights Report: Uzbekistan,* June 2001.

20. Barnett Rubin, interview with the author, July 2001.

21. Yakubov, *Pack of Wolves.*

CHAPTER 8 Namangani and Jihad in Central Asia

1. Information on the importance of these enclaves and Namangani's strategy in 1999 comes from many interviews with Uzbek officials in Tashkent in October 2000 and Tajik IRP leaders in Dushanbe in February 2001, as well as Central Asian and U.N. diplomats from 1999 on.

2. These interviews were conducted in Batken by the author, March 2001.

3. United Nations Integrated Regional Information Network (IRIN), "Interview with UN chief in Kyrgyzstan," Bishkek, August 19, 2001.

4. See Ahmed Rashid, *Taliban: Militant Islam, Oil and Fundamentalism in Central Asia* (New Haven: Yale University Press, 2000). Chapter 9, "High on Heroin: Drugs and the Taliban Economy," deals extensively with the drug trade in Afghanistan.

5. Reported in S. Levine, "Uzbekistan's Crackdown on Radicalism May Fuel the Fervor," *Wall Street Journal,* May 3, 2001; "Tajik, Russian Officials Suggest Tajikistan Is Developing into Drug Production Center," Eurasia Insight, August 14, 2001.

6. General Mylnikov was quoted in the Itar Tass news service, "Bin Laden

Allocates Millions of Dollars for Uzbek Militants," December 14, 2000. See also S. Abdvldavey, "Batken, a Small Episode in a Big Game," *Times of Central Asia*, April 20, 2000.

7. Ahmed Rashid, "IMU Insurgency Threatens Tajikistan Political Reconciliation," *The Analyst*, September 27, 2000.

8. Unnamed foreign diplomat, interview by author, Tashkent, October 2000.

9. G. Bukharvaeva, "Local Communities Uprooted" Institute of War and Peace Reporting, August 19, 2000.

10. B. Ergashev, "Uprooted Uzbek Villagers Abandoned," Institute of War and Peace Reporting, January 31, 2001.

11. Greg Child, "Fear of Falling," *Outside*, November 2000. This provides a thrilling account of the kidnapping according to the four American climbers, although their story was subsequently disputed. The other climbers kidnapped included six Germans, three Russians, two Uzbeks, and one Ukrainian.

12. I am extremely grateful to U.S. reporter and climber John Bouchard for sharing his investigation into the incident with me. All this information is based on his account. Bouchard is writing a book about the kidnapping incident.

13. Bouchard reported that the American climbers sold the magazine rights of their story for $17,500, the book rights to Villard Press for $350,000 and film rights to Universal Studios for a sum that was in the high six figures.

14. BBC monitoring service, "Uzbek Court Charges IMU," October 18, 2000.

15. U.S. State Department, *Uzbekistan: Human Rights Practices*, 2000 (Washington, D.C.: February 2001). Diplomats and local officials in Dushanbe and Tashkent told me in 2000 and 2001 that the losses suffered by both armies were actually in the low hundreds.

16. Ahmed Rashid, "Asking for Holy War," *Far Eastern Economic Review*, November 9, 2000.

17. Ahmed Rashid, "IMU Insurgency Threatens Tajikistan Political Reconciliation," *The Analyst*, September 27, 2000.

18. This information comes from interviews with U.S. officials in Washington in the summer of 2001.

19. Ahmed Rashid, "Uzbek Militants Return to Central Asia," *The Nation*, January 12, 2001.

20. The Taliban refused to give me a visa to visit Afghanistan after my book about them appeared in the spring of 2000. By chance, I traveled with Muttawakil on a U.N. plane, which was dropping him off in Kabul while I continued on to Dushanbe. We had a long, pleasant talk during which

he promised me a visa, but I never got it. He viewed the IMU with great
respect and spoke at length about what he considered the horrendous
conditions of Muslims in Uzbekistan, harshly criticizing President
Karimov.

21. Muhammad Sharif Himmatzoda, interview with the author, Dushanbe,
March 2001.

22. B. Musaev, "Uzbeks Losing Patience," Institute of War and Peace Reporting, April 2001.

23. Islam Karimov, *Uzbekistan on the Threshold of the Twenty-first Century*
(Tashkent: Uzbek Government Press, 1997).

24. Bruce Pannier, "IMU Leader Says Group's Goal Is Return of Islam,"
Radio Free Europe, June 6, 2001.

25. BBC Uzbek service, "Uzbek Militants Claim Kyrgyz Attack," August 1,
2001.

26. David Stern, "Historic Pact Signed with US," *Financial Times*, October
13, 2001; Susan Glasser, "US Operated Secret Alliance with Uzbekistan,"
Washington Post, October 14, 2001.

27. BBC Uzbek service, "IMU Response to Uzbekistan's Granting of Bases to
the US," October 9, 2001.

28. Valdimir Davlatov, "Dushanbe Finally Backs US Campaign," Institute of
War and Peace Reporting, October 12, 2001.

CHAPTER 9 The New Great Game?

1. Milan Hauner, *What Is Asia to Us? Russia's Asian Heartland, Yesterday
and Today* (London: Unwin Hyman, 1990).

2. Strobe Talbott, "Remarks on U.S. Foreign Policy in Central Asia at the
Paul Nitze School for Advanced International Studies," U.S. State Department, 21 July 1997.

3. U.S. Senate, Testimony of CIA Director George Tenet to U.S. Senate
Select Committee on Intelligence, February 8, 2000.

4. U.S. House of Representatives, Speech by Congressman Dan Burton,
March 21, 2001.

5. U.S. State Department, "Centcom Chief General Tommy Franks Round-
table Press Briefing in Tashkent," May 21, 2001.

6. Russian casualties in these battles against the Muslim world have been
high. Russia lost 13,500 soldiers in Afghanistan, 7,000 in the two Chechen
wars, and 200 in the Tajikistan civil war.

7. AFP, "Uzbekistan Asks Russia for Protection Against Terrorism," Tashkent,
May 19, 2000; AFP, "Uzbek President Hits Out at Russia," September 22,

2000. The Collective Security Agreement of the CIS, signed on May 15, 1992, bound nine CIS states (Armenia, Azerbaijan, Belarus, Georgia, Kazakhstan, Kyrgyzstan, Russia, Tajikistan, and Uzbekistan) into a collective security arrangement. The treaty was renewed in May 1999, when Azerbaijan, Georgia, and Uzbekistan refused to sign, forming instead GUUAM with Ukraine and Moldova.

8. AFP, "Uzbekistan Says Taliban Threat Exaggerated," Bishkek, September 26, 2000.

9. N. Megoran, "The Borders of Eternal Friendship: Kyrgyz-Uzbek Relations in 1999," Eurasia Insight, January 2000.

10. Uzbekistan earned $309 million in 2000 from these oil exports.

11. I have explored this new Great Game in much greater detail in my earlier book, *Taliban: Militant Islam, Oil and Fundamentalism in Central Asia* (New Haven: Yale University Press, 2000).

12. Ahmed Rashid, "Unstable Fringe," *Far Eastern Economic Review*, September 9, 1999.

13. AFP, "Six Countries to Fight Terrorism," Shanghai, June 14, 2001.

14. Moheyuddin Kabir, interview with author, Dushanbe, March 16, 2001; Ahmed Rashid and Susan Lawrence, "Joining Foreign Jehad," *Far Eastern Economic Review*, September 7, 2000.

CHAPTER 10 Central Asia and Its Neighbors

1. See Ahmed Rashid, "First the War," *Far Eastern Economic Review*, July 26, 2001, where I explore the concern of many Afghans and the Bush administration that the Taliban leadership is now heavily influenced by bin Laden and his Arab followers.

2. Ahmed Rashid, *Taliban: Militant Islam, Oil and Fundamentalism in Central Asia* (New Haven: Yale University Press, 2000).

3. At a press conference in Islamabad on May 25, 2000, Pakistan's chief executive (later president), General Pervez Musharraf, gave the clearest articulation to date of the reasons for Pakistan's continued backing of the Taliban. He explained that in view of the demographic and geographic pattern, Afghanistan's majority ethnic Pashtuns "have to be on our side. This is our national interest. Pashtuns are represented by the Taliban at the moment, and Taliban cannot be alienated by Pakistan." He added that "we have a national security interest there."

4. "Central Asian Muslims Looking Towards Ummah," *The Nation*, September 18, 1991.

5. At an international antinarcotics conference in London in June 2001, Western officials representing the United States and the United Kingdom, and other antinarcotics agencies, were openly critical of their governments' failure to curb drug-smuggling operations in the Gulf. U.S. and European officials have a better understanding of the dangers posed by Dubai's free port, but they have not yet placed any pressure on the government of Abu Dhabi to do something about it.

CHAPTER 11 An Uncertain Future

1. Barnett Rubin, "Regional Instability in Southern Central Asia," unpublished paper, August 2001.
2. Kazakh government television, monitored by BBC, "Unofficial Figure for HIV-Positive in Central Asia Hits 300,000," August 8, 2001.
3. Anthony Lake, *Six Nightmares: Real Threats in a Dangerous World and How America Can Meet Them* (Boston: Little, Brown, 2000); International Crisis Group, *Incubator of Conflict: Central Asia's Localized Poverty and Social Unrest*, June 8, 2001.
4. "Trouble in Central Asia," *New York Times*, August 17, 2001.
5. International Crisis Group, *Uzbekistan at Ten: Repression and Instability* (Brussels: August 2001); AFP, "Jiang Calls for New Order to Counter US," Moscow, July 17, 2001.
6. International Crisis Group, *Central Asia Fault Lines in the New Security Map* (Brussels: July 4, 2001).
7. Quoted in John Riddell, ed. *To See the Dawn: Baku 1920 — The First Congress of the Peoples of the East* (New York: Pathfinder, 1993).
8. Council of Foreign Relations, Ferghana Valley Working Group Report, *Calming the Ferghana Valley: Development and Dialogue in the Heart of Central Asia* (New York: Century Foundation Press, 1999). See also United Nations Development Project, *UNDP Ferghana Valley Development Report* (New York: U.N. Publications, August 1998), and Soros Foundation, *Soros Foundation Ferghana Project* (Bishkek and New York: Soros Foundation, 1998).
9. World Bank, *Poverty Assessment Report* (Washington, D.C.: World Bank, June 2000).
10. International Committee of the Red Cross, *World Disaster Report 2001* (Geneva: International Committee of the Red Cross, 2001); United Nations Integrated Regional Information Network (IRIN), "One Million People Face Starvation in Tajikistan," Dushanbe, August 29, 2001.

11. Ashraf Jehangir Qazi, interview with the author, January 2001. Qazi has served as Pakistan's ambassador in Moscow, Beijing, and New Delhi, and has extensive experience of the entire region under discussion.

GLOSSARY

Abdullah Saidov *See* Nuri, Sayed Abdullah.

Adolat (Justice) Radical Islamic group in the Fergana Valley. A precursor of the IMU.

Ahmad, Qazi Hussein Chief of the Jamiat-i-Islami party in Pakistan.

Akayev, Askar President of Kyrgyzstan since 1991

Al Qaeda (The Base) Global terrorist network headed by Osama bin Laden.

an-Nabhani, Sheikh Taqiuddin Filastyni (the Palestinian) Founder of the HT.

Basmachi A Turkic term that means "bandit" used by the Soviets to describe both the revolt and Islamic Mujahedeen who opposed the Communist system in Central Asia after 1917.

bin Laden, Osama Exiled Saudi Arabian militant, head of Al Qaeda.

Birlik (Unity) Opposition party in Uzbekistan. Founded in 1988 and banned in 1992, Birlik subsequently established the Human Rights Society of Uzbekistan.

CIS *See* Commonwealth of Independent States.

Commonwealth of Independent States (CIS) A post-independence commonwealth that in 2001 consisted of Armenia, Azerbaijan, Belarus, Georgia, Kazakhstan, Kyrgyzstan, Moldava,

Russia, Tajikistan, Turkmenistan, Ukraine, and Uzbekistan.

CPTJ Communist Party of Tajikistan.

Dostum, Gen. Rashid Leader of the anti-Taliban United Front (also called the Northern Alliance) after the assassination of Ahmad Shah Masood and a leader of the Uzbek minority in northern Afghanistan.

Erk (Freedom) Opposition party in Uzbekistan. A splinter group of Birlik, Erk was founded in 1990 and banned in 1992; it subsequently established the Independent Human Rights Organization of Uzbekistan.

hadith The body of traditions about the sayings and acts of The Prophet Muhammad that delineate proper Muslim behavior and form along with the Koran, the basis for sharia (Islamic law).

hajj The annual pilgrimage to Mecca, a religious rite every Muslim is required to perform at least once.

Hekmatyar, Gulbuddin Afghanistan warlord who founded the Hizb-i-Islami.

Himmatzoda, Muhammad Sharif Leader of the military wing of the IRT.

Hindustani, Muhammad Rustamov Deobandi Muslim leader of an underground Islamic movement in Tajikistan during the Soviet era.

Hizb-i-Islami (Party of Islam) Most extreme party of Afghan Mujahedeens formed to resist the Soviet invasion of Afghanistan; founded by Gulbuddin Hekmatyar.

Hizb-i-Islami Turkistan (Islamic Party of Turkistan) Reputed name change of the IMU, signifying a new mission to bring Islamic revolution to the whole of Central Asia and Xinjiang Province.

Hizb ut-Tahrir al-Islami (HT; Party of Islamic Liberation) Fundamentalist Islamic movement that seeks, through nonviolent means, to restore the caliphate and institute sharia throughout the Muslim world.

HT *See* Hizb ut-Tahrir al-Islami.

Ikhwan-ul-Muslimeen (Muslim Brotherhood) Group established in the 1930s in Egypt that advocated that colonies seek independence from their colonizers and try to form Islamic states.

imam Prayer leader at a mosque who has also acquired some religious learning and has respect and support of the community.

IMF International Monetary Fund.

IMU *See* Islamic Movement of Uzbekistan.

Interservices Intelligence (ISI) Pakistan secret service.

IRP *See* Islamic Renaissance Party.

Islamic Movement of Uzbekistan (IMU) Militant Islamic group founded in 1999 by Tohrir Yuldeshev and Juma Namangani that has declared a jihad against the government of Uzbekistan.

Islamic Renaissance Party (IRP) Islamic political organization founded in the Soviet Union in 1990, with independent branches in the Central Asian republics. The IRP is a legal party only in Tajikistan.

Islam Lashkarlary (Fighters for Islam) Radical Islamic group in the Fergana Valley.

ISI *See* Interservices Intelligence.

jihad The way an individual can become a better Muslim and be of service to society; can also be a call to holy war against non-Muslims.

Jamiat-i-Islami (Islamic Party) Largest religious party in Pakistan.

Jamiat-i-Ulema Islami (JUI; Islamic Ulema Party) Pakistani organization that supports the IMU and the Taliban.

Jiang Zemin President of the People's Republic of China.

Karimov, Islam President of Uzbekistan since 1991.

khilafat (caliphate) The Islamic state established by successors to The Prophet Muhammad that in the early Islamic period after His death united all Muslim lands under a single caliph (*khalifa*), literally "successor to The Prophet."

Khojaev, Jumaboi Ahmadzhanovitch *See* Juma Namangani.

Lali Badakhshan Party of the Pamiri Tajiks who sought greater autonomy during the Tajik civil war.

Lashkar-i-Jhangvi Extremist Pakistani anti-Shia group.

madrassah School where students study Islamic subjects, Islamic law, and the Koran.

Masood, Ahmad Shah Defense minister of Afghanistan until the Taliban takeover; leader of the anti-Taliban forces (the United Front) after 1997; assassinated September 2001.

Mujahedeen Fighter who undertakes jihad for Islam.

mullah Traditional Islamic prayer leader at a mosque.

Musharraf, Gen. Pervez Chief executive of Pakistan, 1999–2001; president since 2001.

Nabiev, Rakhmon President of Tajikistan, 1991–92; although Tajikistan now has a coalition government, the United Nations still recognizes Nabiev as president.

Nahzar-i-Islami (Islamic Knowledge) Illegal Tajik Islamic educational organization, founded by Sayed Abdullah Nuri.

Namangani, Juma Founder and military leader of the IMU.

Nazarbayev, Nursultan President of Kazakhstan since 1991.

NGO Nongovernmental organization.

Niyazov, Saparmurad President of Turkmenistan since 1991.

nomenklatura Ruling Soviet Communist elite.

Nuri, Sayed Abdullah Founder of Nahzar-i-Islami and founding member and leader of the Tajikistan IRP.

ODCCP U.N. Office for Drug Control and Crime Prevention.

pir Title given to the head of a Sufi order.

Rabbani, Burhanuddin President of Afghanistan, 1992–96.

Rahmonov, Emomali President of Tajikistan since 1992.

Shanghai Cooperation Organization (SCO) *See* Shanghai Five.

Shanghai Five Group of five countries (China, Russia, Tajikistan, Kazakhstan, and Kyrgyzstan) that share common borders and are pledged to meet at summit level annually. In 2000 renamed the Shanghai Forum, with Uzbekistan added as a country with ob-

Praise for Ahmed Rashid's *Taliban*

"A must read for anyone wanting to understand America's new war."
Larry P. Goodson, *New York Times*

"A fabulous piece of journalism."
Sebastian Junger, author of *The Perfect Storm* and *Fire*

"[Rashid] knows as much about his subject as any other writer and one could not wish for a better guide to the fabulous complexities of what is one of the most tragic national stories of the past century."
Jason Burke, *Observer* (London)

"Rashid . . . provides the most reliable and absorbing account of the militant Central Asian movement that has given shelter to Osama bin Laden, addressing the Taliban's complicated economic, diplomatic, sociological and military origins."
Lorraine Adams, *Washington Post*

"Virtually the only informed work on the men who, since 1994, have ruled almost all of Afghanistan. . . . [An] indispensable book."
Steve Wasserman, *Los Angeles Times Book Review*

"The standard work in English on the Taliban."
Christopher de Bellaigue, *New York Review of Books*

"Read this remarkable book, and the bewildering complexity of Afghan politics and the deadly overspill of chaos, narcotics, and sectarian violence into the surrounding region will become clear."
Patrick Seale, *Sunday Times* (London)

"[A] valuable and informative work."
Richard Bernstein, *New York Times*

"An excellent political and historical account of the movement's rise to power."
Katha Pollitt, *Nation*